# The Profession
## of
# Local Government
# Management

# The Profession
## of
# Local Government
# Management

## MANAGEMENT EXPERTISE
## AND THE AMERICAN
## COMMUNITY

———

### ROY E. GREEN

New York
Westport, Connecticut
London

**Copyright Acknowledgments**

The author and publisher are grateful to the following for allowing the use of excerpts from:

Roy E. Green, "Local Government Managers: Styles and Challenges," *Baseline Data Report*, vol. 19, no. 2 (Washington, D.C.: International City Management Association, March/April 1987). Reprinted by permission.

Roy E. Green and B. J. Reed, "Occupational Stress and Mobility Patterns among Professional Local Government Managers: A Decade of Change," in *The Municipal Year Book 1988* (Washington, D.C.: International City Management Association, 1988), pp. 32–45. Reprinted by permission.

Laurei S. Frankel and Carol A. Pigeon, "Municipal Manager and Chief Administrative Officers," *Urban Data Service Report*, vol. 7, no. 2 (Washington, D.C.: International City Management Association, February 1975). Reprinted by permission.

Selections from *Encyclopedia of Associations*: 1988. Edited by Karin E. Koek, Susan B. Martin, and Annette Novallo. Gale Research, 1988. Copyright © 1988 by Gale Research, Inc. Reprinted by permission of the publisher.

**Library of Congress Cataloging-in-Publication Data**

Green, Roy E.
   The profession of local government management : management
expertise and the American community / Roy E. Green.
     p.    cm.
   Includes bibliographies and index.
   ISBN 0-275-93276-1 (alk. paper)
   1. Municipal government by city manager—United States.  2. City
managers—United States.  3. County manager government—United
States.  4. Local government—United States.  5. Government
executives—United States.   I. Title
JS344.C5G69    1989
352'.008'0973—dc20        89-3945

Library of Congress Catalog Card Number: 89-3945
ISBN: 0-275-93276-1

First published in 1989

Praeger Publishers, One Madison Avenue, New York, NY 10010
A division of Greenwood Press, Inc.

Printed in the United States of America

The paper used in this book complies with the
Permanent Paper Standard issued by the National
Information Standards Organization (Z39.48-1984).

10 9 8 7 6 5 4 3 2 1

To my mother,
ELIZABETH BECKER GREEN,
and to the memory of my father,
HENRY GREEN,
who have given my life purpose and direction;

and to my wife,
PATRICIA DWYER GREEN,
who has been the source of unending support and confidence

# CONTENTS

# TABLES AND FIGURES

## TABLES

**FIGURES**

# ACKNOWLEDGMENTS

Like all who take on a project of this nature, I have incurred a variety of debts to many people and to several organizations. Each in their own way has been willing to give of their time, expertise, and often some of their scarce resources to help advance this study. I am particularly indebted to the International City Management Association (ICMA) for making available to me their chief administrative officer survey data bases, for allowing me to cite freely from publications that I and others have previously written based on these questionnaires, and for providing me with their mailing list so that additional independent surveys could be conducted. I wish to indicate my appreciation to my coinvestigator on two of these independent studies, Professor B. J. Reed of the University of Nebraska–Omaha, for allowing me to make use of our jointly collected survey data in this study. I am also very appreciative of the clerical support offered by the secretarial staff of the Department of Planning, Public Policy, and Management at the University of Oregon.

Special thanks, however, must go to Evelina R. Moulder, Senior Editor, Municipal Data Service, International City Management Association; Gwen E. Rivkin of the University of Wisconsin–Milwaukee; and Professor James A. Stever of the University of Cincinnati, for their useful comments and suggestions on a number of early chapter drafts. Also appreciated has been the computer and editorial efforts of two of my graduate research assistants at the University of Oregon; Mary Ellen Skinner and Jill Jackson. Of course, all the assistance in the world cannot stop us from exhibiting our own unique shortcomings; and so, those institutions and individuals who have been helpful to me in completing this project are absolved from any of the study's limitations and defects.

# 1

# THE PROFESSION OF LOCAL GOVERNMENT MANAGEMENT: IN PURSUIT OF A DYNAMIC IDEAL

Recently, a member of the new, emerging generation of scholars of public administration remarked:

It seems that city managers are important actors in the modern city. The question, though, is why. Are they important because of their professional qualifications or simply the strategic role that they occupy? . . . Are city managers simply convenient brokers that corporations and other urban interests need for various particularized agendas? Or, are they important because of the professional qualities which they possess?[1]

Traditionally, observes James Stever, professionals have been described as having the following traits:

a scientific or technical education, a supporting professional association, a code of ethics, service to a clientele, [and] a supporting state licensing procedure that regulates both entrance into the profession and prevents quackery. Beyond these traits, the professional, to be truly professional, must be accepted by the public and the clientele served as legitimate. He or she must be regarded as being crucial, seen as a person with somewhat mystical powers. Admittedly, this is a rather stiff test for any group thinking itself to be a profession, but it does offer a criteria to separate out the genuine from the ingenuine.[2]

Thinking about these concerns should give one ample reason to pause. A whole range of important questions are implied by this comparison of an occupation with these traditional standards of professionalism. For example, how do the chief administrative officers of local governments measure up to such standards of professionalism? Is progress being made along the criteria? Is it important that local government managers meet these standards in the first place, and, if so, for whom is it important?

Pushing this reasoning one step further raises another complete set of significant issues about the essence of professionalism among local government management. Can local government managers really be a "professional" in the sense described above? Are they allowed to be or desired to be by the councils and communities that hire them? Or is the literal comparison of this academic criteria of professionalism a misrepresentation or a misapplication of the essential roles that local government managers have come to exercise in the public sector? Does this comparison do harm to the reputation of the field or to the individuals compared? And if the public nature of the occupation represents a significantly different milieu for professionalism, how do managers demonstrate their professional status?

A third set of issues may in fact represent the toughest examination of all professional standards because it focuses on the motivational aspects of the professional. Examples of this line of inquiry might be: Are these chief administrative officers self-conscious about the changing nature of the roles that they play? Are they aware of an evolution in established expectations for the profession? What self-perceptions do they bring into the urban situation? Do they see themselves as technical facilitators, brokers, and mediators? Or, do they see themselves as professionals who have something substantive to contribute? Moreover, to what extent can and do local government managers go beyond a brokering role and impart or attempt to implement their substantive professional judgments onto policy and program issues?

A focus on the general direction of the internal professionalization of managers may ultimately be just as good a predictor of the future as the criteria used externally to measure what roles and functions individuals and their associations are thought to contribute to the professionalism of local government management. However, taking both perspectives together seems to provide the most reasonable approach for furthering our understanding. The challenge posed by both lines of inquiry (the outward attributes of professionalism, and the inward professionalization of practitioners) is unavoidable and important to those of us concerned with the future needs of our communities. This type of approach would serve as a status report drawn from an examination of these perspectives, and should help us to learn more about what local government managers are and might be doing as professionals. These perspectives are also important in terms of what today's trends may portend for the future of local government professionalism and for the leadership and direction of our communities.

There is no shortage of research and commentary on these topics. But a consensus among analysts on the issues has proven to be as illusive and inconclusive as we may consider the answers to be important. And there appears to be an increasing gap in our understanding about what current local government manager's roles, responsibilities, and careers are thought to be—and have now come to be—within our nation's communities. For example, the theory of "corporatism" is a concept with some credence among a number of contemporary analysts who study emerging national trends in U.S. society.[3] Corporatism attempts to explain a perceived reduction in the role and influence of government leadership in the direction and development of our communities by suggesting that the most significant decisions for the United States are made primarily outside the realm of government.

If we were to give credence to corporatism as the dominating principle for understanding and measuring government–private sector relations, then the future of today's local government managers might be viewed as one evolving into that of full-time negotiator. If increased corporatism is the direction that our social and economic system is headed, then local government managers might come to be viewed as but necessary conduits who broker nongovernmental interests into some kind of consensus that can be eventually legitimated by public policy. Such a development would reduce professional management into a quasi-professional status whose members' power is based on timely access to information, rather than their expertise in understanding and using it. James Stever cautions that ''The future of the profession may very well hang on answers to these questions.''[4] I believe that the trends and the reactions of local government managers remain to be ascertained on these important issues, and that the actual roles of local government managers are evolving and will be redetermined through the interplay of community residents, the business sector, other members of the government (civil service and elected), as well as through their own efforts. However, there can be little doubt that international, interstate, as well as the local business community will be active and important participants in the choices made.

## TRENDS IN PROFESSIONAL ROLES

What, then, are some of the emerging major social and economic trends concerning contemporary community life in the United States? What are some of the dominating images that we are using to illustrate and define the issues in order to explain the changes that have been occurring? It has frequently been observed that the forces of community change—economic, demographic, technological, and political—are perpetual, if not predictable. Urban experts possessing an ever-widening assortment of qualifications have provided insights into the various states and stages of community evolution and change by providing histories, projecting futures, and evaluating options for the public and private sectors. We also know that some of the images conflict with each other and have come to divide as well as inform public and private policymakers.[5]

Some analysts argue that public officials charged with the government responsibility for linking public and private interests through local institutions, processes, and cultures play a pivotal role in the evolving community. Dennis Judd, a well-known urbanologist, notes:

Historically, city politics has involved an interplay between government and the institutions of private investment. . . . In local communities . . . governments in the twentieth century have vastly increased their responsibilities. But the growth of the public sector has not eclipsed the power and authority of private institutions to make critical political decisions involving jobs, land use, and investment. . . . Despite the expansion of governmental responsibilities, the private sector has retained control over critical resources. In urban politics, it is the continuities in our history, rather than the changes, that are surprising.[6]

This thesis obviously clashes with that offered by R. Jeffrey Lustig's corporatism theory, in that Judd observes a substantial growth in authority and influence by both the local governmental as well as the business sectors. Judd might well argue that in fact this process was accelerated by the Reagan administration's urban policies.

The succession of George Bush to the presidency in 1989 revealed a carefully measured attempt to transform the style of leadership and to implement a different set of domestic policy consolidation strategies from those of his predecessor. However, the Bush election does not seem to foreshadow any major or sudden shifts away from the Reagan administration's essential federal philosophy toward the devolution of intergovernmental, and public to private sector, urban responsibilities and obligations.

But if some argue that there are important continuities in the relationship between the public and private sectors at the local level, others argue that times and the future are becoming more uncertain. They suggest that immense change has been introduced into public–private sector relationships in even the smallest communities as local, national, and—in fact—global economics, demographics, technologies, and politics influence the community environment. This view holds that the continuing development of professional local government management is inherently tied to and inseparable from the evolution and the redefinition of the community's relationships with its public and private sectors. The realization of either of these two societal forces (the suggested growth in the influence by both public and private institutions in community and individual lives, or a persistent rise in the disequilibrium of international and national corporatism without a counterbalancing protective authority from public institutions) would portend significant change for the future.

In addition to the historical and contemporary analyses represented above, a number of intriguing descriptions of U.S. community life have been developed by a number of other futuristic thinkers. They have also reviewed our history and current circumstances to portray and project different images of our future. Most of their projections are based on examinations of current circumstances, but analyzed within various frameworks (time and scope) of past patterns of change. Three different groups of views about the direction, importance, and impact of government on the current and future well-being of community and economic development are represented by John Naisbitt, Katherine L. Bradbury et al., and the International City Management Association (ICMA) Committee on Future Horizons of the Profession.

Recognizing the inherent linkage between community change and the future of its own members, the International City Management Association commissioned a Committee on Future Horizons of the Profession (1978–79) to study and prognosticate about what shape and direction these developments might take, and what the implications might be for the profession of local government management. One of the most significant conclusions drawn in the committee's final report was that, as the community meets change, so the responsibilities of professional managers will be changed. The committee's findings—presented in the publication, *The Essential Community: Local Government in the Year 2000*—observed that "in the past the focus has been on the technology of service delivery, the analytical skills of administration, and the strategies of direction from the top down," but then suggested that in the future the primary role of the manager will become that of the broker or negotiator," . . . to direct an organization or group of people without dominating it."[7]

John Naisbitt offers another view by identifying ten "megatrends" that he argues are transforming an industrialized U.S. society into one increasingly dominated by an information (processing) economy. Naisbitt's ten megatrends can be summarized as the interrelationship of two interactive sets of factors: (1) a change in the fundamental and technological nature and basis of the U.S. economy—linked to an increasing interdependence with the global economy at even the most local levels of society—and (2) a decentralization and redefinition of power, choice, and responsibility from national levels of public and private institutions that are now devolving toward the local, private, and individual levels. Contends Naisbitt, the new type of local leadership will be those individuals willing to function as facilitators, not as order givers.[8] Many observers might see this as a troublesome set of projections for the future of professional local government management.

A less optimistic perspective for the future of large communities is the body of research represented by the work of Katherine L. Bradbury et al., in their book *Urban Decline and the Future of American Cities*.[9] Defining urban decline as a loss of population and jobs, they focus on the circumstance and future of larger cities. But of broader interest to us is that Bradbury et al. conclude that changing community circumstances are resulting from many of the same factors as mentioned by earlier analysts: the interdependent nature of changing international, national, and local economies; and the resulting shifts in jobs and population. However, they view the role and impacts of government policies and programs quite differently from those previously mentioned. Bradbury et al. suggest that, while government policies may help to soften major societal trends, they will not often be able to alter their basic nature or course. In some instances, increasingly scarce community resources make the socially and politically painful choices of retrenchment and triage an unavoidable necessity and responsibility for community leadership.

While concluding that local government needs to reform those institutions and practices that perpetuate or aggravate the problems of urban decline, Bradbury et al. also suggest that

there are valid reasons for public policy to intervene in the current processes of urban change. The adverse situations in which many cities find themselves are not solely the result of their incompetence or of "natural" market forces working themselves out. Rather, those situations are strongly molded by political institutions, legal regulations, social prejudices, and market imperfections. The process of decline itself sets in motion nonmarket responses which inefficiently aggravate it. Yet market forces are extremely powerful; so it would be folly to try policies that ignored their constructive roles in guiding the form and structure of economic change.[10]

It would seem that Bradbury et al. envision a need for a more substantively involved role for government and its policies, programs, and leadership—even when the tasks are not pleasant—than either R. Jeffrey Lustig or the Horizons 2000 Task Force projects to be likely, or John Naisbitt sees as inevitable.

While a relationship between the private sector and the public sector certainly has always existed, there is reason to believe that the balance of roles and responsibilities of local public officials continues to change, but not necessarily according to any of the forecasted directions. And in this manner, we might benefit from viewing professional local-government managers, in themselves, as reflectors and unique observers of the evolution of local government and its relationship to the private sector. It would seem that part of the answer to the question about what local professional management is becoming might be found in what and how it has developed up to today. It may also be that the future of the profession is most likely to be found within the seeds of current experiences and perceptions—that is, if we can identify the right signposts marking the pathways of their careers, their roles, and their relationships to communities served.

## THE COMMUNITY AND ITS RELATIONS WITH GOVERNMENT

Over the years there has been a great deal of study on U.S. community life and on its politics and governments. The studies have been conducted by academics of many disciplines, by a host of professional associations, by various and sundry research and nonprofit institutions, as well as by government officials, agencies, committees, and commissions charged with managing the interests of the public. Reports of their findings have been followed with varying degrees of interest by students and the general public (whose attitudes and opinions have been duly, frequently, and competitively reported in public opinion polls). The focus of many studies undertaken shortly after World War II was concerned with the "community power" structure—that is, who makes the effective decisions in local communities. This line of investigation splintered into an academic debate over methods for determining who actually controlled this power (an elite group or a plurality of competing groups). The debate was occasionally accompanied by a special interest in the role of the city manager. Finally, though, this much-researched issue focus seemed—as much as anything—largely unresolvable and was superseded by ongoing national demographic events.

Paralleling postwar demographic shifts, the next era of analysis focused on a different dynamic of community life; the explosion of the suburbs. Of particular interest were their proliferating populations, mounting demands for services, and the resulting multiplication, overlap, and interrelationship of governmental jurisdictions and finances straining to keep up. Researchers worked to track and identify the causes, directions, impacts, and future implications of the Baby Boom era and generation. Reformation of local government became a focus; and studies were made on the social as well as political demise of the "machine," and on the nature of newer forms of participation in public affairs. The effects of local nonpartisan elections and the increase in the numbers, types, and impacts of public interest groups were mapped and evaluated for public policy impact. Local government managers—particularly the city manager—were already being identified for their unique, quasi-political leadership role, and for their relationships with their elected councils and other community groups.

The mid–1960s erupted with the unrest of U.S. urban centers. James F. Sullivan and Charles R. Adrian have suggested that "the succession of summer ghetto riots that began in 1965 seems to have marked a change both in directions of research and in the actual power configurations and decision processes of urban government."[11] New research initiatives were made to study the urban racial disturbances and the impacts of government programs to resolve differences. Alienation from local government, and the feelings of intracommunity isolation, became the target of much study. This era of research was marked by a heavy use of survey research to examine resident feelings toward their communities as well as their governments, and also to assess the public and private regardingness of their public officials (elected, appointed, and civil service). A rather radical new theory of public administration—the so-called new public administration—was proffered in the early 1970s as a framework for balancing the interests of traditionally underrepresented groups (utilizing the federal courts and protections within the civil service) in counterbalance to influence of the middle and upper classes as represented in elected and appointed positions of the legislative and executive branches. The concepts generated much discussion—but little measurable impact on the operations of government in the United States.

Reformed communities (those with nonpartisan elections, council–manager forms of government, and at-large elections) were also studied in the 1960s and 1970s in an attempt to evaluate how well and how differently they had met the policy challenges that were also confronting the traditionally governed (strong or weak mayor–council) communities. Political scientists and sociologists were often divided in their conclusions—the latter frequently finding that the form of government made no difference in the types of urban policies that were realized; and the former frequently finding that reformed communities were in fact less responsive to these types of community divisions, due in part to the homogeneous nature of the constituencies most often served by the council-manager type of government.[12] The next generation of research would focus on changes in the federal intergovernmental relations system.

The Johnson administration's War on Poverty initiatives transformed a federal aid system from one that had relied almost exclusively on state and local governments as the primary partners for defining local need and interpreting and administering federal urban policies and programs, to one where state and local governments were often viewed as being suspect in their ability and willingness to identify and represent various sectors of local public interest. Some research went so far as to suggest that many of the new Great Society programs were structured either to bypass state and local governments through direct aid schemes to individuals and the quasi-governmental and nonprofit sector, or to regulate urban policies and programs through a system of crosscutting federal mandates imbedded in existing and new grant-in-aid programs.[13]

Simultaneous to these developments, the U.S. Supreme Court was rendering a whole series of decisions implementing the "one man, one vote" principle in a move to enforce the Voting Rights Act of 1965. The Court's decisions expanded the application of this principle to congressional districts, then to state and local government jurisdictions, as well as to the operations of political parties. These judicial opinions were attempts by the high court to redress—on the basis of fundamental Constitutional and legal rights—many of the alienating and participation-inhibiting obstacles reported during the 1950s and 1960s and highlighted by the Civil Rights Movement and the years of urban unrest.[14]

The research of the 1960s and 1970s tracked public interest in the evolving demands for direct citizen participation in local public affairs. Most of the decentralization efforts of local governments were reported to be in response to the period of urban unrest and to the sense of general public alienation that had grown out of the 1950s and 1960s. Many resulting investigations concerning community isolation from government decision-making processes were initiated by federal, state, and some locally sponsored commissions—as well academic researchers—and were widely reported by the mass media. The expansion in policy scope and financial impact of federal grants-in-aid programs in the 1960s and 1970s were closely followed—with analyses focusing on how well the various new programs were meeting program goals, as well as on public expectations. There was a recurring pattern to the findings reported. Most of the research found that inefficiencies, conflicts, and unpleasant and unintended consequences had resulted from the sudden growth in the federal grants-in-aid system.[15]

A number of grant reform efforts were undertaken toward the end of the Johnson administration to reduce the density of regulation, and the ostracization of general-purpose local governments. The notion of the "block grant" was

introduced in the late 1960s to provide greater on-site discretion to local communities for problem identification, definition, and solution. However, these
efforts are reported to have often led to increased levels of competition between
general-purpose jurisdictions (municipalities and counties) and federally funded
regional–planning and coordination bodies and nonprofit organizations.[16]

The balance between the benefits and costs of this dual system for addressing
community-level problems remains a contested issue. Some analysts have argued
that its duplicative and competitive nature was in part responsible for the unofficial—but real—recategorization (increasing federal regulation) of the block
grant programs.[17] Efforts to reform the federal grants system became more
pronounced as programs multiplied and overall funding levels increased, and as
presidential administrations changed. The Nixon administration's New Federalism reforms were an effort to reduce direct federal intervention into state and
local affairs, and to place a renewed emphasis on involvement by state and local
governments in federal urban policies and programs. New Federalism touted the
streamlined use of block grant techniques for existing federal categorical programs, and promoted for passage the general and special revenue-sharing programs. Both approaches were designed to allow substantial discretion to
community governments for meeting locally determined goals and needs.[18]

Federal contributions to urban development programs peaked in the mid–
1970s. The presidential campaigns and elections of two former governors—
Jimmy Carter and Ronald Reagan—have been viewed as resulting primarily from
a popular desire to modify and, in different contexts, reduce the extensiveness
of direct federal regulation and involvement in state and community affairs. The
Carter administration's efforts are largely seen by researchers as attempts to
increase and improve the coordination and operation of intergovernmental relationships (particularly the grants-in-aid system), while leaving mostly intact
the program goals and financial support provided by the federal government.[19]
By contrast, the Reagan administration attempted to implement a much more
fundamental set of reforms through a reduction in both regulation and funding
for the federal grants-in-aid system.

As part of its New, New Federalism initiatives, the Reagan administration
promoted an economic and political philosophy that attempted to reduce federal
levels of taxation and regulatory burdens in as many ways as possible. Cut backs
in the numbers and types of federal urban-assistance programs were sought and
partly won from Congress. These policy initiatives were promoted as methods
to generate economic and locally responsive community development, as a strategy for restructuring state–local resources and capabilities and as a vehicle for
freeing public–private sector cooperative ventures at the community level. For
the remaining urban programs, the Reagan administration tried to reduce federal
regulations imposed by attempting to further ''block'' remaining grant programs,
and to reduce regulation within otherwise unaltered categorical programs.[20]

Some differences in emphasis (for example, in the attempts at creative use of
the federal tax code) are likely to evolve and to distinguish the Reagan admin-

istration's and the Bush administration's policies toward federal relations with state and local governments (and the communities they serve), as well as in the emphases placed upon federal strategies for promoting public-private sector solutions to pressing domestic issues and problems. New urban policies could easily be articulated by the Bush administration that are more than semantically different from those of the Reagan years. For example, President Reagan's preference for private sector revitalization and governmental privatization initiatives may have led to quite different urban policy decisions, reactions, and consequences than are implied by President Bush's evocation of the American civic culture, organized within and shouldered by the nonprofit sector—but now potentially buttressed by the availability of federal tax incentives (the so-called "thousand points of light" initiative).

This difference in emphasis might also be revealed by the appointment of former Congressman Jack Kemp to be Secretary of the U.S. Department of Housing and Urban Development. Kemp's selection could be viewed as evidence of President Bush's decision to consolidate, promote, and further develop federal-urban policies in a matter compatible with, yet distinctive from, those pursued by his predecessor. Then Congressman Kemp's early sponsorship of the federal "enterprise zone" legislation as an experimental free market approach to solving some of the problems of urban economic distress—a legislative proposal endorsed by presidential candidate Ronald Reagan during a campaign swing through the Bronx in 1980—was also endorsed by President Bush in his first address before Congress in 1989. The Bush endorsement was of some potential import due to the fact that the concept's essential tax incentives and deregulatory features were left largely unrealized as a result of the Reagan administration's philosophical dilemma over later support of the Tax Reform Act of 1986; although later a programmatically weakened federal enterprise zone program was passed by Congress and signed by President Reagan during the waning months of his administration.

The assumptions, desirability, and short- and long-term impacts of the Reagan administration's changes are the focus of much current research and community interest. Fundamental change has no doubt occurred during these years, but only some of the most immediate consequences have been realized by local communities and their governments. And in the interim, local government leaders— elected and professional—will continue to wrestle and be responsive to dividing and competing technological, social, economic, and political events and changes as they lap over the nation and its individual communities.

More than a decade ago, Sullivan and Adrian concluded from their review of urban research that there was substantial pressure being placed on local government managers to adapt and to make changes in their roles as professionals. The calls to change still have a familiar ring to us today:

What the studies since about 1965 have hinted at, in most cases probably without the authors' being fully conscious of the implications, is that the council–manager plan is under pressure to change and that the role of the manager as spelled out in the period from about the time of the Great Depression through the 1950s is no longer suitable. . . . Development of a new pattern of city politics, a new patronage based on federal aid, and federal pressures for greater and broader participation in decision making at the local level, all seem to suggest a change in the roles of both the manager and the political side of city government represented by the council members and the mayor. In the changes that seem to be taking place, it appears that managers are being forced to learn new roles and to undergo the trauma of seeing their discretionary powers reduced; council members are beginning to act more like old-time power and patronage brokers on behalf of neighborhoods and ethnic groups; and mayors may be the greatest beneficiaries of the changes in terms of increased formal power, status and public attention.[21]

What seems so dramatically different today from the time of their research is the list of forces thought to be driving the need for change. The outcomes that they projected remain to be assessed—that is, the forecasted role alterations projected for various community leadership positions.

## PROFESSIONALISM, EXPERTISE, AND GOVERNMENT MODERNIZATION

It has long been suggested that political machines and the political conditions and processes thought to cause and accompany them were somehow peculiar to a past era of American history. Until more recently, many students viewed the significance of political machines as interesting artifacts important only for marking an early stage in U.S. political and social development. Most scholars who argue that we are now in the post–political machine era have suggested that there was an intrinsic linkage between the U.S. free-market economic system, our history of rapid industrialization–urbanization, the turn-of-the-century influx of divergent, deprived, and befuddled immigrants, and our tumultuous partisan electoral process. They contend that most of these community political features have been fundamentally changed—reformed, if you will—which ultimately has led to the passing away of political machines.

While these characterizations may be pertinent to assessing the variations in the form and functioning of political machines found operating in the United States during the nineteenth and early twentieth centuries, the traditional description of political machines obfuscates aspects of machine-type politics that may well continue today. Machine-style politics as a permutation of yesterday's political machine may well continue to challenge the integrity of today's local governments and the values and roles of professional local government managers. There have been many urban scholars who have documented that the unwanted side effects of political machines had much to do with the original desire to modernize local government by developing and promoting professional quality management.[22] Today, some of the most important values that communities may seek to receive from their professional chief administrative officers are likely to be found in their standards for conduct, as well as in their contemporary administrative skills. Both would seem to be important in maintaining the integrity of local government processes. In this vein, the contrast in values between, on the one hand, political machines or machine-like politics—which focus primarily on narrowly defined (selfish) interests and outcomes—continues to be sharply differentiated from, on the other hand, a concern for community and legally legitimated processes and outcomes.

Analysts have argued that the opportunity for the development of political machines is inherent to the routine processes of any government at any time— that is, administrative discretion over the distribution of divisible and scarce public resources and privileges. For example, as late as the mid–1970s Raymond Wolfinger argued that there has been a premature pronouncement of death for political machines in the United States. He disagrees with those who argue that the council–management form of government, including an experienced professional public manager with an advanced degree, will be sufficient in itself to constrain these types of encroachments on the proper functioning of local government. Wolfinger counters the "form over process" view by suggesting that much of the administrative discretion over public resources and privileges—once in the control of political parties—has not been lost to posterity, but to governmental bureaucracies through civil service reform and the ensuing merit systems.[23] It is of interest that aspects of both structural reforms were being nationalized in the 1960s and the 1970s through a growth in federal urban grants-in-aid programs (with their crosscutting mandates) and the one-man, one-vote Supreme Court decisions.

The essence of machine politics is the unethical *tactics* that they employ and the view of government that they represent, and not just the illegality or inefficiencies that may result from their final financial or policy *choices*. To put it another way, machine-type politics can be viewed as being inconsistent with official and publicly accepted values for doing the public's business, and therefore they are deemed corrupt and unsanctionable. Wolfinger considers that political machines might indeed continue to exist—although in a much less obvious, centralized and organized fashion.[24]

Studies done on corruption and inefficiencies in local government generally contend that, even today, a requisite condition for the emergence and maintenance of political machines is the presence of a socially or economically disadvantaged segment of the political community.[25] The studies argue that this segment seeks a way out of its current circumstances by offering power or money for access and upward mobility. However, others suggest that a more fundamental precondition for the existence of political machines is a desire by any segment of the community to protect or promote certain privileges and resources singly available to them in the public domain when either official access to or confidence in using approved channels are limiting to them. In other words, the challenge to publicly accepted norms for government decision making may come from the influential as well as those viewed as economically or socially disadvantaged.

And therefore, the incentives offered by contemporary political machines are not necessarily limited to those who have been seen as traditionally deprived.

A third dimension of the discussion on contemporary machine politics attempts to differentiate political machines from machine-like politics. We raise the distinction here only because the resolution or eradication of political machines may not necessarily result in the elimination of machine-type politics and the extralegal benefits and privileges that selected groups may receive from it. For example, newer forms of unethical influence—frequently referred to as white-collar crime—may involve controlling the access or timely distribution of information concerning important community policy decisions for the benefit of selected interests.

The distinction between political machines and machine-type politics is usually drawn using as a test the presence, durability, and continuity of an organization of individuals. Wolfinger has argued that the durability and continuity of a permanent organization of individuals is not a necessary condition for a political machine to exist. Today's machines—he argues—need not be highly structured, nor centralized.[26] Rather, the potential for centralization would seem to be correlated to the extent of shared or delegated administrative discretion. In this view, the necessity for structure would be a function of community size and complexity.

If this view be correct, then the new political machine may—in reality—be composed of networks of episodically active individuals who can be characterized by their knowledge of, access to, and experience in exploiting the various fields of administrative discretion over public resources and privileges. Their intent would be to violate or circumvent officially approved channels of access for ultimate personal reward. One of the important challenges faced by communities and their professional government managers may not be whether or how often actual political machine organizations or established networks of individuals exist in competition with the doctrines of fairness and equality of access, but whether machine-type politics exist and work in a less obvious—but pervasive—manner. Professionalism—as represented in administrative capacity, knowledge of ethics, and negotiating skill may be of premium value both to local government managers and to their communities.[27]

Historically, we know that the "good government" reformers who were promoting the council–manager form of government made every effort to elevate and promote the occupation of city manager as a unique profession. This effort was made in response to a belief that certain public interests can be identified as being superior to individual or particular group interests in a community. It was advanced that the best way to solve most problems is to minimize political divisions in the community. This strategy for community conflict reduction has been described as the promotion of "expertise over politics"—a process by which as many community problems as possible would be defined as technical, and therefore sound, expert judgment could be applied to their resolution.[28] In pursuit of this goal, another team of urban researchers—Stone, Whelan, and Murin—have observed that "even where professional city management has not been instituted atop the administrative branch of government, the trend is to provide the mayor with a chief administrative officer (CAO) or an assistant under some title who excels in the skill of management."[29] This trend offers perhaps one of the most profound tests of the reformers' strategy for using expertise to overcome politics outside the council–manager form of government. It may be measured by the degree to which the individual manager is considered to be a professional—the expert—on the basis of formal education and professional training, and not by virtue of being a member of any particular electoral or special interest coalition in the community.

Many of the issues and dilemmas that confront professional local government managers today have been confronting them since the council–management experiment began around the turn of the century. It is perhaps the nature of these dilemmas that gives vitality and meaning to the occupation, and that defines its prospective status as a profession. Professional local government management is concerned with helping communities deal with their dilemmas. We continue to relearn that, ultimately, public or private institutional control over the direction or impacts of major international and national–let alone local and personal–socioeconomic trends are too complex and subtle for final mastery or solution. Therefore, expectations for controlling the present and the future course of events have always been frustrating for professional local government managers, even when the public's best interest is clearly in their hearts.

While there are processes that have always been outside the ultimate control of any government or system of governments—or, in fact, any private set of institutions—most serious students of the field would agree that both public and private institutions represent important organized processes for the aggregation of interests, and are influential. A vision of good government has been shared by many. And by definition, those who claim to be reformers are those who would choose to eradicate political machines, and reform and eliminate machine-type politics in whatever the form of government and wherever it is operating. In recent years, there has been an increasing awareness among those who would reform local government that they might try to improve its operations through the employment of professional public managers, but not necessarily through the adoption of the council–manager form of government. Current government reform and modern thinking seems to emphasize a concern for the knowledge-based authority of the professional manager, and has resulted in furthering discussions about outlets for its proper development and use.

What are the role consequences for professional local government managers in the continuing process of modernization? We refer the reader to a prognosis made recently by Stone, Whelan, and Murin:

Technical expertise is hard to cope with. Modern governance calls for a high degree of expert decision making, and we are unable to dispense with it. Experts, by the nature of the situation, know more about their work than ordinary people do; and modern life has become so technically complicated that a wide variety of experts is necessary. Yet we have long since learned that experts, professionals, and other holders of administrative office are neither all wise nor disinterested and impartial participants in the decisions they make.[30]

From the local government's perspective, the problem-solving needs of its administrators can be seen in light of who has responsibility for a given cluster of governmental obligations (full-time professionals, or part-time elective or appointive officials) and what the responsible officials' relationship is with their local government (in-house staff versus adjunct or shared staffing). These factors would seem to influence the level and nature of specializations required by government administrators. Concern for the local government officials' administrative responsibilities—both in rural as well as in urban communities—has grown, along with an increase in the demands placed on the governments that they serve. The demands on local government administrators are not only the requests made by local citizens and their elected representatives for the maintenance of service, but also the new demands now being made by other levels of government to expand administrative responsibilities into the evolving field of intergovernmental policy formulation and implementation. This trend appears to have been enhanced rather than reduced by the Reagan and the early Bush administrations initiatives.

The reform movement of the first half of the twentieth century began by adopting the ideology of scientific management, but soon confronted the realities of human relations, and then evolved into a midcentury era of accommodation— a so-called New Realism.[31] The reform movement operating in the second half of the century seems to have added another set of issues associated with the need for new forms of managerial expertise. And it has also come to be concerned with the evolving influences and authorities derived from them. These issues have raised many concerns over the placement, use, and legitimacy of these new skills and knowledge—concerns from within as well as from outside the profession. Moreover, these issues are being raised during a period of public debate over the nature and role of government responsibilities and capacities. However, it is worth noting that local government management is not the only profession to be confronted with such dilemmas. Consider for a moment the changes occurring in medicine, law, accounting, and education.[32]

## THE WORKING PROFESSION AND THE IDEAL

Richard Stillman's review in *The Rise of the City Manager* represents perhaps the most thorough, historical assessment of the origins and growths of the council–manager plan, the development of the city management profession, and the succeeding generations of dilemmas that city managers have faced individually and as a group up to the mid–1970s.[33] Stillman's identification of two major dilemmas facing city managers may represent a fulcrum point in the twentieth century for professional public management. As issues, they are relevant because they have continued to present quandaries for managers and because they have evolved and been transformed by events of the past ten years into quite different dilemmas. In both ways, they continue in some form today and are worth briefly updating for what they suggest about local government management as a professional pursuit.

The first dilemma identified by Stillman relates to the increase in social responsibilities of local government. He attributes this increase in local responsibilities to the social, economic, and political problems of the 1960s, and of the myriad of federal urban programs designed to solve them. John Naisbitt and others suggest that the megatrends of the 1980s confronting today's public administrators have superseded most of the problems enumerated by Dwight Waldo and referenced by Stillman for the 1960s and 1970s periods. The newer issues have evolved, but not necessarily after resolution of any of the earlier problems. Science and technology, and the personal and ethical reactions to new concerns raised by new creations and capacities, continue to confront the manager and their fellow citizens today. Changes also continue unabated in the fields of social, economic, political, and criminal activity, and are still characterized by variations among groupings familiar to us: race, sex, age, and occupation. The impact of the devolving of the global economy to the local level, the diminution of the federal aid program system, and the greater emphasis on privatizing many heretofore publicly operated or funded programs may not have altered the categorization of these problems, but it certainly has altered the nature and scope of responsibilities placed on local communities and their leadership to meet them.

A second dilemma confronting local government managers was identified as that which pertains to urban administrators operating under the council–manager form of government. The academic and political battle continues over what the pros and cons for the council–manager plan are, and whether it represents a more desirable form of government. The so-far unresolvable debate is centered on two basic arguments. The first argument revolves around the significance and implications of research evidence offered by analysis of the relatively middle-class and frequently suburban communities where the council–manager form of government is most often found. The second argument centers on the unique quasi-political role played by managers within a typically nonpartisan political system (a combination that represents a minority of the national's local governments). Concern has often been focused on perceived disparities and inadequacies in managers' education and training—which are identified relative either to the realities of their changing community-leadership roles or to the requirements placed on them as administrative and technical experts. This dilemma may—like the first one—always be with us. As we noted earlier, the issues raised in this fashion persist, and some are becoming the focus of reform or modernization efforts in themselves.

This writer proposes that one strategy for getting out of the discussion enigma over which is the best form of government is to simply move beyond it. Although it is not clear that the issue will ever be resolvable—important as that may be—this problem should not impede us from further investigating the role played by the ideal of professionalism in government management. In pursuing this approach we direct our attention toward the attributes and changing roles of the professional local-government manager. And in this way we can assess the status of local government management as a profession, how and where it might be identified, and what types of difference it may make to the communities in which such managers serve. As we have seen, this strategy cannot assume a static community environment, and we are now removing it from the confines of the form of government in which it was incubated and nourished as an emerging profession.

There is tension caused by the two continuing dilemmas identified by Stillman. But these occupational stress factors also seem to be compounding as traditional responsibilities and expectations are being replaced or added to with new community expectations for expertise and service. Again, local government management seems not to be unique in this regard, when compared to other professions.[34] At the beginning of this chapter, we summarized a number of dimensions often equated with professionalism as it has evolved from the traditional professions of the ministry, law, and medicine. Professions are not static; even the oldest of them continue to wrestle with time and change. Rather, all professions are perpetually in the process of becoming more—or becoming less—amidst a whole variety of values linked with their professionalism. Just how emergent do candidate occupations need to be before being able to make a legitimate claim for professional status? And is there a process whereby a new or different skill acquisition and its practice may indicate an improved degree of professionalization, or a step toward deprofessionalization? Does, for example, the increasing perception that local government managers are becoming more involved in public–private sector bargaining and negotiation indicate—by definition—that they are behaving in a less professional fashion?

These issues represent a crucial set of questions that seem related to the possession and use of changing knowledge specialties. It is here that I believe many academic chroniclers of professionalism make the mistake of using the traditional professions as a readily available mechanism for establishing a sliding scale of traits—or criteria trends—which actually may be unrelated to the categories of expertise associated with another field's responsibilities. The traditional criteria can be simply put: "To be truly professional, [one] must be accepted by the public and the clientele served as legitimate. He or she must be regarded as being crucial."[35] Within this most fundamental context, standards for education, professional associations, codes of ethics, and licensing should be evaluated in terms of how they sort and screen applicants and candidates. Particular structures and processes for improving specialized knowledge and for ensuring its integrity and uniform application in the public interest have often been confused for being equivalent to achieving and maintaining a certain

**Figure 1.1**
**Viewing Local Government Management as a Profession**

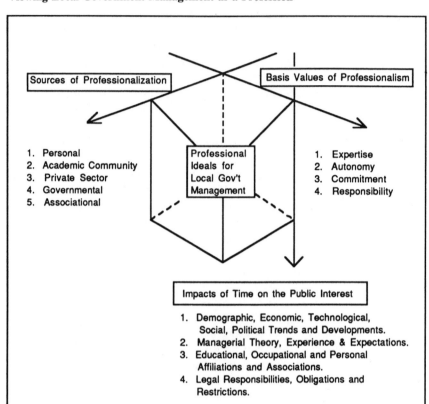

"professional" level of performance. At least part of this confusion seems to be caused by the myopic assumption that structures, procedures, and standards ought all to be found along similar organizational dimensions in every occupation, and in the same preparatory sequence. Typically, this means as they are found in the traditional professions. Questioning this assumption then raises the more difficult task of looking for alternative sources or locations for control and regulation of those occupational practices claiming status as a profession.

Figure 1.1 will help us to organize and structure this broader inquiry into the professional characteristics of local government management. It is a framework for viewing, describing, and understanding just how, when, where, and why there is a profession among those who are the chief administrative officers of local levels of government, and for evaluating the research in progress and reported about them. The framework has three dimensions, displayed as a cubic illustration: (1) On one plane is the traditional and cumulative index (values) for assessing the profession's relative features as a profession; (2) the second plane represents a dimension that suggests how changes in these features might over time impact on the perceptions and realities of professionalism in the context of the broader public interest; and (3) on the third plane is an array of the possible and changing sources of professionalization that may alter the development, promotion, accreditation, and viability of numerous policies and programs designed to institutionalize professional standards of behavior. These three basic dimensions of professionalism are graphed to illustrate how they might relate to each other, while also providing an arrangement for juxtaposing and comparing the attributes of managers who are currently in the field, but who began their careers at different times and have followed different career paths. In this way, Figure 1.1 attempts to provide a visual representation for considering local government managers not only according to the traditional criteria for professionalism—but also in view of different sets of catalysts for professionalization, as well as in terms of established and changing professional norms.

In the chapters to follow, we will be describing and analyzing in some detail the three dimensions encompassing professionalism within the field of local government management. In order to make comparisons with other research done on other professions—as well as that done on professional local government management—the writer has adopted from Howard Vollmer and Donald Mills's classic collection of case studies and essays on professionalization the following simple terminology. *Profession* will refer to "an ideal type of occupational organization which does not exist in reality, but which provides the model of the form of occupational organization that would result if any occupational group became completely professionalized." The term *professionalization* will be used to refer to "the dynamic process whereby many occupations can be observed to change certain crucial characteristics in the direction of a 'profession,' even though some of these may not move very far in this direction. It follows that these crucial characteristics constitute specifiable criteria of professionalization." *Professionalism* will refer to an "ideology and associated activities that can be found in many and diverse occupational groups where members aspire to professional status." And finally, *professional groups* will "refer to associations of colleagues in an occupational context where we observe that a relatively high degree of professionalization has taken place. 'Professionals,' then, are those who are considered by their colleagues to be members of professional groups."[36] Each of these terms has been used as a way to focus on a particular aspect of local government management; and as a consequence, each identifies the theme and substance of at least one complete chapter.

## THE NEED TO TAKE STOCK

There has been a need for more thorough empirical study of the contemporary world of the professional local government manager. This can be seen in the increasing gap in our understanding about what their current roles, responsibilities, and careers ought to be—and have now come to be—within our nation's communities.[37] New and potentially productive research approaches toward the study of local government management have often been frustrated by a lack of appropriate field data and have—to some extent— apparently been thwarted by the historical dominance of two inhibiting types of questions: (1) Whether a manager in any governmental position should be considered truly and distinctly a professional, especially when contrasted to private sector careers such as physician, attorney, certified public accountant, teacher, and so forth;[38] and (2) whether research in the field should move beyond the current academic penchant for making virtually all empirical research on professional government management a litmus test of the historical arguments for preferring one model of government over another.[39]

The current debate over the accuracy and appropriateness of educational admissions tests and graduation requirements, and the private sector as well as general public concern over the validity of governmental and associational certification or licensing processes (even for the traditionally acclaimed professions), should also raise new questions about the suitability of using any single or simple definition of professionalism to represent a generic standard for all occupations.[40] Changing times require new frameworks of perception, understanding, and solution. New skills and techniques are needed by government managers so that communities can effectively meet their widely varying challenges. But the implications of these changes may be important for the profession's overall public credibility, which may go beyond the practical application of individual specializations and the exercise of historical responsibilities.

Essentially, this study is directed toward: (1) assessing the nature of current and changing professional leadership patterns emanating from different types of local communities; and (2) assessing the role that managers—selected according to specific criteria of education, skill, and experience—have been playing and might play to meet the future. This volume represents the culmination of an interest in documenting the evolution of the local government management profession and in conducting an independent analysis of societal and political influences on the profession during the past decade and a half—utilizing four merged national survey data bases that cover this period.

A secondary goal is to expand and update the historical assessment of the profession done by Richard Stillman in *The Rise of the City Manager* (published in 1974) and the earlier work done by Richard Booth, *Council-Manager Government in Small Cities* (published in 1968). Furthermore, my analysis of the survey information comes midway through the period of projections made by the Horizons 2000 Task Force Committee formed by the ICMA to undertake an assessment of the then current condition of the profession and communities served, and their visions about what the future might hold for both communities and managers by the year 2000. In fact, three of the four surveys analyzed in this study occurred after the committee report was published. The committee began its work in 1978 and completed it the following year. In achieving my own objectives, the focus of the committee study has been expanded (where possible) to include county managers and council-of-government directors—utilizing the revised and expanded ICMA recognition criteria for governments, which now include general managers.

For the author, this volume represents a long-term personal teaching interest (instructional and curricular efforts), a research interest (academic and technical), and a community-service interest (current as well as past federal, state, and local government service). It is the final leg of a three-year research project and agenda, and the culmination of nearly ten years of personal interest in teaching and writing about the field of professional local government management. We shall begin by looking at the personal and professional characteristics of local government managers who were selected for holding the position of city manager or general manager in one of the communities recognized by the ICMA, but who are not necessarily members of the association.

## NOTES

1. James A. Stever, Director, Graduate Program in Public Administration, the University of Cincinnati, letter to the author, November 3, 1987.

2. Ibid.

3. R. Jeffrey Lustig, *Corporate Liberalism: The Origins of American Political Theory 1890–1920* (Berkeley: University of California Press, 1982).

4. Stever letter.

5. Roy E. Green, "Local Government Managers: Styles and Challenges," *Baseline Data Report* 19, no. 2 (Washington, D.C.: International City Management Association, March/April 1987), p. 1.

6. Dennis R. Judd, *The Politics of American Cities: Private Power and Public Policy* (Boston: Little, Brown, 1984), p. 1.

7. Laurence Rutter (for the ICMA Committee on Future Horizons of the Profession), *The Essential Community: Local Government in the Year 2000*, Municipal Management Series (Washington, D.C.: International City Management Association, 1980), p. 127.

8. Stever letter.

9. Katherine L. Bradbury, Anthony Downs, and Kenneth A. Small, *Urban Decline and the Future of American Cities* (Washington, D.C.: Brookings Institution, 1982).

10. Bradbury, Downs, and Small, *Urban Decline*, p. 296.

11. James F. Sullivan and Charles R. Adrian, "Urban Government Research: A View of Three Decades," *National Civic Review* 66, no. 9 (October 1977), p. 438.

12. The difference in conclusion has also separated political scientists. See the contrast between Robert L. Lineberry and Edmund P. Fowler, "Reformism and Public Policies in American Cities," *American Political Science Review* 61, no. 3 (September 1967), pp. 701–16; and David R. Morgan and John P. Pelissero, "Urban Policy: Does Political Structure Matter?" *American Political Science Review* 74, no. 4 (December 1980), p. 1,005.

13. David B. Walker, *Toward a Functioning Federalism* (Boston: Little, Brown, 1981).

14. See John J. Harrigan, *Political Change in the Metropolis*, 3rd ed. (Boston: Little, Brown, 1985), for an excellent review of the research literature on the impact of the U.S.

Supreme Court with regard to the issues of civil rights, the Civil Rights Movement, urban unrest in the 1960s and 1970s, voting rights, and citizen participation.

15. Two of the most important and thought-provoking studies in the area were written by Aaron Wildavsky, *Speaking Truth to Power: The Art and Craft of Policy Analysis* (Boston: Little, Brown, 1979); and Theodore J. Lowi, *The End of Liberalism: The Second Republic of the United States*, 2nd ed. (New York: W. W. Norton, 1979).

16. This argument is the heart of Wildavsky, *Speaking Truth*; and Walker, *Functioning Federalism*.

17. See Lawrence D. Brown, James W. Fossett, and Kenneth T. Palmer, *The Changing Politics of Federal Grants* (Washington, D.C.: Brookings Institution, 1984).

18. See Walker, *Functioning Federalism*; and Brown, Fossett, and Palmer, *Changing Politics*.

19. For a critical assessment of the difference in assumptions and strategies underlying the Carter administration and the Reagan administration approaches to correcting the overburdened federal system, see John L. Palmer and Isable V. Sawhill, eds., *The Reagan Experiment: An Examination of Economic and Social Policies under the Reagan Administration* (Washington, D.C.: Urban Institute Press, 1982).

20. Many of the philosophical goals and rationales for the Reagan administration's first grant-reform proposals were set forward by Claude E. Barfield, in *Rethinking Federalism: Block Grants and Federal, State, and Local Responsibilities* (Washington, D.C.: American Enterprise Institute for Public Policy Research, 1981). The Urban Institute undertook a systematic assessment of domestic reforms during the Reagan administration's first four years in office in a project called the Changing Priorities Project. It contains published reports on housing assistance for older Americans, medicaid, other issues concerning older Americans, wage inflation, federal housing policy in general, state and local fiscal relations in the early 1980s, the deficit dilemma, housing finance, and public opinion during the Reagan administration, among others. For a summary assessment of the first four years of intergovernmental and grants-in-aid reform, see the project's final pre–1984 election report by John L. Palmer and Isable V. Sawhill, eds., *The Reagan Record: An Assessment of America's Changing Domestic Priorities* (Cambridge, Mass.: Ballinger Publishing, 1984).

21. Sullivan and Adrian, "Urban Government Research," p. 443.

22. See Clarence N. Stone, Robert K. Whelan, and William J. Murin, *Urban Policy and Politics in a Bureaucratic Age*, 2nd ed. (Englewood Cliffs, N.J.: Prentice-Hall, 1986); for somewhat different perspectives on how and why the evolution occurred, see also Harrigan, *Change in Metropolis*; and Judd, *Politics of American Cities*.

23. Raymond E. Wolfinger, "Why Political Machines Have Not Withered Away and Other Revisionist Thoughts," *Journal of Politics* 34 (May 1972), pp. 365–98.

24. Ibid.

25. Although much debated and since amended, this argument was most clearly stated in the work by Edward Banfield and James Q. Wilson, *City Politics* (New York: Random House, 1963). For a more recent assessment of the linkage between social mobility and political machines, see Raymond E. Wolfinger, *The Politics of Progress* (Englewood Cliffs, N.J.: Prentice-Hall, 1974).

26. Wolfinger, "Why Political Machines."

27. See Stone, Whelan, and Murin, *Bureaucratic Age*; for somewhat different perspectives on the impacts and results of local government reform and modernization efforts, see also Harrigan, *Change in Metropolis*; and Judd, *Politics of American Cities*.

28. Stone, Whelan, and Murin, *Bureaucratic Age*, p. 112.

29. Ibid., p. 115.

30. Ibid., p. 183.

31. See Richard J. Stillman's *The Rise of the City Manager: A Public Professional in Local Government* (Albuquerque: University of New Mexico Press, 1974), for a systematic review of the schools of thought that have—over time—dominated the preparation, work, and professional associations of public administrators generally, and city managers in particular.

32. Barry Bozeman has identified a number of key issues in this sphere of concern for public management, see his *Public Management and Policy Analysis* (New York: St. Martin's Press, 1979). A very different perspective on these issues has been described in a study undertaken by the information Industry Association; see Forest Woody Horton, Jr., ed., *Understanding U.S. Information Policy: The Information Policy Primer* (Washington, D.C.: Information Industry Association, 1982).

33. Stillman, *Rise of City Manager*, pp. 99–112.

34. For an overview of these concerns within the traditional professions, see Bruce Jennings, Daniel Callahan, and Susan M. Wolf, eds., *The Public Duties of the Professions* (Hastings-on-Hudson, N.Y.: A Hastings Center Report, Special Supplement 17, no. 1, February 1987), and Michael Davis, "The Use of Professions," *Business Economics* 22, no. 4 (October 1987), pp. 5–10.

35. Stever letter.

36. Howard M. Vollmer and Donald L. Mills, *Professionalization* (Englewood Cliffs, N.J.: Prentice-Hall, 1966), pp. vii–viii.

37. A sample of questions concerning what is happening at the community level and to local government managers are included in Dennis F. Thompson, "The Possibility of Administrative Ethics," *Public Administration Review* 45, no. 5 (September/October 1985), pp. 555–61; Phillip J. Cooper, "Conflict or Constructive Tension: The Changing Relationship of Judges and Administrators," *Public Administration Review* 45, Special Issue (November 1985), pp. 643–51; Michael S. Deeb, "Municipal Council Members: Changing Roles and Functions," *National Civic Review* 69, no. 8 (September 1979), pp. 411–16; and Jeff S. Luke, "Finishing the Decade: Local Government to 1990," *State and Local Government Review* 18, no. 3 (Fall 1986), pp. 132–37.

38. There is a current widespread interest in issues associated with professionalism in the public sector; and along with this growth in interest has come an expansion in written commentary. See, for example, Robert T. Golembiewski, "The Pace and Character of Public Sector Professionalization: Six Selected Questions," *State and Local Government Review* 16, no. 2 (Spring 1984), pp. 63–68; David N. Ammons and Joseph C. King, "Professionalism and Local Government Administration," *American Review of Public Administration* 16, no. 4 (Winter 1982), pp. 386–401; Robert B. Denhardt, "Public Administration: Sub-Field? Profession? Discipline?," *American Review of Public Administration* 16, no. 1 (Spring 1982), pp. 15–21; and Garth N. Jones, "Rise and Fall of a Professional Ideal: Particulars Concerning Public Administration," *American Review of Public Administration* 16, no. 4 (Winter 1982), pp. 305–19.

39. See Harry P. Hatry, "Would We Know a Well-Governed City If We Saw One?" *National Civic Review* 75, no. 3 (May/June 1986), pp. 142–46; and David B. Walker, "Intergovernmental Relations and the Well-Governed City: Cooperation, Confrontation, Clarification," *National Civic Review* 75, no. 2 (March/April 1986), pp. 65–87.

40. To compound the issue further, Allan Bloom's book, *The Closing of the American*

*Mind* (New York: Simon and Schuster 1987), goes one step further to criticize most bachelor degree programs as having lost their liberal arts character in lieu of an increasing emphasis on preprofessional preparation—a development that Bloom finds very worrisome. On the other hand, the professions themselves have come under increasing governmental scrutiny for antitrust practices, see—for example—William L. Trombetta, "The Professions under Scrutiny: An Antitrust Perspective," *Journal of Consumer Affairs* 16, no. 1 (Summer 1982), pp. 88–111.

# 2

## RESOURCES OF THE PROFESSION: ITS PEOPLE AND THEIR CAREER PATHS

This chapter describes the range of personal, educational, and occupational career characteristics of the chief administrative officers who are serving in communities recognized by the International City Management Association.[1] The term *recognition* refers to a formal process established by the ICMA for identifying communities that provide a legal framework conducive to the practice of professional management. An essential component of such criteria is that recognized communities must provide for an appointed position of overall professional government management.

Throughout this volume, I refer to professional local government management as encompassing city, village, town, and township managers; county managers; chief administrative officers (CAOs); and executive directors (EDs) of councils-of-government (COGs).[2] Although there are differences between the jobs of these various managers, they are grouped together here because of the common responsibilities that are recognized in the positions by the ICMA. In the latter regard, the ICMA formally recognized in 1969 the similarities between the city manager and the position of CAO by setting forth criteria for an overall general management position, as it was applied first to county government, and then to COGs and leagues.[3] In light of the discussion in Chapter 1, it is worth noting that in recent years substantial discussion has been occurring within the ICMA over the purposes and consequences of identifying communities with city managers or general managers versus identifying or recognizing the positions of city management or general management without direct reference to form of government. This discussion concerns the basic mission of the association and how it will view local government management as a profession. We will look more closely at some of the issues associated with this discussion in Chapter 5.

In Chapter 2, the focus will be on the chief administrative officers serving in the recognized communities. I will utilize them as a reference group composed of managers who would most likely be considered by themselves and by others with similar positions or responsibilities to be professionals and colleagues. It is important for the reader to bear in mind that the focus on this group does not imply that they are statistically or otherwise representative of all full-time, appointed local government managers (let alone citizen, part-time, or elected managers). Nor does this volume's focus indicate any special status for the group being analyzed other than as the common reference group mentioned above.

In this regard, a careful review of the research literature suggests that such an approach is reasonable and is shared by many other students whose interests focus on the development of professions. That is, when researchers are comparing professional status across vocational groups, "managers serving in ICMA-recognized jurisdictions" is the government service occupation most frequently cited as being the most professionally developed.[4] At first glance, this may seem to be a case of the drunk man looking for his dropped keys under a lamp post merely because the light is located there. In reality, however, we are looking at these particular managers not only because there is some light where they are (in the form of longitudinal survey information), but also because we feel that at least some of the keys concerning professionalism in local government management can in fact be found there. They are an important reference group.

A good deal of direct evidence for the analysis in this chapter—and most of the chapters that follow—will be based on my independent assessment of manager characteristics as they were manifested in a series of CAO surveys conducted by the ICMA in 1973–74, 1980, and 1984. These data will be supplemented with the responses from two surveys conducted separately by the author as part of an academic team in the years 1978 and 1986–87. In the latter studies, only a 50 percent sample of the ICMA-recognized communities were surveyed.

Table 2.1 arrays the cumulative distribution of U.S. municipalities and U.S. counties by population group, by geographic region, and by metropolitan status as abstracted from the *1984 U.S. Census of Governments*.[5] This distribution of municipal and county governments allows us to make a comparison with ICMA's enumeration of recognized municipalities and counties. We can see from the table that ICMA's list of recognized governments includes a little more than one-third of all counties and municipalities counted by the U.S. Census Bureau as having populations above 2,500.

Table 2.1 also illustrates what the typical response-rate pattern is for an ICMA-directed CAO survey (sent to a 100-percent sample of recognized governments). In the specific instance of the 1984 study, the overall response was 63.8 percent. For all three of the ICMA surveys—as well as for both Green–Reed surveys included in this analysis—the response rate never dropped below 50 percent of the mailed sample. This high rate of response was present regardless of the geographic region of the country, the metropolitan location of the government, the form of government recognized, or the population size of the jurisdiction (with a single survey exception for those recognized communities with less than 2,500 population, and another exception for the representative town meeting form of government). The survey-based analyses below represent responses from at least a 15-percent sampling of the Census Bureau's total enumeration of county and municipal governments (with over 2,500 population). Appendix A provides a more complete summary of the survey response-rate patterns for the surveys used in this study. This appendix also includes a description of how the survey responses were matched by community identification number—making selective longitudinal comparisons of individual manager responses possible between the surveys. For this important reference group of professional managers from U.S. local-level government, the data allow us to discuss with confidence a broad range of important topics.

## THE USE AND DUTIES OF PUBLIC PROFESSIONALS

The use and duties of professions and how they come to serve the public interest are ethical and functional matters. These matters are associated with how professionals utilize the particular expertise that defines their field. Let us assume for the moment that such a distinctive field of expertise does exist for general managers in local governments. Michael Davis of the Center for the Study of Ethics in the Professions at the Illinois Institute of Technology makes explicit the distinction between the narrow welfare of professionals themselves or their associated group interests, and the general welfare—which "refers (more or less) to a certain number of individuals voluntarily organized (primarily) to benefit others by assuring that those so organized will provide a certain service in a certain way."[6] Davis observes that, in a perfect market, professions would be pointless because all market participants would be rational, fully informed, and fairly endowed with resources.

Noting—however—that the marketplace for various types of expertise is rarely perfect, Davis argues,

Information is often hard to get, unevenly distributed, or difficult to digest. And perhaps just as important, most markets impose significant costs on "third parties." . . . These facts often are appealed to in order to justify regulating the market. Because professions are just another means of regulating the market, these facts also may be appealed to in order to justify professions. Or, at least, they may be if it can be shown that we are better off with a profession than with new laws.[7]

Davis was using economically rigorous concepts to focus on the role of the marketplace in distributing various types of professional expertise. The thrust of his argument was that, as our society has grown more complicated, the need for professionals who can digest, translate, and utilize various strategic skills and knowledge bases on the public's behalf has grown, as well. This need for experts who can understand a complicated subject matter, accurately recast its essence for others holding different frames of reference, and propose and ad-

**Table 2.1**
**Cumulative Distribution of U.S. Municipalities, Counties, and ICMA-recognized Jurisdictions with the CAO Survey Response, 1984**

| | All Cities | All Counties | All "Recognized" Governments* (including Cities, Counties & COGs) | | |
| --- | --- | --- | --- | --- | --- |
| | | | No. Surveyed (A) | No. Responding | % of (A) |
| Total | 6976 | 3041 | 3697 | 2360 | 63.8 |
| **POPULATION GROUP:** | | | | | |
| (1) Over 1,000,000 | 6 | 20 | 30 | 21 | 70.0 |
| (2) 500,000 - 1,000,000 | 17 | 48 | 50 | 31 | 62.0 |
| (3) 250,000 - 499,999 | 34 | 88 | 77 | 54 | 70.0 |
| (4) 100,000 - 249,999 | 113 | 218 | 173 | 112 | 64.7 |
| (5) 50,000 - 99,999 | 278 | 374 | 247 | 169 | 68.4 |
| (6) 25,000 - 49,999 | 613 | 611 | 436 | 307 | 70.4 |
| (7) 10,000 - 24,999 | 1532 | 957 | 911 | 611 | 67.1 |
| (8) 5,000 - 9,999 | 1739 | 448 | 793 | 510 | 64.3 |
| (9) 2,500 - 4,999 | 2271 | 176 | 605 | 358 | 59.2 |
| (10) Under 2,500** | 373 | 101 | 375 | 187 | 49.9 |
| **GEOGRAPHIC REGION:** | | | | | |
| (1) Northeast | 1948 | 196 | 802 | 454 | 56.6 |
| (2) North Central | 2021 | 1051 | 879 | 634 | 72.1 |
| (3) South | 2046 | 1376 | 1219 | 731 | 60.0 |
| (4) West | 961 | 418 | 797 | 541 | 67.9 |

**METRO STATUS: MUNICIPALITIES**

| | | | | | |
|---|---|---|---|---|---|
| (1) Central | 431 | (NA) | 327 | 245 | 74.9 |
| (2) Suburban | 3690 | (NA) | 1730 | 1117 | 64.6 |
| (3) Independent | 2855 | (NA) | 1328 | 821 | 61.8 |

**METRO STATUS: COUNTIES**

| | | | | | |
|---|---|---|---|---|---|
| (1) Metro | (NA) | 673 | 137 | 86 | 62.8 |
| (2) Nonmetro | (NA) | 2368 | 101 | 58 | 57.4 |

**FORM OF GOVERNMENT:**

| | | | | | |
|---|---|---|---|---|---|
| (1) Mayor - Council | 3776 | (NA) | 724 | 457 | 63.1 |
| (2) Council - Manager | 2523 | (NA) | 2425 | 1578 | 65.1 |
| (3) Commission | 177 | (NA) | 21 | 11 | 52.4 |
| (4) Town Meeting | 419 | (NA) | 124 | 74 | 59.7 |
| (5) Rep. Town Meeting | 81 | (NA) | 21 | 11 | 52.4 |
| (6) With County Administ. | (NA) | 643 | 238 | 144 | 60.5 |
| (7) County W/out Administ. | (NA) | 2398 | (NA) | (NA) | (NA) |

*Limited to municipalities recognized by the International City Management Association as providing for the council-manager plan or providing for a position of overall general management.

*Source:* This table was constructed by the author from "Inside the Year Book," *Municipal Year Book 1985* (Washington, D.C.: International City Management Association, 1985), Tables 3 and 4, pp. xvii, xviii, and from Mary Schellinger, "Local Government Managers: Profile of the Professionals in a Maturing Profession," *Municipal Year Book 1985* (Washington, D.C.: International City Management Association, 1958), Table 1.1, p. 182.

minister the resulting governmental policies and programs in that environment suggests that—over time—there will be an inevitable increase in the level of CAO responsibilities. Other analysts, however, insist that increasing—or at the least changing—particular expertise requirements can also lead to knowledge and skill substitution or replacement. Change in expertise in this occupational context may be changing the nature of the job itself—and perhaps away from the values associated with the existing profession.

The crux of the matter—then—is to distinguish (using the data at hand) between the delegation of managerial responsibilities that stems from the availability of various types of expertise (often called *specialization*), and the culture-driven expansion in required types of expertise (via continuing professional education) that may result in a greater sharing of responsibilities. From the perspective of the general welfare, the prerogatives associated with professional status are derived from a legitimate need on the part of the public to receive services (provided and utilized in a fair and equitable manner) based on a level of knowledge and skills that may not otherwise be available to them as members of a community. In return, professionals can expect to be ''shielded from pressures that otherwise might lead them to take advantage of those they serve, and protect third parties from undesirable externalities.''[8]

On the other hand, Bruce Jennings—an associate for policy studies at the Hastings Center—draws an important distinction separating the public duties of the traditional professions from those in public administration. He contends that public administrators share with other professions an obligation to use their expertise to serve both the good of the community as a whole and the well-being of individual members of the community.

But in public administration this obligation takes on a special form and character. To a greater degree than other professionals, public administrators are responsible for the integrity and legitimate functioning of the process through which the common good is collectively defined. Other professions should serve the community; public administration must serve the community of communities.[9]

Davis had been referring to the growing influence that all professions are inheriting as a consequence of their knowledge-based, strategic position in an ever more complex society. Jennings, however, was profiling an important difference between the extensiveness of the public duties required from public administrators and from their private-sector counterparts. On the other hand, Barry Bozeman captured a third and crucial dimension of the comparison—linking public administration with the traditional professions, while at the same time recognizing its uniqueness. Bozeman—a well-known information management specialist—examined the nature and utility of the expertise required by public managers, and noted,

One of the implications of change and complexity for the public manager is that there will be a built-in obsolescence in any training or education for public administration. It is not clear how one might best cope with this problem: perhaps in-service training and development programs, perhaps periodic retooling in some educational institution, perhaps we will simply depend on the individual's ability to grow with the job. But we can be pretty sure that today's skills will rarely equip the public manager to deal with a wide spectrum of tomorrow's challenges. The best approach to encourage adaptability may be to avoid dogma. . . . Public managers must collect concepts, theories, and experiences and apply them in unique combinations to pressing problems. This is the art of public administration, and future shock will not reduce the need for that art.[10]

It would seem that professional expertise brings with it particular assumptions as to its use. The legitimate exercise of expertise can be recognized through a determination of how, when, where, and why it is used. In fact, George Strauss has delineated the four basic values of *expertise*, *autonomy*, *commitment*, and *responsibility* as summarizing professionalism for any field. I would suggest that the last three values are associated with use of the first.[11] This distinction between expertise and the values associated with its use (autonomy, commitment, and responsibility) requires that an inquiry be made into what the profession's particular specialities, skills, techniques, knowledge, or experience are and how they might be characterized for public administration in general, and for local government management in particular.

The basic inquiry then raises two subissues of concern to those who contend that the public administrator—and, in particular, the professionally high-profile reference group of managers serving in ICMA-recognized communities—are in fact professionals. In the first instance, a question can be raised as to whether there is indeed a unique body of knowledge, skills, or expertise that can be attributed to public managers as they are currently found in the field. The second question is whether—in Jennings's words—''[public administration] needs a clearer conception of its proper ethical mission in a democracy, and a new language for articulating that conception and for interpreting it in concrete cases and practical dilemmas.'' As Jennings contends,

Duties, values, and the ends of the profession tend to be overwhelmed by a concentration on instrumental techniques and professional means. Public administrators readily analyze their own behavior and that of their peers in terms of bureaucratic constraints and political pressures; they are less accustomed to thinking in terms of the values that are internal to, or constitutive of, the practice of their profession.[12]

In later chapters, I will investigate more fully some of the major ethical constraints involved in public administration. For the moment, let us focus on the substantive issues of expertise in local government management. From this perspective, I will consider elected local officials and the government apparatus (the civil service) to be the most directly affected consumers of manager expertise. It is for this professional capacity—this expertise—that communities compete with each other when they select their local government managers.

Figure 2.1 helps us to visualize managers in this qualitative context by moving

**Figure 2.1**
**Career Pathways of Professional Local Government Managers**

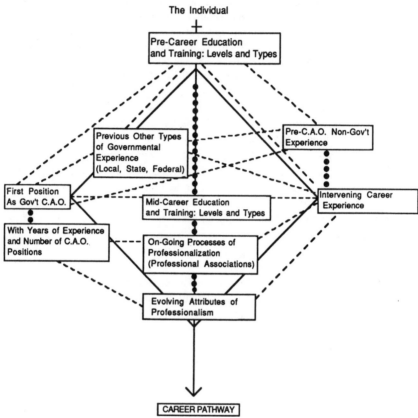

us closer to the career experience of the individual manager. Figure 1.1—by contrast—depicted an overview of local government management as an occupational field within an overall framework of professionalism (see Chapter 1). Figure 2.1 outlines the major occupational pathways associated with local government managers during the course of their careers. Its objective is to identify various types of career-impacting events and choices in a way that may suggest explanations for the variations in behaviors and attitudes reported by local government managers during their careers.

## PROFILING THE MANAGERS: GROUP NORMS AND CAREER PATHWAYS

Attempts have been made at different times during the past three-quarters of a century to draw a profile of the typical city manager based on prevailing characteristics. For example in the 1930s, the first extensive survey of city managers was undertaken by Clarence E. Ridley and Orin F. Nolting.[13] This was followed in 1964 by one of the first major comprehensive studies conducted by the International City Management Association.[14] There are, however, a number of more timely and comprehensive national survey efforts available to us. They include studies conducted by Richard Stillman (also referred to as the "Maxwell School survey" in some reports) in 1971; by the ICMA in 1973–74, 1980, and 1984; and jointly by the author with B. J. Reed in 1978 and 1986–87.

By the mid–1980s the average local government manager surveyed could be characterized as being

a white male getting ready for his forty-third birthday. He got his bachelor's degree, worked for a while, and then went back to school to get an advanced degree. He is married and a member of the Democratic party. He's been in his current position just about four and a half years, but has been in the profession just over nine years. He took a break between his first and second manager jobs.[15]

However, over the past decade and a half of national survey research, the profile characteristics of the professional local-government manager have changed in a number of important ways. Managers have gotten somewhat younger as a group from the time of the 1973–74 survey (43 years) to the 1984 survey (41.6 years)—while at the same time the proportion of very young managers under 30 has been somewhat reduced, with "88% of the managers responding to the 1984 survey [being] between the ages of 30 and 60." The number of women in the profession has increased from 1 percent of the managers in recognized communities in 1971 to 3 percent in 1980 and up to 5 percent by 1984—while the percentage of married managers has somewhat decreased from 96 percent in 1973–74 to 91 percent in 1980, and was reported to be down to 89 percent in 1984 (a rate still substantially above the national average). While there continues to be a slight tendency for managers with partisan preferences to identify with the Democratic party, there has been a substantial increase since the 1973–74 survey in the proportion of managers describing themselves to be independent (37 percent in 1973–74, 45 percent in 1980, and 47 percent in 1984). Generally, there have been only marginal shifts in the racial composition (about 1 percent were from the total of the African American, Native American, and Asian American groups).[16] And while the number of ICMA-recognized local governments has increased from 3,326 entities in 1978 to 4,027 (including cities, counties, COGs, and leagues) by the end of 1986, their metropolitan status (central city, suburb, and rural), regional distributions, and sizes of populations served has remained proportionately stable across the nation.[17]

It is in the educational and career patterns of these local-government managers where the most dramatic, fundamental, and professionally significant changes have occurred. The Stillman study of 1971 reported that 69 percent of the surveyed managers had bachelor's or master's degrees.[18] By the time of the 1974

ICMA survey, 76 percent reported having a bachelor's or master's degree—which has since risen to a reported 88 percent at the time of ICMA's 1984 study. Most impressively, "of that figure, 30% hold bachelor's degrees, 57% hold master's degrees, and 1% hold doctorates." But—equally important in terms of career development patterns—more than one-fourth (27 percent) of the managers reported in 1984 that they had obtained their master's degree after the age of 30.[19]

Also significant is the tabulation of academic majors for the highest level of education completed by the time of the 1984 ICMA survey. Sixty-five percent of responding managers with at least a bachelor's degree reported their majors to be in public management, administration, or planning. Another 13.3 percent majored in politics, government, or history; while 10.3 percent identified business or accounting as their areas of specialization (untabled responses). When majors were tabulated exclusively for managers with master's degrees, the 1986–87 Green–Reed survey revealed that 75.6 percent of the respondents had identified a concentration in public administration. The fields of political science and urban studies (when combined) was identified by another 5.1 percent, while business represented 2.6 percent. No other major was identified in either the 1984 or 1986–87 surveys as representing two or more percent of the respondents.[20]

While the data in Table 2.2 categorize college majors somewhat differently, we can clearly see that substantial change has taken place during the past 50 years in the managers' areas of specialization (at the bachelor degree level). This increase in reported majors is associated with the development and growth of public administration as a separate academic discipline, and with the concomitant growth in programs and degrees available from a widening array of U.S. colleges and universities. In this latter regard, the *1984 Directory: Programs in Public Affairs and Administration, A Survey Report of the Member Institutions of NAS-PAA,* published by the National Association of Schools of Public Affairs and Administration (NASPAA), reports that approximately one-third (32 percent) to one-fourth (23 percent) of all graduates with a master's degree during the years 1977 to 1983 have been placed in local governments.[21]

As one might expect, there are substantial majorities of local government administrators with bachelor's and master's degrees who have concentrated their academic preparation in the field of public administration. This proportion becomes even higher when the separate—but historically associated—fields of political science, government, and urban studies are included. Including these latter groups in with the aggregate schooling in public administration is not without some merit. Many smaller institutions of higher education do not offer separate degrees in public administration, but do offer course work in the field under the substantively associated programs of political science, government, urban studies, and even history.[22]

These reports of a steady rise in the achievement of advanced degrees should also be viewed within the context of the managers' job tenure and mobility histories. The mixture of study and work experience is an ingredient that most

**Table 2.2**
**Undergraduate College Majors**

| MAJOR FIELDS | 1974 ICMA Survey | 1971 Maxwell Survey | 1964 ICMA Survey | 1934 Ridley-Nolting Survey |
|---|---|---|---|---|
| Liberal arts.................. | 4% | 39% * | 4% | 6% |
| Engineering.................. | 18 | 33 | 32 | 77 |
| Public administration........ | 11 | 12 | 40 * | 3 |
| Political science............ | 34 | ... ** | ... ** | ... ** |
| Business administration...... | 14 | 14 | 13 | ... ** |
| Agriculture.................. | 1 | 2 | ... ** | ... ** |

*Includes political science.
**Data not reported or not applicable.

*Source:* Laurie S. Frankel and Carol A. Pigeon, "Municipal Managers and Chief Administrative Officers: A Statistical Profile,"
*Urban Data Service Report* 7, no. 2 (February 1975), Table 12, p. 8.

professions consider important, and is often formally required as an internship in many college professional credentialling programs. Changes in the nature of the mix—as part of the formal education process, and as part of career development pathways—can often indicate fundamental changes in the evolution of a profession.

The 1984 ICMA survey indicated that, on average, managers had served in their current positions for 5.4 years. But length of tenure tends to be highly associated with size of community served and the age of the manager. The responses from the 1984 survey indicated that more than two-thirds (71 percent) of the managers were in their current positions for less than six years (35 percent for two years or less) and that "the percentage of managers age 30 or less who have been in their current jobs for [only] 1 or 2 years is just over five and a half times greater than the percentage of managers 60 or over who have been in their position for that amount of time." As one might expect, when age and years of experience in the field increase, so does the average length of tenure. But of special interest is that 91 percent of the managers responding to the 1984 survey indicated that, while they had served in three or fewer positions, the average tenure for the first position was consistently shorter than the average tenure for later career appointments.[23]

There are a number of key personnel and occupational factors that may be part of the career development process explaining this pattern. For many, the desire for in-service upward occupational mobility may conflict with an immediate desire to complete a graduate degree. Again, data from the NASPAA survey report of member institutions strongly suggests this to be the case. The report notes that "the percentage of pre-service, on-campus and male students have increased" during the period 1979 through 1983; but it also reports that, on average, two-thirds of those enrolled in graduate programs are reported to be in-service and part-time while attending classes.[24] It is not inconsequential, however, that most graduate course work is offered only on the central campus of the college or university. How managers resolve the dilemma over sequencing these two career choices may become increasingly associated with the rate and course of an individual's career development.

One important explanation for the linkage between education and career path was offered by ICMA's director for research, Mary Schellinger. She observed,

Whether it is the recent emphasis on advanced degrees [by the hiring community officials] or the radical changes in the way governments do business that has driven managers back to school to learn new skills, many managers have earned their advanced degrees at an age that is beyond the traditional age for a student going straight through school without a work break between degrees.[25]

Equally significant from the individual manager's perspective may be the possibility that his or her first experience with—or position in—public service (as CAO or otherwise) or else a new awareness or concern over professional security and mobility may also serve to motivate the manager to seek additional academic training and credentials.

The timing and source of entry and reentry into the field of full-time local government management represents a significant aspect of manager career development patterns. There are trends, but no single route appears to dominate. These multiple career pathways, however, have also been commonly associated with a lack of professionalism in the field. A recent report from the 1986–87 Green–Reed survey outlined the most typical pathways taken by chief administrative officers for entry into the field:

Responses from . . . [the] survey indicate that approximately 38% had either been an assistant manager or a department head before advancing. . . . Twenty-six percent had made basically horizontal moves [from non–ICMA recognized community positions, or from other levels of government], 15% from the private sector (private/profit making and consultant). . . . Fully 77% of the respondents had at least some government experience prior to becoming a manager. This [proportion] increases to almost 85% if military and education experience are added.[26]

As the most likely occupational points of entry, the above represent a substantial shift from the findings of earlier published research. One report written in 1971 indicated that only 29 percent of the survey respondents had been employed in "government service" prior to entering (city) management.[27]

The 1986–87 Green–Reed survey pattern also indicated that important changes had occurred from the time of the 1971 national-sample survey administered by Richard Stillman. Respondents to the Stillman questionnaire reported that nearly one-half (47 percent) of the managers had come directly from a business occupation.[28] The 1986–87 survey respondents indicated that only about 15 percent had come directly from business. Based on the 1986–87 study, we were able to conclude that, "increasingly, applied local experience is required for most positions of chief administrative officer, in practice if not by governmental policy. Horizontal entry, even when substantial managerial experience has been gained in some other nonlocal governmental capacity, seems to be declining."[29] This evolution of premanager pathways seems to be increasingly dominated by those who have made specific preparations for public service careers.

One of the most professionally suggestive response patterns revealed by the 1986–87 survey data surfaced when managers were queried about their alternative career interests.

[Only] 17% of [the] respondents chose "other government service" as an alternative occupational preference . . . only 21% so indicated when purely "political" positions were considered as an additional option, reaching a modest total of only one-third (34%) if teaching were added as an alternative. These figures remained equal to those that [had been] obtained in [the] 1978 survey of city managers.[30]

We concluded after reviewing the preferences from both the 1978 and the 1986–87 surveys that most managers (nearly two-thirds of those reporting at each time) would not seriously consider an alternative position in the public sector if they were to opt out of being the CAO for a local government. However, what we did find was that, "consistent with results from [the] 1978 survey, the 1986–87 respondents indicated a very strong preference for an alternative career in business . . . (58% if you add consulting as a separate entrepreneurial activity)."[31]

Responses from this reference group of local government managers seems to indicate clearly that they feel being a chief administrative officer for a community represents a significant—perhaps the pinnacle—professional and career achievement in government service. As a measure of esprit de corps, these responses evoke a sense of strong professional and occupational commitment. The responses also suggest that, if these CAOs were to consider leaving the profession, it would most often mean to leave public service altogether in order to pursue a substantially different set of occupational goals. This pattern toward business and industry, however, may represent more than just an occupational coincidence resulting from the local government manager's work experience with the private sector.

The 1984 NASPAA survey report of member institutions indicates that "the placement figures for master's graduates in the *1984 Directory* are relatively stable except for Local Government, which shows a decline, while Business and Other [or unclassified] categories show increases." The latter's placement figures are up from 8 percent to 12 percent for business and industrial placement and up from 1 percent to 16 percent for the unclassified positions, while local government placements are currently down 9 percent from their reported high of 32 percent in 1979 and 1981. The placement of M.P.A. (master's degree in public affairs/administration) graduates in local government positions still represents the single largest category of employment (at 23 percent); but, as alternatives, unclassified and business or industry placements run only slightly behind the state and national government placements (at 17 percent each) by 1 percent and 5 percent, respectively.[32]

For M.P.A. graduates (recalling that well over one-half of the managers serving in ICMA-recognized governments have a master's degree, and three-quarters of those have M.P.A. degrees), the increasing marketability of their degrees in the private sector currently represents an alternative career-growth sector. From the marketplace perspective, the need for additional government managers seems likely to remain at significant—but relatively constant—levels as long as government staff sizes remain around their current levels. This projection includes current turnover rates as well as the increases due to any growth in newly authorized positions. Therefore, there is reason to believe that, for those interested in a career in local government, the marketplace will increasingly require managers (in the smaller communities as well as in the larger) to have an advanced college degree. And if current trends continue, that degree will increasingly be the master's in public affairs/administration.[33]

## ACADEMIA, EDUCATIONAL UTILITY, AND PROFESSIONALISM

What individuals interested in public service careers actually receive—and what they should receive—from their academic preparation has been and continues to be an intensely discussed set of issues. Important differences are present among and between practitioners and scholars in the field. David Ammons and Joseph King—two interested and well-informed local public officials—have summarized the current critical arguments questioning the substance and lack of uniformity in the educational preparation of local CAOs. Ammons and King note,

Administrators come from a wide range of educational backgrounds. Increasing numbers have a graduate degree, but those degrees are earned in a variety of fields and for about one-half of all administrators, the maximum educational attainment remains a bachelor's degree. Many managers are educated in public administration, a field that is difficult to equate with the study of law and medicine in terms of specialized theory and knowledge. In fact, as more managers move toward public administration for preparation, they increasingly abandon the study of civil engineering—the academic base of many of their predecessors—with its specialized theory and knowledge. Despite growing exposure of the occupation as a whole to programs of public administration, many city managers have taken different preparatory routes to their management posts, making it difficult to contend that the education of local government managers is standardized.[34]

A competing viewpoint to that offered by Ammons and King is argued by R. Richard Riggs of the Kansas Corporation Commission. Riggs contends that

while requiring PA practitioners to absorb the available knowledge is a feature absent from the current scene . . . there seems little doubt that a distinct body of inquiry labelled "Public Administration" does, in fact, exist. This is not a self-evident fact. . . . Some authors see the lack of curricula consensus among schools of public administration as indication that . . . there is no base of specialized knowledge. This argument, though, leads more reasonably to the conclusion that—far from there not being enough knowledge to sustain a profession—there is in fact so much knowledge and so many paradigms and frames of reference, that it is merely cataloging and organization of the available data which remain to be done.[35]

Still another point of view toward these concerns is represented by a team of European academicians who visited 13 U.S. universities in 1980. They selected institutions, public affairs and administration departments, and schools thought to be representative of the breadth and diversity of programs offered in the United States. As a subgroup of U.S. universities, however, the institutions that they chose to visit represented some of the most prestigious centers of higher education in the nation. Their intention was to "see and judge for [themselves] the immense training effort undertaken by American Universities for the Civil Service."[36] For our purposes, their observations represent an alternative and independent viewpoint—separate from any vested domestic interest.

At each institution, these European public administrationists interviewed deans, professors, and students, and reviewed the evolution of curricula and programs. In line with what my own survey of the literature had previously suggested,[37] they confirmed that

public training in the USA is far from being a single, fixed model but is varied and continually being questioned. [The] courses most frequently offered [are] of the following types: Theory and behaviour of organization, administration and public management; analysis of public policies, finance and public accountancy, City and State problems, quantitative methods, economic science.[38]

But this team of European scholars also determined that public administration is not a discipline in the sense that political science or economics is considered to be: "It is rather an applied social science and must be continually renewed by findings coming from all such sciences, and others as well, even including Geography and Anthropology." They viewed the plurality of programs as a "continuing and highly effective process of continuous redefinition of curricula which is peculiar to American universities."[39] And the Europeans seemed to infer that wisdom could be found in this diversity; they concurred with an interview comment made by the well-known public administrationist Aaron Wildavsky, who said, "There are many lessons to be drawn from the condition underlying these experiments and the ensuing consequences. The key, for judging schools for Public Affairs [in the United States] is to be found in attentive comparisons, not in concentration on a single model."[40] Wildavsky's view makes clear reference to an increasingly important role in the marketplace for professionals with training from the various university public affairs/administration programs.

On October 3, 1986, the Council on Postsecondary Accreditation (COPA) Board granted to NASPAA recognition as a specialized agency for accrediting master's degree programs in public affairs/administration. No other agency had ever been approved as the accrediting body for M.P.A. programs before that date. Accreditation in the United States is a system for recognizing educational institutions and professional programs for levels of performance, integrity, and quality. This process certifies programs that meet a standardized degree of confidence—set by the appropriate educational community—for the use and benefit of the publics that they serve. The authority to accredit M.P.A. programs—little noted outside most university circles—represents a substantive as well as symbolic step toward meeting the traditional criterion of professionalism for standardizing educational preparation.[41]

However, it is one of the unique and significant features of the United States that accreditation of educational institutions and professional programs is extended primarily through nongovernmental and voluntary institutional or professional associations. In Europe, program accreditation is most often extended through the national government or one of its agencies.[42] One major objective of the nongovernmental accreditation process in the United States is to allow the marketplace to have a direct influence on the kinds of professional expertise being produced. This arrangement attempts to be sensitive to the needs of the general and specific publics who will be served, as well as benefiting individuals within the profession who meet its qualifications.

In the specific case of the M.P.A. programs, it is NASPAA that applied for and was recognized as the accrediting agency. The accrediting process requires institutions and programs to examine their goals, activities, and achievements; to consider the expert criticism and suggestions of a visiting team; and to determine internal procedures by acting on recommendations from the accrediting body. Accreditation status is reviewed on a periodic basis. In this case, M.P.A. programs are to be reviewed at least once every seven years. As it stands today, all accredited M.P.A. programs must offer course work in at least the following common curriculum components: political and legal institutions and processes; economic and social institutions and processes; organization and management concepts, including human resource administration; concepts and techniques of financial administration; techniques of analysis, including quantitative, economic, and statistical methods; and an internship program.[43]

However, within this required framework, there is retained by the individual institution considerable flexibility as to the particular substance and viewpoints covered. Likewise, individual institutional prerogatives in areas of program specialization or concentration (for example, in local government management) are protected; and in fact, diversity and program experimentation beyond the core components are encouraged. The NASPAA Standards also require program sensitivity to the variety of students seeking admission to and graduation from the M.P.A. program. That is to say, M.P.A. programs are to develop their program objectives with a view to serving pre-service, in-service, full-time, and part-time students.[44]

Joseph Uveges conducted a study of the impacts of NASPAA's voluntary standards and peer review process for a ten-year period (1975–85). This ten-year period preceded the association's recognition as the official accrediting agency for M.P.A. programs. Uveges surveyed 202 NASPAA member institutions that offered master's-level degrees in public affairs and administration, and received 104 useable responses. Questions were raised about each of the six major topical sections corresponding to the NASPAA Standards: program jurisdiction, curriculum, faculty, student qualifications and services, supportive services, and off-campus programs.

In sum, Uveges concluded,

If the intent of those who developed and promoted the use of the MPA Standards was to have an impact upon the curriculum of master's level programs in public affairs and administration, and to provide support for the increase in program autonomy necessary to provide direction to public administration education, they have had some success. In these two areas the Standards are perceived to have had some impact and to have been of some benefit to NASPAA members. However, the intensity level of the impacts perceived [by those responding to the survey] is relatively low, perhaps indicating a degree of caution and concern at the program level resulting in a selective use of those portions of the Standards most helpful to meeting program needs and most amenable to solution within the resource and power capabilities of those programs.[45]

While some changes have been made in the M.P.A. standards as well as the peer review process, the Uveges report indicated that standardization of program structure, process, and curriculum was developing even before there was an official accreditation process.

Significant as the NASPAA/M.P.A accreditation process may come to be, we must still acknowledge that—by definition—local government managers are not required by law or any professional association policy to possess an advanced, specific degree. Nevertheless, the CAO survey information that we have been reviewing clearly indicates that the trend toward more education—and specifically, in the field of public administration—is likely to continue among at least this well-respected reference group of local government managers. And this trend is likely to continue despite what Ammons and King see as the unfortunate preference of managers toward educational preparation in the field of public administration. Their explanation for the trend is that,

simply because city councils increasingly expect managers to have a graduate degree, more managers expect their assistants and department heads to be so educated (and those are the routes to the top for many managers), and perhaps because young persons desiring to excel in administration perceive an association between education and excellence.[46]

## PROFESSIONAL LITERACY: ANOTHER VIEWPOINT ON EDUCATIONAL UTILITY

What does it mean to be literate as a professional in today's world? The increasing proportion of professional local government managers with advanced college degrees, and the growth in public administration as their preferred—or at least elected—concentration, represent a long-term trend of major import. Perhaps echoing the message of E. D. Hirsch's book, *Cultural Literacy: What Every American Needs to Know*,[47] the survey evidence suggests that communities and their elected officials are coming to expect from their chief administrative officers increasingly higher professional qualifications. These qualifications may be viewed as a desire or an attempt by managers as well as communities to secure the type of professional literacy that is associated with advanced collegiate degrees. The national standardization of M.P.A. program performance, integrity, and quality is an attempt to move in that direction.

By adapting the notion of "literacy," I mean to suggest that *professional*

*literacy* and its standardization are the acquired capacities or abilities to understand the context of the more precise and technical information associated with
current and changing occupational responsibilities. This standardization of assumed knowledge is crucial to sharing and using information and innovation in
an increasingly complex social, economic, technological, and political community environment.

However, the move toward greater professionalism in the overall field of local
government management should not be taken to mean that all communities desire
or have the same need for professional management—nor for the same type
(skills, experience, and knowledge) of professional manager. One need only
consider the recent explosion in the para- and semi-professions in medicine, law,
and even the ministry to see variations within the marketplace of expertise,
expectation, and cost. By the same token, the diversity and variety in the desire
for professionalism in local government management should not be taken to
mean that there is no such thing as a profession within the field of local government management. If members of a profession are continually involved in a
process of adapting to needs and dilemmas by acquiring new skills, experience,
and knowledge (professionalization) in order to maintain a professional level of
performance (professionalism), then all professions are perpetually in pursuit of
an evolving ideal.

In this regard, the issues associated with who, how, and when licensing or
certification (and relicensing or recertification) of professionals are most usefully
discussed in terms of the public's as well as the profession's interests. Many
current concerns over certification are associated with the nature and substance
of the procedures, and are now extensively and often critically being reviewed
within some of the most widely recognized and traditionally established occupations of medicine, accounting, the law, elementary and secondary education,
and even the ministry.[48] For occupations within the public sector, the issues
present many dilemmas—too numerous and complex to discuss in detail here.

But at least one significant point should be made with regard to the traditional
requirement that professionals pass some type of licensing or certification examination. The corollary to this convention is that certification must be through
a centralized and standardized procedure. Here I mean "traditional requirement"
in the sense that the professions of medicine, law, and the ministry—among
others—have long since established licensing or certification processes to control
entry and to maintain qualifications within their fields. I am also using "conventional" in the sense that scholarship on the development of professions has
regarded this precedent of licensing as a criterion. It is much easier for the
academic observer—and maybe for the general public—to recognize such a
centralized procedure if it is administered either by the government or else by
an agency or association recognized by the government. But the essence of any
licensing or certification process is not whether it is centralized—but whether it
is present, enforceable, and standardized in practice. Officially recognized licensing procedures may not always be an accurate surrogate criterion useful for

identifying an occupation that has developed to the point of functioning as a genuine profession.

The essence of licensing and certification is a concern over the measurement of expertise. This concern typically takes form through a dual focus on competency and performance. Determinations or expectations for competency and performance of CAOs in local governments lend themselves only partially to written or independently examinable criteria (one form of standardization) that, at the same time, can be reviewed by an authority outside the individual communities served (that is, centralization). This discussion should not be construed, however, as meaning that there is no need for professionals in the field. Nor should it be construed as meaning that there is inadequate expertise to be mastered, nor a recognizable profession already operating in the field.

External sources of accountability imposed on local government managers include a wide range of provisions from federal and state constitutions and statutes, various intergovernmental agreements and programs, as well as local ordinances and codes. One way or another, CAOs are either sworn to uphold or are nonetheless legally bound to comport with a substantial and complex array of standards for competency and performance of professional duties. These include fiduciary, bonding, risk and liability management, and other financial responsibilities; civil service and other personnel rights; political participation restrictions on managers and other personnel (the "littler Hatch Acts"); competitive bidding regulations and other due process restrictions; freedom of information and privacy proscriptions; as well as other public service laws and ordinances. These multiple sources of accountability also serve to illustrate the telescoping zones of federal, state, and local standards that govern the official behaviors of local government managers. The main point is that, while the CAOs of local governments are not—as members of the profession—required to undergo a centralized and singularly comprehensive licensing or certification process before entry into the field, their behavior once they are on the job is governed by expectations for competency and performance that are quite rigorous. And it is worth noting that some of the public service laws and ordinances may actually serve as effective screening devices for those seeking positions as professional local government managers. One example of this type of screening is when managers must become bonded for certain official responsibilites.

Thus, when comparing criteria and tests for competency and performance among professions, one can make a strong argument that significant standards for local government managers do—in fact—currently exist. These legal and community-established standards are clearly enforceable, and satisfy two of the major purposes for formal certification procedures. That professionals must undergo performance reviews at regular intervals is a process that does not escape the local government manager, either.

Chief administrative officers are appointed and serve at the pleasure of a majority vote of a council or commission. With the election of each new council/ commission or on negotiation of the managers' contracts, or at junctures in between, their measures are taken in an informal style; and many managers have formally scheduled evaluations, as well. With regard to the telescoping standards of federal, state, and local legal or programmatic standards, performance auditing and program evaluations are frequently mandated and are normally quite thorough. These audits and evaluations often involve an appraisal of the manager beyond that narrowly prescribed by the individual program, or on the particular responsibility. And there is clear evidence that such procedures are taken very seriously by managers—evidenced in the frequent survey reports of how time-consuming, intensive, and distracting the procedures have become. The cross-cutting mandates of many federal and state aid programs and of various interlocal agreements are appropriate illustrations of this type of audit and evaluation procedure.

## LINKING THE TWO TRIBUTARIES: EDUCATION AND EXPERIENCE

On the face of it, there may be little reason to question why there has been a shift toward the academic discipline of public administration as the most appropriate and useful preparation for public service. It would seem obvious enough. But once we subject the matter to consideration, there is an important and related issue that must be addressed. As we have already seen, the nature and focus of the discussion can undergo many metamorphoses. The initial issue that we considered was whether there exists enough pertinent theory and skills to support a standardized knowledge base for a profession in local government management. The NASPAA/M.P.A. accreditation authority, standards, and process would suggest there is national academic recognition that a sufficiently rigorous and unique knowledge base does, in fact, exist.

However, another important issue has been raised about the future course of public administration. Is there sufficient communication between practitioners and academics to maintain and further stimulate a distinctive development of the profession? The nature and continuity of the relationships between those who assist in the preparation of future professionals through teaching and conducting research (let us call them *public administrationists*), and those who are most often the appliers and practitioners of a field's expertise and skills (let us call them *public administrators*) may be regarded as still another measurement of a profession's development.

What we have here is a double-edged condition: The issue is not simply whether professional local government managers must have a specific set of university credentials to be deemed professional, but also whether those who instruct them during their formal education need to have that same professional degree. As a complement to this, there are others who debate whether some experience with the rigors of the public administrator's actual environment should be required of the faculty in addition or as an equivalency to the M.P.A. degree. In the current academic marketplace, the work-history credentials of college and university professors are most often being scrutinized right along with their research qualifications (typically, at the doctorate level). With some variation, this dual research-and-experience requirement is the case with most educators in the traditional professions of the ministry, law, and medicine.

As we have witnessed in our references to the published research, some of the most insightful work done in public administration has been done by public and private sector managers while in service. They were faced to develop their own ideas, perspective, and understanding whenever the available academic research and commentary have been lacking or inappropriate to their particular circumstances and problems.[49] In this vein, Robert McGowan has observed,

While individuals are frequently associated with landmark events and discoveries . . . the emergence of many ideas, concepts, and theories are the result, in large part, of professions. . . . Defined as organized groups which constantly interact with society through networks of formal and informal relationships, professions serve as a useful vehicle for molding theory, institutionalizing training and practice, and developing a self consciousness among individuals [and] professionals.[50]

McGowan includes in his concept for professional development those who are practitioners as well as those who are academics. Both—he seems to suggest—are necessary for the maintenance of an active and legitimate profession. It is worth noting that a great deal of valuable research has been done by both, and can be found in many publications inside and outside the journals of academia. Being able to comprehend and evaluate the research and writings of the other side for one's own professional responsibilities is a "humanware" problem that is an important objective of professional education and literacy.

The natural (and ultimately desirable) tension between and among educators and researchers on the one hand, and practitioners on the other, can at times be disconcerting for those preparing for—as well as those already in—public service. Many would paraphrase Gloria Grizzle's desire when she says,

Both instructors and practitioners should commit themselves to designing curricula that provide the analytic skills that M.P.A. students need. What seems most lacking is an appreciation among instructors of the skills that practitioners deem essential coupled with an appreciation among practitioners of their responsibility to share with M.P.A. programs, on a continual basis, their opinions about the skills that M.P.A. students need to acquire.[51]

While the relationships between the academic community and local government managers remain largely informal, there are signs of a maturing structure and growing continuity in this vital area. As formal training in the field of public administration becomes more common as the in-service credential of choice, its concepts and notions are more likely to develop into the professional language by which academic practitioners will communicate ideas and experience without substantial additional occupational cost.

There appears to be little systematic data about the impact of public service experience on public administration faculties, or their approaches to instruction. But for the first time in 1983, NASPAA analyzed "the academic fields and discipline from which faculty members (including adjuncts) regularly offer courses taken by PA/A graduate students." It found that public administration led the field, but represented only about one-quarter (24 percent) of the faculties responding to the survey. Other fields represented were—in rank order—political science (18 percent), economics and business administration (both with 10 percent), health services (5 percent), statistics, mathematics, law, planning, urban affairs, and sociology (each with 4 percent), computer sciences (3 percent), psychology (2 percent), and other (8 percent).[52]

It is clear from these data that graduates in M.P.A. programs are taught by multiple-disciplinary faculties. How this relates to the orientation and array of course content cannot be distilled from the survey information. But in the sections to follow, we will get some idea of the perceived usefulness that managers have reported for indivdual educational fields as preparation for their careers. The reader should remember that this kind of analysis needs to be distinguished from an assessment of any particular array of interdisciplinary courses taught within an individual M.P.A. program.

Is there order within such diversity? Let us begin our review of the linkage between educators and practitioners by asking local government managers to evaluate the utility of various educational fields typically associated with public management, and to assess the utility of those educational experiences in their own careers. In fact, respondents to the 1984 ICMA/CAO survey were asked to assess how useful they believed a variety of different educational areas actually are for becoming a modern manager, chief administrative officer, or executive director of a local government. Table 2.3 displays the responses.

Aggregating the "essential" with the "very useful" responses, the city or general managers from these communities ranked budgeting and finance first (93.6 percent), administration—including organizational theory—second (83.7 percent), public relations third (81.1 percent), and personnel fourth (78.1 percent) as the most important fields of education for a career in local government management. What is particularly striking about the responses is the large separation between the perceived strength for educational utility found in these four fields and the next most highly rated field: economics (identified by 60.9 percent as essential or very useful). A course-related internship was the only other educational area identified by over 50 percent of the 1984 respondents as being essential or very useful (so identified by 60.1 percent of the respondents).

The survey responses arrayed in Table 2.3 may also illustrate an important distinguishing feature that separates the occupational experience of local government managers from the analytical and research training and experience of college faculty members. When comparing the combined "marginally or not useful" survey tallies with the proportions identifying the "essential or very useful," the fields of statistics, sociology, and political science were perceived to be the three educational areas least useful to the modern manager (each was

Table 2.3
Usefulness of Educational Areas for the Modern Manager, 1984

| Field of Education | Essential | | Very Useful | | Useful | | Marginally Useful | | Not Useful | | Respondent Total | |
|---|---|---|---|---|---|---|---|---|---|---|---|---|
| | No. | % (a) | No. | % (a) | No. | % (a) | No. | % (a) | No. | % (a) | No. | % |
| Political Science | 256 | 11.1 | 606 | 26.3 | 982 | 42.6 | 408 | 17.7 | 55 | 2.4 | 2,307 | 100.0 |
| Administration/ Organization Theory | 1,103 | 47.4 | 846 | 36.3 | 321 | 13.8 | 57 | 2.4 | 2 | 0.1 | 2,329 | 100.0 |
| Psychology | 243 | 10.5 | 842 | 36.3 | 888 | 38.3 | 307 | 13.2 | 37 | 1.6 | 2,317 | 100.0 |
| Sociology | 95 | 4.1 | 525 | 22.8 | 1,025 | 44.4 | 576 | 25.0 | 86 | 3.7 | 2,307 | 100.0 |
| Economics | 450 | 19.4 | 966 | 41.5 | 708 | 30.5 | 182 | 7.8 | 19 | 0.8 | 2,325 | 100.0 |
| Public Relations | 984 | 42.3 | 901 | 38.8 | 368 | 15.8 | 69 | 3.0 | 2 | 0.1 | 2,324 | 100.0 |
| Systems Analysis | 212 | 9.2 | 783 | 33.9 | 977 | 42.3 | 310 | 13.4 | 29 | 1.3 | 2,311 | 100.0 |
| Urban or Regional Planning | 223 | 9.6 | 805 | 34.7 | 1,017 | 43.8 | 255 | 11.0 | 20 | 0.9 | 2,320 | 100.0 |
| Personnel | 845 | 36.3 | 972 | 41.8 | 462 | 19.9 | 44 | 1.9 | 4 | 0.2 | 2,327 | 100.0 |
| Budgeting and Finance | 1,570 | 67.2 | 617 | 26.4 | 139 | 6.0 | 9 | 0.4 | 1 | 0.0 | 2,336 | 100.0 |
| Statistics | 141 | 6.1 | 565 | 24.4 | 1,004 | 43.4 | 543 | 23.5 | 60 | 2.6 | 2,313 | 100.0 |
| Information Technology | 300 | 13.0 | 820 | 35.5 | 881 | 38.2 | 282 | 12.2 | 24 | 1.0 | 2,307 | 100.0 |
| Course Related Internship | 603 | 26.5 | 765 | 33.6 | 617 | 27.1 | 255 | 11.2 | 37 | 1.6 | 2,277 | 100.0 |

*Note*: Percentage totals may not equal 100, due to rounding.

*Source*: Compiled by the author from responses to "A Profile of Local Government Manager/Chief Administrative Officer/ Executive Director—1984," the survey instrument administered by the International City Management Association, Washington, D.C., in that year. The survey question was: "How useful do you believe the following educational areas are for becoming a modern manager/CAO/ED?"

identified by at least one-fifth of the managers as marginally or not useful). The occupational utility of psychology, systems analysis, urban and regional planning, and information technology received a more diverse assessment by responding managers than did statistics, sociology, and political science; but clearly, there was no consensus among the responding managers about the comparative utility of the former.

However, it is also important to note that all of the academic disciplines listed were rated by substantial majorities of managers to be of at least some usefulness. This supports the common expectation that most managers view any college education as being generally beneficial. These findings might also suggest that a careful review be made of core curriculum requirements for M.P.A. programs, particularly when local government management is the focus or concentration of the program.

Table 2.4 allows us to compare the 1984 average rating given by managers—grouped by their own major fields of study (for highest level of education completed)—with their assessments of various educational areas listed on the 1973–74 ICMA survey. The data arrayed in Table 2.4 allow us to take our analysis closer to the actual educational experience of each manager. The mean scores for each field of education could range from 1.00 (scored by the manager as being essential) to 5.00 (scored as being not useful) on both the 1973–74 and the 1984 ICMA surveys.

Note—first of all—that, of the nine individual majors listed on the 1984 survey (including "other" as a category), the overwhelming preference for educational field of preparation was public management/administration/planning. This major represented 65.2 percent of all who responded, and more than doubled the next four sets of majors combined. The next four sets of majors were ranked in descending order as: (2) politics/government/history, (3) business/accounting, (4) engineering, and (5) other social science. When these four were combined, they represented another 31.2 percent of the managers. Taken together, these five groupings of academic majors represented 86.4 percent of all the managers responding to the 1984 ICMA survey.

A second important conclusion to be derived from Table 2.4 is that—regardless of personal specialization (with the exception of the very small number of managers with liberal arts or geography majors, and the residual "other" category)—the responding managers identified the same four most-valued educational fields, and the same three least-valued fields. For the five most frequently identified areas of educational specialization reported by managers who were active in 1984, there was some modest variation in the strength of the values associated with the fields of administration, public relations, and personnel. However, in both surveys, budgeting and finance as a set of skills was ranked as the educational area with the greatest utility for the modern government manager.

Furthermore, when the responses from the 1984 survey instrument are compared with the responses to the 1973–74 survey in Table 2.5, they indicate that there has been a strong continuity in these assessments of educational utility

**Table 2.4**

**Perceived Usefulness of Educational Areas for Becoming a Modern Manager, 1973–74 and 1984**

| Manager's Major at Highest Level of Education Completed | Field of Education | | | | |
|---|---|---|---|---|---|
| | Pol.Sci. Avg. | Org.Th. Admin. Avg. | Psych. Avg. | Soc. Avg. | Econ. Avg. |
| (1) Politics, Govt, Hist. | 2.36 | 1.81 | 2.60 | 3.10 | 2.48 |
| (N) = | 253 | 252 | 253 | 251 | 251 |
| (2) Public Mgt, Admin, Plan | 2.70 | 1.70 | 2.59 | 3.00 | 2.32 |
| (N) = | 1,238 | 1,249 | 1,243 | 1,241 | 1,246 |
| (3) Bus, Accounting | 2.95 | 1.63 | 2.58 | 3.07 | 2.28 |
| (N) = | 194 | 195 | 193 | 195 | 195 |
| (4) Engineering | 3.21 | 1.76 | 2.94 | 3.27 | 2.48 |
| (N) = | 78 | 78 | 79 | 79 | 79 |
| (5) Science | 3.20 | 1.74 | 2.95 | 3.30 | 2.30 |
| (N) = | 20 | 19 | 20 | 20 | 20 |
| (6) Social Science | 2.91 | 1.84 | 2.43 | 2.77 | 2.28 |
| (N) = | 74 | 73 | 74 | 74 | 75 |
| (7) Geography | 2.86 | 2.00 | 2.71 | 3.00 | 2.57 |
| (N) = | 7 | 7 | 7 | 7 | 7 |
| (8) Liberal Arts | 2.78 | 2.44 | 2.44 | 3.11 | 2.33 |
| (N) = | 9 | 9 | 9 | 9 | 9 |
| (9) Other | 3.00 | 2.11 | 2.71 | 3.19 | 2.29 |
| (N) = | 27 | 28 | 28 | 27 | 28 |
| Total in 1984 Survey | 2.72 | 1.73 | 2.60 | 3.03 | 2.34 |
| (N) = | 1,900 | 1,910 | 1,906 | 1,903 | 1,910 |
| Totals for 1973-74 Survey | 2.00 | 1.30 | 2.10 | 2.30 | 1.90 |
| (N) = | 1,622 | 1,655 | 1,607 | 1,578 | 1,616 |

*Note*: Grouping managers by their own fields of specialization for their highest level of education completed, an average score was computed by the author from the respondents' usefulness assessments for each educational area based on a five-point scale: essential (1), very useful (2), useful (3), marginally useful (4), and not useful (5).

*Source*: On the 1973–74 and 1984 ICMA/CAO surveys, the respondents were asked, "How useful do you believe the following educational areas are for becoming a modern manager/CAO/ED?"; and in 1984, they were also asked to indicate their own "major or area of specialization for all degrees completed."

| Pub.Rel. Avg. | Sys.Ana. Avg. | Urb/Reg Plan. Avg. | Pers- onnel Avg. | Budget. Fin. Avg. | Stat. Avg. | Inf. Tech. Avg. | Course Intern. Avg. |
|---|---|---|---|---|---|---|---|
| 1.93 | 2.78 | 2.55 | 1.95 | 1.45 | 2.99 | 2.56 | 2.05 |
| 252 | 253 | 251 | 251 | 253 | 253 | 252 | 251 |
| 1.88 | 2.61 | 2.54 | 1.85 | 1.40 | 2.93 | 2.54 | 2.05 |
| 1,245 | 1,240 | 1,245 | 1,247 | 1,252 | 1,241 | 1,237 | 1,231 |
| 1.69 | 2.49 | 2.69 | 1.83 | 1.23 | 2.73 | 2.36 | 2.80 |
| 194 | 195 | 195 | 194 | 196 | 195 | 192 | 187 |
| 1.72 | 2.58 | 2.65 | 1.96 | 1.57 | 3.12 | 2.54 | 2.92 |
| 79 | 78 | 78 | 79 | 79 | 77 | 79 | 74 |
| 1.80 | 2.79 | 2.80 | 1.55 | 1.10 | 3.05 | 2.89 | 2.45 |
| 20 | 19 | 20 | 20 | 20 | 20 | 18 | 20 |
| 1.75 | 2.64 | 2.65 | 1.99 | 1.57 | 3.00 | 2.58 | 2.64 |
| 75 | 73 | 74 | 73 | 75 | 73 | 73 | 69 |
| 1.43 | 2.71 | 1.86 | 1.86 | 1.86 | 2.71 | 2.86 | 2.00 |
| 7 | 7 | 7 | 7 | 7 | 7 | 7 | 7 |
| 2.33 | 3.11 | 2.56 | 2.33 | 1.78 | 2.78 | 2.67 | 2.44 |
| 9 | 9 | 9 | 9 | 9 | 9 | 9 | 9 |
| 1.93 | 2.93 | 2.75 | 2.21 | 1.50 | 3.32 | 3.00 | 2.86 |
| 27 | 28 | 28 | 28 | 28 | 28 | 28 | 28 |
| 1.85 | 2.63 | 2.57 | 1.87 | 1.40 | 2.94 | 2.54 | 2.20 |
| 1,908 | 1,902 | 1,907 | 1,908 | 1,919 | 1,903 | 1,895 | 1,876 |
| 1.50 | 2.20 | 1.90 | 1.50 | 1.20 | 2.30 | (NA) | 2.00 |
| 1,653 | 1,589 | 1,622 | 1,639 | 1,659 | 1,598 | (NA) | 1,563 |

**Table 2.5**
**Comparison of 1973–74 and 1984 ICMA/CAO Survey Responses Concerning Educational Usefulness**

| Educational Area | 1984 Survey Average | 1984 Survey Rank | 1973-74 Survey Average | 1973-74 Survey Rank | Change in Proportion | Ranked By Change in "Average" Score | Change in Position of Rank from 1973-74 Score to 1984 |
|---|---|---|---|---|---|---|---|
| Political Science | 2.7 | 10 | 2.0 | 7-8 | +0.7 | Tied 10-12 | Down 2 Positions |
| Administration | 1.7 | 2 | 1.3 | 2 | +0.4 | Tied 3-7 | Same |
| Psychology | 2.6 | 7-9 | 2.1 | 9 | +0.5 | 8 | Same |
| Sociology | 3.0 | 12 | 2.3 | 11-12 | +0.7 | Tied 10-12 | Same |
| Economics | 2.3 | 6 | 1.9 | 5-6 | +0.4 | Tied 3-7 | Same |
| Public Relations | 1.9 | 3-4 | 1.5 | 3-4 | +0.4 | Tied 3-7 | Same |
| Systems Analysis | 2.6 | 7-9 | 2.2 | 10 | +0.4 | Tied 3-7 | Up 1 Position |
| Urban/Regional Planning | 2.6 | 7-9 | 1.9 | 5-6 | +0.7 | Tied 10-12 | Down 1 Position |
| Personnel | 1.9 | 3-4 | 1.5 | 3-4 | +0.4 | Tied 3-7 | Same |
| Budgeting/Finance | 1.4 | 1 | 1.2 | 1 | +0.2 | Tied 1 & 2 | Same |
| Statistics | 2.9 | 11 | 2.3 | 11-12 | +0.6 | 9 | Same |
| Information Technology | (2.5) | (NA) | (NA) | (NA) | (NA) | (NA) | (NA) |
| Course-related Internship | 2.2 | 5 | 2.0 | 7-8 | +0.2 | Tied 1 & 2 | Up 2 Positions |
| **Mean of Area Averages** | **2.32** | (NA) | **1.85** | (NA) | **+0.47** | (NA) | (NA) |

*Note:* Average scores were calculated based on the five-point scale offered for each educational area. However, scalar values varied somewhat between the two studies, 1973–74/1984: Essential/Essential (1), Useful/Very Useful (2), Marginal Use/Useful (3), No Use/Marginally Useful (4), and Irrelevant/Not Useful (5).

*Source:* Compiled by the author from responses to a "Profile of Manager/Chief Administrative Officer 1973," and "A Profile of the Local Government Manager/Chief Administrative Officer/Executive Director—1984," the survey instruments administered by the International City Management Association, Washington, D.C., for those two years. The questions were identical: "How useful do you believe the following areas are for becoming a modern manager/CAO/ED?"

over time. That is, the same four most-valued educational fields were identified despite the decade separating these two surveys. While this finding may seem like common sense to some, the consistency in findings does have considerable significance. The lack of change is particularly striking when contrasted with the proportion of managers who reported being trained as civil engineers (33 percent) in the 1971 Stillman survey. And the stable pattern is particularly impressive when we consider the occupational mobility of the managers over this time frame, the expansion in the number of ICMA-recognized communities with general managers, and the changes that have inevitably occurred in the circumstances of most—if not all—communities.

The responses displayed in Table 2.5 also indicate that two educational fields had reduced rankings in perceived usefulness from 1973–74 to 1984. They were political science (down from a tie for seventh and eighth to tenth position) and urban and regional planning (down from a tie for fifth and sixth to a tie for seventh and eighth positions). Two other areas had elevated rankings for perceived usefulness over the same decade of time. Course-related internships (up from a tie for seventh and eighth to fifth position) and systems analysis (up from tenth to a three-way tie for seventh through ninth positions). While there appears to be no single or simple explanation for these changes, the topical and methodological emphasis of published research in each of the fields (including the utility of internships) may correspond to a shift in perceived knowledge applicability for actual government management. The professional challenges faced by teachers, researchers, and practitioners may move into and out of sync with each other. That is to say, it would appear that, as the challenges faced by managers continue to evolve, so also do the thrusts of research and writing in the various multiple-disciplinary fields related to public affairs/administration programs.

While representing only a modest statistical difference, managers with a major in the area of public management/administration/planning showed a slightly higher value for "personnel" over "public relations" as essential or very useful fields than was true for the overall respondent pattern found in either 1973–74 or 1984. But overall, local government managers consistently seemed to conclude that there is comparatively less educational utility from a package of skills known as "policy analysis" and from the social science disciplines of political science and sociology than conventional wisdom might hold to be true. Rather, there seems to be a higher value placed on many of the traditional fields associated with local government management (budgeting and finance; administration, including organizational theory; personnel; and public relations) as being the foci of the managers' need for intensive, formal educational preparation. The consistency in the assessments most likely indicates a continuity in local-government manager responsibilities, and also an awareness by officials of the changes that have been occurring within these fields of specialized knowledge.

We should not conclude our consideration of the information arrayed in Table 2.5 without discussing the pattern of across-the-board decline for the perceived usefulness of all 12 educational areas listed. The decline between 1973–74 and 1984 averaged slightly less than one-half point (0.47) for all fields as measured on the five-point scale. This is a significant reduction! At first blush, the pattern could be interpreted as one more piece of evidence in the widespread criticism being levelled at all aspects of U.S. education. Some would add that, in the interdisciplinary and widely varying world of M.P.A. programs, expectations might have initially been too high regarding what a two-year professional degree can accomplish. After graduate-managers had some opportunity to compare their raised expectations with the increasingly complicated world, one would expect to see a certain amount of additonal criticism. The tension is between the nature of training offered and the types of expertise actually demanded by in-service experience—whether changing needs are being clearly identified and described, and how college and university programs should adjust to the changes. Remember that flexibility and responsiveness are two of the objectives that have been ascribed to the U.S. system of nongovernmental accreditation for college and university degree programs.

However, there is at least one other important alternative—and perhaps supplementary—interpretation of this declining pattern in perceived educational utility. As the marketplace for local government managers becomes increasingly dominated by individuals who do possess the more advanced college degrees, the perceived usefulness to the individual manager seeking entry or mobility within the field may be reduced as the distinctiveness (rarity) of having achieved a particular level or type of education is reduced. From this perspective, the unofficial marketplace standards for professionalism in the field of local government management can be viewed as effectively being raised and broadened, while the perceived individual usefulness of an advanced degree—in terms of singularly guaranteeing placement and career mobility—has been reduced.

Earlier we noted a growth in the proportion of managers having advanced degrees, and their increasing amounts of pre-CAO government experience. It would seem that the marketplace is demanding ever higher standards of those who would pursue a career in this field. In any case, both the high-expectations and the market-pressure explanations for the reduced educational assessments are linked and simultaneously represented across the 12 fields of education compared between 1973–74 and 1984. That is to say, managers measure the usefulness of their college training in light of how well it has helped them to deal with changing occupational responsibilities—success at which allows them to consider various career options.

## POSTGRADUATION: PUBLIC ADMINISTRATIONISTS AND LOCAL GOVERNMENT MANAGERS

We can identify at least two important areas of continuous professional-level association between public administrationists and local government managers. The first is the growing need for continuing professional education. The second is a countervailing professional need for the insights, the perspectives, and—increasingly—the shared resources and capacities of the other group. These two interests may also be considered measures of an occupation's evolving professionalism. Recognition of the saliency of these matters for local government management may in itself be evidence of the maturation in professionalism of the field—that is, a sharing of the same challenges that all professions are confronting today.

At this point, it may be useful to consider Milton Stern's perspective (as dean of university extension at the University of California, Berkeley):

Changes of cultural attitude have been hard pressed to match the speed of the veritable post-industrial revolution that has overtaken the country. That, most of all, is why CPE [continuing professional education] has become a paradoxical necessity for people already educated beyond others in society. Society, in fact, requires continuing education. . . . In effect, our country is in the process of extending compulsory education . . . to the end of professional careers. We may embark upon second or third careers, and second or many marriages, but the continuing certainty of our lives, at least for active professionals, will be lifetime education.[53]

If it be true that this is an ever-intensifying requirement placed on today's professionals, then the question becomes: How can form be harnessed to the pursuit of function? That is, as Dean Stern asks, "Who shall develop, organize, provide for, control, and profit from the continuing education of professionals in our society?"[54] Stern sums up the current condition of continuing professional education when he observes,

The professional sector is not only the largest growth area of continuing education today, but it is the least known for several reasons: (1) its growth has occurred both in and out of traditionally recognized institutions and organizations; (2) most frequently, it has developed spontaneously in a typically American self-help or mutual package (that is, it has been organized by temporary combinations of entrepreneurs, professional societies, universities through professional or continuing education arms, government, business—in combinations of two or even three kinds of providers); (3) only lately has anything like comprehensive data collection or record keeping been attempted.[55]

The data in Table 2.6 "resemble" Stern's "remarks" about the condition of continuing education for most professions. His statement is specifically apropos to the field of continuing education for public sector managers, and appears to be no less true for local government managers. Table 2.6 arrays responses to the 1973–74 and the 1984 ICMA surveys on the issue of CAO participation in continuing education programs. Managers were asked what types of work-related courses or training programs they had participated in within the previous three and two years, respectively. The survey items effectively cover five of the ten years separating the two studies. Three categories of continuing education pro-

**Table 2.6**

**Manager Participation in Continuing Professional Education Programs, 1970–73 and 1982–84**

| Type Educational/Training Program | No. Responding (A) | 1973-74 Survey No. | % of (A) | Avg. % Per Yr. (B) | No. Responding (A) | 1984 Survey No. | % of (A) | (1984 Survey) Avg. % Per Yr. (C) | Average % Increase (B-C) | Rank By % Increase |
|---|---|---|---|---|---|---|---|---|---|---|
| **UNIVERSITY BASED:** | | | | | | | | | | |
| (1) Enrolled in specific university degree program | 1744 | (172) | 9.9 | 3.3 | 2360 | (180) | 7.6 | 3.8 | +0.5 | 5 |
| (2) University course for credit | 1744 | (175) | 10.0 | 3.3 | 2360 | (243) | 10.3 | 5.2 | +1.9 | 2 |
| (3) Non-credit university course | 1744 | (377) | 21.6 | 7.2 | 2360 | (376) | 15.9 | 8.0 | +0.8 | 3 |
| **ASSOCIATION BASED:** | | | | | | | | | | |
| (4) ICMA correspondence course | 1744 | (141) | 8.1 | 4.1 | 2360 | (170) | 7.2 | 3.6 | -0.5 | 6 |
| (5) ICMA workshop | (NA) | (NA) | (NA) | (NA) | 2360 | (414) | 17.5 | 8.6 | (NA) | (NA) |
| (6) ICMA conference | (NA) | (NA) | (NA) | (NA) | 2360 | (899) | 38.1 | 19.1 | (NA) | (NA) |
| (7) State association sponsored program | (NA) | (NA) | (NA) | (NA) | 2360 | (1415) | 60.0 | 30.0 | (NA) | (NA) |
| **PRIVATE SECTOR/GOV'T/NON-ICMA BASED:** | | | | | | | | | | |
| (8) Seminar/Institute lasting one to two days | 1744 | (1323) | 75.9 | 25.3 | 2360 | (1688) | 71.5 | 35.6 | +10.3 | 1 |
| (9) Seminar/Institute lasting three or more days | 1744 | (1163) | 66.7 | 22.2 | 2360 | (831) | 35.2 | 17.6 | -4.6 | 8 |
| (10) Other | 1744 | (85) | 4.9 | 1.6 | 2360 | (105) | 4.4 | 2.2 | +0.6 | 4 |
| (11) None | 1744 | (215) | 12.3 | 4.1 | 2360 | (153) | 6.5 | 3.3 | -0.8 | 7 |

*Note*: Percentages may not total 100, due to rounding.

*Source*: Compiled by the author from the 1973–74 ICMA/CAO survey where the respondents were asked if in the past three years they had taken any courses or participated in any training programs related to their work; and from the 1984 ICMA/CAO survey, where respondents were asked to recall their participation over the past two years. In both instances, the managers could select all programs that were applicable. Three programs have been designated as not applicable (NA) because they were not listed on the 1973–74 questionnaire.

viders were offered for review: private seminar or institute (entrepreneurial), ICMA (a specific professional society), and university-based course work.

Similar to professionals in other fields, local government managers report regular participation in various types of continuing educational programs. In each of the two surveys, over 95 percent of the managers said that they had participated in at least some type of in-service training or education for each relevant year. And the rate of participation has increased. Only an average 4.1 percent of these CAOs reported that they had not participated in some type of program during the years 1970–73. The nonparticipation rate was reduced even further to an average 3.3 percent during the period 1982–84.

A second factor to be gleaned from the data pertains to the preferences shown among the various types of continuing education programs available to in-service local government managers. The respondents to the 1984 questionnaire indicated a clear preference for four types of training programs listed among the ten possibilities. Two were offered as ICMA-affiliated programs and two were sponsored by other nonuniversity-affiliated institutes or seminars. A concern for brevity, specificity, and timeliness of topic are suggested by these four preferences. One- and two-day seminars or institutes and state association (ICMA)–sponsored programs were clearly the two most frequently preferred. Perhaps this is true because they tend to be most responsive to the immediate, technical types of responsibilities and concerns facing the managers.

This interpretation of the 1984 survey responses is buttressed by another observation. The three least-preferred types of continuing education programs (ICMA correspondence courses, enrollment in a specific university degree program, and taking a university course for credit) involve often rigorous, broad-ranging, and time-consuming course work and course evaluation processes. However, when comparing the 1973–74 and 1984 survey responses, we should note that there were at least 90 in-service managers (from the ICMA-recognized governments) enrolled per year in university degree programs, which are not counted in the figures in Table 2.6. The level of degree program enrollment is not so modest as might at first appear. This total does not include the growing numbers of individuals who are in university programs preservice (as full-time students or as part-time students with non-CAO occupations), nor managers taking a leave of absence from their profession to pursue their educations.

While the list of continuing education programs on the 1984 ICMA survey was not identical to the list on the 1973–74 questionnaire, seven of the categories were offered on both instruments (ICMA workshops, ICMA conferences, and state association–sponsored programs were not listed on the 1973–74 instrument). The responses arrayed in Table 2.6 indicate that the greatest percentage of increase was a five-fold preference increase shown for one- and two-day seminar or institute programs (with a 10.3 percent increase in participation) over the second greatest: university courses taken for credit (with a 1.9 percent increase in participation). Interestingly, the latter increase is shown to be from among one of the least utilized forms of continuing education.

Why the university course taken for credit has increased is hard to surmise from the survey data available for this study. It may reflect an occupational dilemma increasingly faced by many in-service managers. Unlike the rise in utilization of one- and two-day seminars and institutes, which tend to be more technical in nature, the university course work taken for credit outside a degree program may be resulting from increased community or marketplace pressures on managers to show progress toward securing more expertise and credentials. The selection of nondegree course work may reflect a variety of complicating factors in the lives of managers who are in service and seeking to demonstrate progress toward obtaining the appropriate training and degrees.

Examples of such complicating career factors might be: the availability and proximity of access to a desired degree program; rising educational costs, which may limit the attraction of managers to unique course offerings or which lead managers to take course work from a wide range of academic disciplines; occupational security and career mobility concerns; the issues associated with college credit transfer; and, finally, uncertainties caused by long absence from the processes of formal education. The existence of the latter factor is somewhat supported by the observation that there have been modest participation declines in the extended-session (more costly and time-consuming) technical seminars and institutes. There has also been reported a reduced participation in the ICMA correspondence course program, perhaps because it is unacceptable for degree credit at many colleges.

The second pattern of association between public administrationists and local government managers is the countervailing occupational need for the insights, perspectives, and—increasingly—the resources and capacities of the other. The ultimate relevancy of information sharing and advice giving would seem dependent on the nature and extensiveness of the interrelationship between these two components of the profession. This is true for no less a reason than that they are found in two different organizational settings, and are therefore responding to different occupational stimuli. But they do share a common—albeit different— interest in local government management.

From the local government officials' point of view, there has often been frustration over the nature, extensiveness, and timing of college- or university-based expertise. Peter Szanton reviewed the experience of the university urban research centers, the urban observatories, the information systems consortium, the urban technology systems, and a variety of other local government–academic joint efforts in the 1960s and 1970s—Szanton himself being a major foundation executive responsible for funding several of these experimental efforts. What he found most often was that

the academy, concerned with general principles rather than specific situations, valuing originality of insight above utility of conclusion, distracted by the requirements of teaching and basic research, and seeking the approval of academic peers rather than municipal clients, was simply an unsuitable setting for the production of timely, specific and practical advice, and for casting it in terms city officials could absorb.[56]

However, while Szanton's analysis found evidence that the academic culture and its reward structure do often work at cross-purposes with that of municipal needs and circumstances, he also suggested that

disadvantageous as they were, the characteristics of the academic world cannot fully explain the frequent inability of academics to provide useful advice to urban officials since such failure was an outcome typical not only of unversity-based efforts to advise city governments, but [also] of the work of a wide variety of non-academic providers of advice—not-for-profits, research corporations, management consulting firms, and the analytic staffs of manufacturers, for example.[57]

Szanton concluded that a "far better explanation is that city governments are particularly weak and constrained users of any advice, and are sharply limited in their capacity to act on recommendations for change."[58] These dilemmas illustrate the dynamics that are present when the necessities of practical government and the academically driven analytical processes meet in community affairs.

Such issues seem difficult to resolve at the institutional or generic level. On a pragmatic or individual community basis, however, the communication problem may more often be solvable. Separating individual instance from generalization is but one view of this dilemma—which is shared by most, if not all, professions. However—in a manner similar to the approaches taken by other professions—NASPAA as the new accrediting agency for M.P.A. programs (along with other academic and research societies, such as the American Society for Public Administration) is now promoting regular communication and exchanges of information among the academic community, the various associations of governments (for example, the National League of Cities and the National Association of Counties), and various associations of government officials (such as the International City Management Association and the Government Finance Officers Association).

Expansion and the prospects for continuity of relationships between public administrationists and administrators are important development signposts for the profession of local government management. Perhaps this study, too, may be viewed as a modest step in that direction. However, the information from our survey base says that the joint employment of managers by educational institutions and municipalities, and managers who indicated regular involvement in consulting activities, represented a very modest proportion of the reference group (data not shown). Little systematic information is available about the informal or voluntary activities of local government managers in these areas of professional service. The antecdotal evidence indicates, however, that a great deal of activity may be taking place.

## THE PROFESSIONAL MODEL: FUTILITY OR UTILITY?

Writing in 1980, Cyril Houle—a senior program consultant for adult education at the W. K. Kellogg Foundation—argued that, if the traditional professions "are less triumphant than they were in the 1960s, the chief cause probably lies in growing concern about the extent to which the needs for a highly competent and subtle performance of essential services are being met."[59] Houle's concern was further heightened because of what he felt to be a change in the focus of professional pursuits:

In the past, the major search has been for absolutes that would identify those occupations that could properly be called professions. The more widespread modern trend is to ask what principles of action seem most significant to the members of a vocation as they seek to elevate and dignify its work so that it can become accepted by society as a profession.[60]

But at the same time—and as if to suggest the futility of ever achieving professional recognition for any occupation within public administration—it seems that Houle was concurring with an earlier essay written by R. L. Schott in 1976. Schott had suggested that public administration as a field should "become more modest in its claims to professionalism. Such modesty may enhance the quality of its contribution to the practice of public affairs and avoid a frustration of its scholars, educators, and practitioners due to impractical or impossible aspirations."[61] There is an interesting irony here that cuts across all notions about the traditional and the newer professions and their development. How have researchers compared the accommodations that traditionally acknowledged professions make in order to meet the challenge of evolving circumstances and changing times, with those changes made by emerging or new professions seeking to improve their performance and professional standing?

Perhaps where you stand depends on where you sit! For example, how would the following questions be treated if public administration—or, specifically, local government management—were an historically acknowledged profession? Does the bond of public administrationists with public administrators end with the graduation and credentialling of students who share a common interest in public administration? Does the later bond exist only when there is some rare reciprocating (research or consulting) project to be undertaken? It takes but a moment of reflection to note that this is not the case, and could not be true in any occupation claiming to be a legitimate and active profession. It would not be characteristic of a profession whether its researchers, educators, and practitioners were in the field of medicine, law, accounting, the ministry, elementary or secondary education, or local government management.

Presenting a challenge to the many of us interested in professional local-government management, Milton Stern recounts,

It is the independent professions derived from the ancient guilds that have been better able than the civil service to maintain themselves in society and in a rough way to maintain their own integrity. A fundamental question for professionals in our time, as their numbers increase and their work becomes more complex, is whether they will be able to maintain an integrity similar to that of the older "free" professions.[62]

Interpreting the responses to the various surveys introduced in this chapter is not a business to be undertaken lightly. However, these survey data do allow us the opportunity to address at least some of the key assertions that have been made by Houle and by Schott—and that, no doubt, have been felt by many others. For, regardless of whether we consider the professional development of local government managers to be ultimately beneficial to the public—or to those in the occupation, for that matter—the professional model is obviously useful as a framework for marking, measuring, and assessing the nature and direction of careers in the field.

In the next two chapters, I will focus on the outward and inward occupational values of autonomy, commitment, and responsibility among government managers. These chapters scrutinize some of the most unique occupational attributes of CAOs, and how these attributes can be distinguished from those of public servants serving in other capacities or at other levels of government. Also in these two chapters, a study is made of the managers' official activities, responsibilities, and duties, and how their activities can be matched with their personal values, attitudes, and expectations.

## NOTES

1. For a more complete explanation of the recognition criteria used by the ICMA, see their *Who's Who in Professional Local Government Management* (Washington, D.C.: International City Management Association, 1985).

2. See Mary A. Schellinger, "Local Government Managers: Profile of the Professionals in a Maturing Profession," in the *Municipal Year Book 1985* (Washington, D.C.: International City Management Association, 1985), p. 181.

3. See Richard J. Stillman's review of the ICMA decision to extend the recognition process so as to include counties, councils-of-government, and leagues in addition to municipalities, in Stillman's "Local Public Management in Transition: A Report on the Current State of the Profession," in the *Municipal Year Book 1982* (Washington, D.C.: International City Management Association, 1982), p. 161.

4. See, for example, the classification of and comparisons made with city managers by Richard H. Hall, *Occupations and the Social Structure* (Englewood Cliffs, N.J.: Prentice-Hall, 1969); Ronald M. Pavalko, *Sociology of Occupations and Professions* (Itasca, Ill.: F. E. Peacock Publishers, 1971); and Magali S. Larson, *The Rise of Professionalism* (Berkeley: University of California Press, 1977).

5. Cited in the introduction, "Inside the Year Book," in the *Municipal Year Book 1985* (Washington, D.C.: International City Management Association, 1985), pp. xvii and xviii.

6. Michael Davis, "The Use of Professions," *Business Economics* 22, no. 4 (October 1987), p. 6.

7. Ibid., p. 6–7.

8. Ibid., p. 5.

9. Bruce Jennings, "Public Administration: In Search of Democratic Professionalism," in Bruce Jennings, Daniel Callahan, and Susan M. Wolf, eds., *The Public Duties of the Professions*. (Hastings-on-Hudson, N.Y.: A Hastings Center Report, Special Supplement 17, no. 1, February 1987), p. 20.

10. When making these observations, Barry Bozeman was particularly concerned with public management capacity issues as he saw them framed by a "no-growth" society. See his *Public Management and Policy Analysis* (New York: St. Martin's Press, 1979), pp. 361–62.

11. See George Strauss, "Professionalism and Occupational Associations," *Industrial Relations* 2, no. 3 (May 1963), pp. 8–9.

12. Jennings, "Public Administration," p. 18.

13. Clarence E. Ridley and Orin F. Nolting, *The City Manager Profession* (Chicago: University of Chicago Press, 1934).

14. Described by Laurie S. Frankel in *Municipal Managers and Chief Administrative Officers: A Statistical Profile*, Urban Data Service Report 7, no. 2 (Washington, D.C.: International City Management Association, February 1975), pp. 7–8.

15. Schellinger, "Local Government Managers," p. 188.

16. Abstracted from ibid., pp. 181–83.

17. Roy E. Green and B. J. Reed, "Occupational Stress and Mobility among Professional Local Government Managers: A Decade of Change," in the *Municipal Year Book 1988* (Washington, D.C.: International City Management Association, 1988), p. 37.

18. See Richard J. Stillman, *The Rise of the City Manager: A Public Professional in Local Government* (Albuquerque: University of New Mexico Press, 1974), chap. 4, "The Modern City Manager," for Stillman's analysis of his 1971 survey (and specifically Table 4, for a summary of his findings on the educational attainment of managers).

19. Schellinger, "Local Government Managers," pp. 183–84.

20. The tabulation of these figures from the 1986–87 Green–Reed survey and from the 1984 ICMA/CAO survey have not been previously published.

21. See the National Association of Schools of Public Affairs and Administration, *1984 Directory: Programs in Public Affairs and Administration, A Survey Report of the Member Institutions of NASPAA* (Washington, D.C.: NASPAA, 1984), p. xii.

22. There have been a number of fine studies that have surveyed the evolution of public administration as an academic and intellectual enterprise and as an occupational field. See Gerald E. Caiden, *The Dynamics of Public Administration: Guidelines to Current Transformations in Theory and Practice* (Hinsdale, Ill.: Dryden Press, 1971); Nicholas Henry, *Public Administration and Public Affairs* (Englewood Cliffs, N.J.: Prentice-Hall, 1975); Howard E. McCurdy, *Public Administration: A Synthesis* (Menlo Park, Calif.: Cummings Publishing, 1977); and—most recently—James Stever, *The End of Public Administration* (Dobbs Ferry, N.Y.: Transnational Publishing, 1988).

23. Schellinger, "Local Government Managers," pp. 185–87.

24. NASPAA, *1984 Directory*, p. xi.

25. Schellinger, "Local Government Managers," p. 183.

26. Green and Reed, "Occupational Stress and Mobility," p. 36.

27. Reported in a symposium edited by Keith F. Mulrooney, "The American City Manager: An Urban Administrator in a Complex and Evolving Situation," *Public Administration Review* 31, no. 1 (January/February 1971), pp. 6–46.

28. Stillman, *Rise of City Manager*, p. 77.

29. Green and Reed, "Occupational Stress and Mobility," pp. 36–37.

30. Ibid., p. 37. See also Roy E. Green and B. J. Reed, *Occupational Stress and Professional Mobility Patterns among City Managers*, Urban Data Service Report 13, no. 6 (Washington, D.C.: International City Management Association, June 1981).

31. Green and Reed, "Occupational Stress and Mobility," p. 37.

32. NASPAA, *1984 Directory*, p. xii.

33. Ibid.

34. David N. Ammons and Joseph C. King, "Professionalism and Local Government Administration," *American Review of Public Administration* 16, no. 4 (Winter 1982), p. 388.

35. R. Richard Riggs, "The Professionalization of the Public Service: A Roadmap for the 1980s and Beyond," *American Review of Public Administration* 16, no. 4 (Winter 1982), p. 357.

36. A. Dersin, "What Kind of Schools for Public Management? The State of Affairs in the USA, 1980," *International Review of Administrative Sciences* 47, no. 2 (November 2, 1981), p. 151.

37. Universities visited by the Europeans were: the University of California at Berkeley, the University of Southern California, the University of California at Los Angeles, Stanford University, Carnegie-Mellon University, the University of Pittsburgh, American University, George Washington University, Princeton University, Yale University, Suffolk University, the Massachusetts Institute of Technology, and Harvard University.

38. Dersin, "What Kind of Schools?", p. 165.

39. Ibid., p. 154.

40. Quoted in ibid., p. 165.

41. For those readers who might be interested in a more classical discussion of the "professional model," three of the most often discussed works are by William J. Goode, "Community within a Community: The Professions," *American Sociological Review* 22, no. 2 (April 1957), pp. 194–200; Ernest Greenwood, "Attributes of a Profession," *Social Work* 2, no. 3 (July 1957), pp. 45–55; and Edward Gross, *Work and Society* (New York: Thomas Y. Crowell, 1958).

42. See the Council on Postsecondary Accreditation, *The Balance Wheel for Accreditation: Annual Directory, July 1986* (Washington, D.C.: COPA, 1986), p. 1. See also the COPA document, "Provisions and Procedures for Becoming Recognized as an Accrediting Body for Postsecondary Educational Institutions or Programs" (mimeograph).

43. See the National Association of Schools of Public Affairs and Administration, *Standards for Professional Master's Degree Programs in Public Affairs and Administration, Effective September 1, 1986* (Washington, D.C: NASPAA, 1986), p. 3. See also the NASPAA document, *Policies and Procedures for Peer Review and Accreditation of Professional Master's Degree Programs in Public Affairs and Administration*, approved by the NASPAA Executive Council on October 9, 1986.

44. See NASPAA, *Standards for Professional Degree Programs*, p. 3.

45. See the conference paper by Joseph A. Uveges, Jr., "Identifying the Impacts of NASPAA's MPA Standards and Peer Review Process on Education for the Public Service," presented to the Southeast Regional American Society for Public Administration (ASPA) Meeting, October 23–25, 1985, at Charleston, S.C., p. 35.

46. Ammons and King, "Professionalism and Local Administration," p. 398.

47. E. D. Hirsch, Jr., *Cultural Literacy: What Every American Needs to Know* (Boston: Houghton Mifflin Company, 1987).

48. For example, William Trombetta, the deputy attorney general of the antitrust section division of criminal justice for the State of New Jersey, wrote,

increasingly, the professions are coming under the scrutiny of the anti-trust laws. Such anticompetitive forms of professional conduct as group boycotts, arbitrary and unreasonable licensing requirements, barriers to entry and exclusionary practices, price-fixing, stifling of innovative delivery systems, and restrictions on the scope of professional practice are [being] reviewed.

See Trombetta's article, ''The Professions under Scrutiny: An Antitrust Perspective,'' *Journal of Consumer Affairs* 16, no. 1 (Summer 1983), p. 88. Further, the Hastings Center recently completed a two-year project aimed at examining the practicers of law, medicine, social work, journalism, corporate management, and public administration on many of these same issues, but from the perspective of professional ethics. See their report: Bruce Jennings, Daniel Callahan, and Susan M. Wolf, eds., *The Public Duties of the Professions* (Hastings-on-Hudson, N.Y.: A Hastings Center Report, Special Supplement 17, no. 1, February 1987).

49. The contributions range from the classical, theoretical study done by the private-sector executive, Chester Barnard—in his *The Functions of the Executive* (Cambridge, Mass.: Harvard University Press, 1938)—to the more recent public-sector, pragmatic contribution made by Brian W. Rapp and Frank M. Patitucci, *Managing Local Government for Improved Performance: A Practical Approach* (Boulder, Colo.: Westview Press, 1977).

50. Robert McGowan, ''The Professional in Public Organizations: Lessons from the Private Sector,'' *American Review of Public Administration* 16, no. 4 (Winter 1982), p. 338.

51. Gloria A. Grizzle, ''Essential Skills for Financial Management: Are MPA Students Acquiring the Necessary Competencies?'' *Public Administration Review* 45, no. 6 (November/December 1985), p. 843.

52. NASPAA, *1984 Directory*, p. xii.

53. Milton R. Stern, ed., *Power and Conflict in Continuing Professional Education* (Belmont, Calif.: Wadsworth Publishing, 1983), p. vii.

54. Ibid., p. 9.

55. Ibid., p. 6.

56. Peter Szanton, *Not Well Advised* (New York: Russell Sage Foundation, 1981), p. x.

57. Ibid., pp. x–xi.

58. Ibid.

59. Cyril O. Houle, *Continuing Learning in the Professions* (San Francisco: Jossey-Bass Publishers, 1980), p. 26.

60. Ibid., p. 27.

61. R. L. Schott, ''Public Administration as a Profession: Problems and Prospects,'' *Public Administration Review* 36, no. 3 (1976), p. 258.

62. Stern, *Power and Conflict*, p. 11.

# 3

## FROM OUTWARD PROFESSIONALISM: OCCUPATIONAL VALUES AND ASSOCIATED ACTIVITIES . . .

As we begin our trek over the terrain of professionalism in the field of local government management, I am reminded of a certain solace once offered to me by a university mentor. I was attempting to sort out some of my confusion with a research project; he examined my predicament and then related an Old Chinese curse to this effect: "May you live in interesting times." Seeing that I was puzzled by his approach to my dilemma, the professor went on to say that "you have to learn how to live with ambiguity in order to be a social scientist." I am not sure that, at the time, I knew what he meant; today I recognize that the most interesting questions are often simply put, but the most difficult to answer. Perhaps the professor was suggesting that my dilemmas be the inspiration for my career. In fact, this ironic motivational approach may provide the intrigue that drives the chief administrative officers of local governments!

Early in this book, we set up a substantial agenda of important as well as interesting issues about occupational status and its characteristics for our particular field of interest. We established three sets of questions for examining the professionalism of CAOs in our survey sample recognized ICMA communities: First, it is important that local government managers meet standards of professionalism, and if so, for whom? Second, are local government managers really expected to be professionals in the traditional sense? That is, do they desire to be, and are they expected to be by the variety of administrative (and community) constituencies that they serve? And third, what sort of motivational dimensions are characteristic of those who have chosen local government management as a career. Are CAOs "self-conscious" about the evolving—perhaps changing—nature of role expectations that they must meet? To what extent can and do local government managers go beyond a negotiating/brokering role and impart or attempt to implement their substantive professional judgments into policy and program issues? This latter question—in particular—has provoked much concern and has been the source of much confusion among those interested in the future of professional management in the public sector.[1]

The preceding chapters reviewed the literature describing the requirements for a professional model and also summarized the ICMA and Green–Reed survey data, which profiled the career paths of individuals who currently serve local communities in the capacity of CAO. This review has identified a number of central themes that set the stage for the following analyses. The first of these themes is recognition of a continuity in the basic categorization of occupational dilemmas thought to be facing local government managers: the ever-changing social responsibilities of local government, and the often suggested "identity entrapment" of professional government managers within the debate over expectations for the council–manager plan. A second theme has been more narrowly identified as a concern over what government management expertise might include, as distinct from the values directly associated with the council–manager plan. The third theme—professional accountability, responsibility, and commitment (which we may summarize as a concern for professional ethics)—was only profiled earlier, pending elaboration and analysis in this and the following chapters. This theme refers to the underlying principles that legitimate and help to animate the "mystical" art and craft of the occupation, as measured against standards of the traditional professions.[2]

The status associated with the identification of any occupation as a profession is in the values that it is thought to represent. By definition, professions and professionals are not and do not want to be perceived as value neutral—or, worse yet, valueless. The overview given in earlier chapters was associated with the breadth of legitimate roles necessary for a profession to exist. These may be generically described as a profession's claim to and record of utilizing authority—based on accepted values of expertise, autonomy, responsibility, and commitment. It is within this theme of professional ethics that there reigns so much confusion, and to which we now turn.

## PLAYING THE PROFESSIONAL ROLES OF A CAO

O. P. Dwivedi has recently written a cogent article linking the concepts of professionalism with the values of public responsibility and accountability. Analyzing the deterioration of the machinery of government in a number of developing countries after their independence from colonial powers and then comparing them with the standards and practices of the more established democratic nations such as the United States, Dwivedi concluded that, while there are vast differences in the conditions among these nations,

the more cases relating to the misuse of power and authority are brought to public attention, the more worried becomes the public [everywhere]. . . . Consequently, there is a demand for a cleaner administration and improved moral fibre in public officials, the responsible use of power and authority, and administrative accountability.[3]

This was the basis for the reform movement at the turn of the century in the United States—in which the target was to increase political responsibility by

reducing patronage, nepotism and the use of political power for private gain . . . based on the foundation of civil service neutrality, ministerial responsibility and non-interference in day-to-day operations of departments and agencies, civil service anonymity, and the merit principle of managing personnel functions.[4]

In this regard, Dwivedi identifies and illustrates a number of significant dimensions for considering the proper role and balance of professionalism in a democratic system of government. He notes—as we have earlier—that

the complexity and diversity of the modern State has resulted in a large increase in the powers available to government in pursuit of collective interests of the society. . . . Thus, the administrative State has emerged in which public servants play the roles of crusading reformers, policy makers, social change agents, crisis managers, programme managers, humanitarian employers, interest brokers, public relations experts, regulators of economy, bankers and spokesmen for various interest groups including their own associations. These roles are in addition to the traditional functions of government such as maintaining law and order, providing education and social welfare, managing health programmes, operating transportation and communication facilities and organising various cultural and recreational events.[5]

James Svara—however—recalls that, in the United States,

For almost 100 years, those interested in public affairs have grappled with the perplexities of the relationship between policy and administration. Woodrow Wilson's formulation, simplified over time as the dichotomy of policy and administration, defined the terms for discussing the relative roles and proper contributions of elected officials and appointed staff in policy making for half a century. Since 1945, the model of separate spheres of authority has been attacked, rejected, and seemingly destroyed. The challenge has been three-pronged: conceptual, with redefinition of the key terms accompanying the behavioral movement in political science; empirical, as the evidence mounted of extensive contributions of administrators to policy; and normative, expressed most dramatically in the New Public Administration[6] which proclaimed that administrators should make policy to promote values rarely advanced by elected officials. Yet, despite the challenges, the dichotomy model has persisted for two reasons. First, it is partially accurate in describing the relationship between elected officials and administrators. Second, the model provides a normative base, rooted in democratic theory, for assessing the appropriateness of behavior.[7]

What seems so profound about Wilson's formulation for modernizing government is that his framework is still such a touchstone of reference, controversy, and confusion (and—at times—personal concern) for those interested in the future development of the field, especially those facing their own career choices. For example, Richard Stillman cites Norton Long's comment that managers are—in reality—"politicians for hire," and Karl Bosworth's summary that they are " 'politicians' who derive their considerable influence within city hall and the community at large from their control over budget preparation, personnel appointments, and formal as well as informal council advisory functions"; and then Stillman concludes with his own assessment:

Managers cannot totally embrace either role of professional or politician. If managers became neutral experts without reference to the political facts of life, they would jeopardize their own survival, but if they became politicians without responsible knowledge or expertise in urban affairs, they jeopardize their credibility and worth to the public they serve. In short, managers cautiously and continuously tread a middle ground between the two poles of politics and expertise.[8]

While the major intent of the late-nineteenth-century reform movement was to eliminate executive corruption and provide more checks and balances, Samuel Bowles reported that, from the outset, implementation of conflicting reform principles had a number of unanticipated consequences. Bowles characterized these consequences as producing such "an ingenious combination of checks and balances and mingling of power, that nobody could be to blame for anything, and everybody did it, and everbody said it was you and not I, and everybody was right."[9] Analyzing the reformers' reactions to the unanticipated repercussions of their initial thrusts at municipal reform, Buckwalter and Legler discovered that "subsequently, three significant and somewhat inconsistent treads appeared near the turn of the century, all advocating public accountability: the decline of council committees, the ascendance of the absolute executive appointment power, and the long ballot. In this process, several municipal officers began to be viewed as city overseers: comptroller, treasurer, auditor, and city attorney."[10]

Buckwalter and Legler contend that, even with adoption of the council–manager plan of government, there was

eventual conflict between these two reform concepts, checks and balances on the one hand and centralized professional management on the other, [which] produced a range of managerial authority in council–manager cities. The confounding point for the chief administrative officers is whether these other professionals are to be considered as only government "watchdogs" or as members of a local government management team. City attorneys, auditors, comptrollers and treasurers are often independently appointed by the council or commission, in some circumstances even popularly elected, with a direct link to the other elected officials, in manager–council governments as well as mayor–council systems. And these exceptions to the doctrine of centralized appointing authority have been part of the council–manager plan for local government from its earliest introduction.[11]

Nevertheless, James Svara has suggested that there does remain an important reality to Woodrow Wilson's arguments and model. Part of that reality can be found in how widely the symbols and vocabulary utilized by Wilson (who originally directed them as promotional devices to a selected audience of intellectuals and government officials) have permeated the language and structures of today's community affairs. As a continuing set of symbols for "good government," his model continues to have real and identifiable meaning beyond its actual success or failure as a proscription for government reform, or its accuracy as a predictor of professional behavior for government officials. One need only consider the proscriptive and legal definitions in a common listing of city manager responsibilities to appreciate the influence of the politics/policy–administration model.

For example, Doyle Buckwalter and J. Ivan Legler have observed that

regardless of the size of city organizations, writers for the International City Management Association (ICMA) and the National Institute of Municipal Law Officers (NIMLO) and most state and city codes concur that city managers have the following primary responsibilities:

(1) to serve as the chief administrative officer;

(2) to provide for all aspects of the personnel function;

(3) to prepare budget and appropriate financial documents;

(4) to serve as the prime law enforcement officer;

(5) to attend council meetings; and

(6) to provide studies and recommendations for the council.[12]

And this influence was felt not only through adoption of the council–manager plan of government, but also through the advent of professional general-government managers operating within the mayor–council systems.

However, from other points of view, this continuing Wilsonian influence is neither an accurate description of the reality in which local government managers work, nor is it useful as a behavior guide for professionals serving in the field. There are a host of researchers who contend that there has been a fundamental change–a metamorphosis—in the types of basic, essential responsibilities that chief administrative officers are now expected to perform. For example, James Svara contends that

understanding the relations between elected and administrative officials in council–manager cities is hampered by inadequate models for assigning responsibility for governmental functions. Practitioners tend to view their roles in terms of the traditional model based on dichotomy of policy and administration and, though aware of exceptions, are uncomfortable with them. Scholars, on the other hand, having rejected this model, see extensive overlap and have difficulty recognizing limits of the policy-making role of the manager.[13]

A growing number of practitioners, as well, have reported that these changes in professional role-playing are occurring.[14] They say that managers are now expected to become "economic entrepreneurial leaders" and "mobilizers of community resources," as well as the "strategic planners" and the "administrative innovators"—among other observed and suggested roles. Many analysts—like James Stever—would argue that if these new role expectations are actually replacing the traditional functions of professional local government managers, then this change represents a fundamental departure from the CAOs' traditional progression toward a professional-level career.

James Svara has developed a new approach for redressing the current confusion in the literature over—on the one hand—the scholar's emphasis on how authority is shared in communities employing professional local government managers, and—on the other hand—the manager's desire for normative guidance in daily decision making. While testing his new model is empirically outside the scope and capacity of this study, the approach that Svara has developed does show a new maturation and appreciation of reality. That is, it recognizes that authority—even within the professional team of local government—is always shared somehow. The questions have always been: how, with whom, and following what guidelines for proper behavior? Svara's formulation—dubbed the *dichotomy-duality model*—is based on a "separation of responsibility for the definition of mission by elected officials and the mangement of programs by administrative staff. Policy and administration—which fall between mission and management—are viewed as the shared responsibility of elected officials and staff, with each having a legitimate role in both functions.[15]

## THE SYMBOLIC VALUE OF PROFESSIONALISM

Because of our approach to studying managerial commitment to public accountability and responsiblity, we must be mindful that we are in fact looking at and analyzing community affairs primarily through the eyes of local government managers. Needless to say, how the CAOs in local governments have, over time, actually interpreted and attempted to use their legal authority as well as their expertise should provide substantial insights into the professional tendencies of those in the occupation. Interpreting the survey responses of our sample of local government managers realistically—and within the broader context of professional expectations—represents a formidable task.

To assist us in this interpretation of the roles, activities, attitudes, opinions, and values of local government managers, we can organize our thinking along the lines suggested by Murray Edelman in his analysis called *The Symbolic Uses of Politics*.[16] Edelman provided some useful insights, as well as some important reservations, that are appropriate to our focus on the expected value frameworks associated with the roles of CAOs. These expectations pertain to those held not only by the managers themselves, but also by their administrative constituencies. Reactions to the satisfaction or frustration of these expectations lie at the heart of the legitimation issues. The expectation and worth of values represented by and associated with professionalism (long considered an essential criteria for legitimation) in the management of public affairs are represented through ideas and objectives of CAOs as they participate in shaping a community's future. Managers do this by creatively directing the community's political and social procedures. A symbolic premium is placed on ethical behavior, which cross cuts and legitimates expertise, autonomy, responsibility, and commitment. Ultimately, codes of ethics rest on a consensus as to what the most important principles are and on a consistent and widely shared interpretation of the codes' meaning and application.

Because the managers in our sample are largely serving in council–manager governments, our typology of these values must be selective. A review of the literature will turn up ample warning that this reformed type of government tends to be present in the more moderate-sized, homogeneous, and less politically divided ("expertise over politics") communities. Notes Edelman:

The unimodal structure [of mostly shared community values] encourages a maximum of democratic procedures, forms, and structuring because political parties [to the extent in which they exist] and private power groups will predictably move in the same direction. . . . A multimodal scattering of values is the opposite extreme. In this situation a very large part of the population is likely to see some merit in both sides of the argument: to be ambivalent and at the same time free to explore the possibilities of alternative courses of action.[17]

Nevertheless, while we are constrained to the sample of professional managers for which we already have survey information, we must also recognize the possibility that some of the basic values expected within these communities may well vary for other reasons (and potentially be reflected in the survey responses). For example, the survey base includes not only council–manager governments, but—beginning with the 1980 CAO survey—also a broader array of recognized local governments that have "general managers" in their service. And to the extent that the ICMA chooses to expand further (perhaps "relax" is a more appropriate term) its formal requirements for recognizing governments with general managers, there may be increased diversity in the community characteristics represented.

Another example of how communities may come to change their expectations regarding CAOs was identified by Alan Saltzstein. After conducting an intensive four-city study, Saltzstein reported,

It is likely . . . that the division of authority between council and manager varies considerably among different actors, in different communities and on different issues. If so, it follows that how authority is divided affects the type of manager the council desires. . . . Political structure is frequently assumed to be an important intervening variable in analyzing the policy-making process. . . . Mayor–council governments, for instance, are thought to have a stronger input from elected officials than council-manager governments.

The data presented here suggest that this may be a simplified notion of the process; it is probable that the division of authority varies considerably regardless of structure. . . . Knowing the perceived division of authority . . . may help a manager better to relate his actions to the goals of the council.[18]

In fact, after reviewing a number of recent studies on local government professionals, John Nalbandian argues that—even in what appear to be the most homogeneous of communities—we should view

communities as aggregations of people with competing values, galvanized from time to time in public policy debates, and given the increasingly active roles of professionally-trained department heads linked to citizen constituencies, one ponders the future roles of chief administrative officers and elected officials. My sense is that, despite their visibility and public voice, in actuality the role of the elected official in governing today's communities is diminishing. While governing bodies retain authority in their community, they appear to have less and less a claim to legitimacy–that underlying sense of the rightness and wrongness of public policy and governmental process. Legitimacy has shifted from authoritative bodies back to the community-at-large and to ad hoc interest groups which pop up to force the public policy agenda. This is why the administrative apparatus of responsive local governments is becoming rooted in the community, as the direct source of legitimacy today.[19]

But Murray Edelman again cautions us to keep in perspective the concepts of professionalism in government service, as well as community leadership in general. He concludes that,

once the forms of symbolic interplay in politics are specified and their political functions examined, it becomes clear that some common social psychological mechanisms tie them together. Role-taking is one central theme, especially powerful in influencing the behaviors of public officials and political leaders. A continuing tension between threat and reassurance is another central theme, explaining the reactions of general publics [and among community leadership] to political symbols.[20]

There is important contemporary research evidence supporting this argumentation. For example, Glenn Abney and Thomas Lauth conducted a national survey of all municipal department heads in communities with populations of 50,000 and over in 1978. They found

that although councilmanic intervention continues despite the efforts of the municipal and executive reform movements, reform institutions have nevertheless been successful in structuring the patterns of intervention in such a manner as to preserve the "informational" purposes of intervention without significantly threatening the reform goal of "neutrality" in municipal administration. . . . Reform cities tended to have less intervention than non-reform cities and to have intervention characterized by fewer attempts at what we called "procurement."[21]

Further substantiation is found in Kenneth Greene's random-sample survey of city managers, public works directors, police chiefs, code enforcement officials, and welfare directors in 70 New Jersey municipalities (populations ranging from 10,000 to 100,000) in 1979 and 1980. Greene concluded,

First, administrators' attitudes toward contacts are an important linkage between citizens' requests and agencies' actions. This study suggests that a major reason for the non-responsiveness of agencies to contacts is the professional-technocratic orientation of administrators. Second, attempts to make administrators more responsive must consider the importance of expertise and professionalism to administrators. . . . The data reveal that administrators' decision-making orientations are stronger determinants of their receptivity to citizens' and elected officials' contacts than resource flexibility. . . . Administrators' receptivity is related primarily to their conception of municipal administration. The majority (75 percent) embrace a professional-technocratic view of decision making. . . . Administration is not part of a larger, more political, process, but should be removed from politics. . . . Their commitment to technical standards of judgment explains their reluctance to cooperate with elected officials and to compromise with citizens.[22]

Edelman offers this insight:

Research on leadership suggests that "leadership" may be the wrong word. The word connotes an individual free to choose his course of action and about to induce others to follow his lead because of his superior intelligence, knowledge, skill, and the force of his personality. The emphasis in modern leadership theory is rather upon the willingness of followers to follow. . . . Leadership is a complex and subtle thing, and we are learning to look for its dynamics in mass responses, not in static characteristics of individuals.[23]

After Buckwalter and Legler's review of survey data from nearly 500 city managers and city attorneys (conducted in 1985–86; their study also included 20 in-depth interviews of city managers and city attorneys), they concurred with the earlier researchers by noting that "success of the city manager–city attorney relationship is contingent on achieving a high level of mutual respect, both personal and professional [which can occur only if there is] an appreciation of the expectations of each profession for the other." However, their information also made clear that,

[while] managers and attorneys recognize each other as the ranking, professionally-trained municipal officials . . . , on the whole, city attorneys view their city managers as receiving significantly less rigorous college training. Attorneys conclude that the core skills of legal training—issue formulation and case analysis—are the most important skills lacking in management training. The managers, conversely, identify the lack of emphasis on the management skills of administrative integration/coordination and on budgeting as the noticeable weaknesses of legal training.[24]

We might conclude form this assessment that both the managers and the attorneys are desirous of establishing and maintaining their own occupation's status within the executive branch of the local government—while at the same time recognizing the professional and necessary role of the other.

Finally, Murray Edelman also seems to have anticipated the research impasse over policy and service comparisons made between the manager–council and mayor–council approaches to local government. Edelman argues that forms of government may indicate and be linked to the political diversity among communities, but they are not necessarily linked to any particular direction in their policy and program outcomes. He does contend, however, that forms of government are important because

they mold the very personalities of the actors. . . . We should expect, then, that a person's values, style of life and of political action, and expectations of others' roles would be shaped by his social setting. . . . Clearest, apparently, are the definition of the self as a participant in a prevailing institution or as expendable. . . . A significant difference in scope appears, then, between the settings that influence political acts and those that shape the self and its responses to political events and institutions.[25]

Viewed from this perspective, career mobility patterns may represent a unique feature of the CAO career system—an institutional feature that allows the community to periodically change the authority balance between its chief administrative officer, other government oversight professionals, and the city council, as well as their respectively developed constituencies—and also indicate the professional mobility aspirations of the managers themselves.

John Nalbandian's review of recent ICMA publications seems to support this perspective:

Councils place strong pressures on city managers and chief administrative officers to take an active role in developing public policy. . . . Amidst pressures to take a public and visible role in various aspects of community development, the chief administrative officer in council–manager cities is embarked on a new search for role legitimacy. . . . That is, in the search for legitimacy, it is no longer valid merely to organize one's administrative structure and processes according to the value of efficiency as a means to promote equitable service delivery. Now, the administrative structure and process itself must, to some greater extent, mirror legitimate community values.[26]

Directly linked to this description of expectations for idealized forms of government is Edelman's conception about the supporting roles of constitutions, public laws, and ordinances. These—he argues—give legal stature to and legitimize public expectations about particular government forms: "To formulate a law is essentially a job of constructing a setting in the sense of building background assumptions and limits that will persist over time and influence the quality of political acts but not their content or direction."[27] Taken as a whole, "political acts and settings, leadership, and language all influence legitimations and assumptions about" what government officials can do and become.[28]

An analysis of the symbolic uses of politics also seems to support indirectly the significance and value of professional literacy (discussed in Chapter 2) within public administration as an informal professional criterion for a career in local government management.

> The magical associations permeating language are important for political behavior because they lend authoritativeness to conventional perceptions and value premises. [There are] four distinctive styles which pervade the governmental process: hortatory, legal, administrative, and bargaining language styles. . . . They manifestly deal with authority, persuasion, and participation.[29]

This is the very stuff of governmental politics, policy, and administration.

Language styles also identify the territorial imperatives associated with each of the three major sets of local government officials: elected officials (hortatory-style communications); the chief administrative officer (administrative-style communications); and the other council- or commission-appointed members of the professional management team: the government attorney, auditor, comptroller, and auditor (legal-style communications)—plus their shared bargaining-style of communications ("like hortatory language, it involves an effort to gain support for a political position; but the two styles are fundamentally different in respect to the occasions of their use, the parties involved, and the meanings conveyed by the respective media. . . . The bargainer . . . offers a deal, not an appeal. A public reaction is to be avoided, not sought."). It is in this latter arena of government communications—bargaining—that professional ethics is most likely to be prized and also suspected, because "the meaning of this activity is sometimes the view that the public interest is being safeguarded by knowledgeable sages . . . and sometimes the view that unscrupulous "interests" are plotting for private gain at the public's expense."[30]

After this review, one may very well come to have a different sense of the imperatives that drive the managers' need for and growth in bargaining/negotiating skills. Such skills seem to be in part required and are certainly often mentioned as being expanded by today's CAOs in order to maintain effectiveness in meeting their traditional responsibilities. This creates an additional role as leadership facilitator, whose responsibilities for the procedures and processes of the executive branch of government must be coupled with those of the council, the other professionals inside and outside the executive branch, and their respective administrative constituencies.

## LEVELS OF EXPERTISE

We know that expertise in any field is crucial to the definition, identification, and authority (credibility) of the profession, and that it is a multifaceted concept. For our purposes, it is most operationally appropriate to describe expertise as "know-how"—which suggests not only a body of knowledge, but also an appreciation for how, when, and where it may be applied.[31]

The analysis in Chapter 2 linked education and experience as two of the main tributaries leading to the development of professional expertise. After a review of the ICMA and the Green–Reed survey data, it was suggested that, for individual managers, the mixture of study and work experience is an ingredient important for the development of individual professional careers. It was also suggested that changes in the nature of the mix—as part of the formal education process, or as part of a career development pathway—could be an important indication not only of the changing opportunities available to individual managers, but also of fundamental changes occurring in the evolution of the profession.

The data arrayed in Tables 3.1, 3.2, and 3.3 allow us to consider the latter issue more directly. Table 3.1 displays the average ratio of expertise for each of the 1973–74, 1980, and 1984 ICMA surveys as well as for the 1986–87 Green–Reed survey. There were two stages to the development and analysis of our measure of expertise. First, a separate ratio of expertise was calculated for each responding manager for each survey year. *The ratios of expertise were produced by dividing the number of academic years typically credited for the manager's highest achieved educational diploma or degree by the number of calendar years of full-time CAO local-government experience.* For example, the ratio of expertise could range from 19 (managers with a law degree or a Ph.D. degree and in the process of obtaining their first year of experience), to 12 (managers with a high school degree and the same one year of experience), to 1 (managers with equal numbers of years of education and CAO experience)—and even to a very small fraction or decimal (although never reaching zero), because the number of years of CAO experience that a manager has accumulated can sometimes dwarf the number of years of formal education. This circumstance is quite possible for a senior manager, even considering the number of academic years necessary to earn a Ph.D. or law degree.

A second step in the analysis was to categorize the ratios of expertise by a variety of career monitoring variables thought to be closely associated with personal (individual) development and professionalism. The categories used were: salary, average number of hours worked per week, level of educational achievement, age, total years of CAO experience, number of CAO positions held, years in current position, and sex. When a complete category of data are missing for an individual survey year, it is because adequate data were unavailable to compute that group's ratios.

Admittedly, this measure of expertise does not include nongovernment experience and non-CAO types of government experience. Nor does it give education credit to those with less than a high school diploma, to those who have earned multiple degrees at the same level, and to those working on the next higher degree but who have not yet completed all the requirements. But—like a plumb line used to determine verticality—this ratio of expertise makes visible the balance between academic years of education and calendar years of experience for our entire sample at various points in time, and in comparison to a number of important career-development factors.

When comparing the available 1973–74 and 1984 ratios of expertise with a standard grouping of manager salaries, we see two trends appearing. First, there is evidence supporting the analysis of Chapter 2 that there has been an increase in the overall proportion of managers who have sought and been awarded higher degrees of formal education. Interestingly, this pattern is indicated by consistently larger ratios of expertise (over the 1.00 balance point) shown across each salary category, as well as between the overall average ratios per survey.

The second trend is a reduction in the size of average ratio of expertise—in both the 1973–74 and 1984 surveys—when managers' salaries increase. As the ratio gets closer to 1.00, the manager has gained in experience, which begins to catch up to his or her years of formal education—and the ratio even goes below 1.00 for five managers in the earlier survey. This is clearly consistent with the salary expectations and patterns in other professions. That is, with more advanced and specialized education and training plus increasing years of occupational experience, managers can generally expect to receive—and communities, to pay—higher salaries for CAO expertise. This salary pattern seems to be present even as the marketplace for professional local government managers continues to become more competitive (and after allowing for national cost-of-living adjustments).

When ratio of expertise is compared for respondents to the 1980 and 1984 ICMA surveys across standard categories of hours that the managers reported working per week, a somewhat puzzling pattern appears. For the 1980 survey, the ratios of expertise generally become smaller (closer to 1.00) as the managers' hours worked increase, with the exception of those managers who reported working more than 60 hours per week. However, the differences between the ratios in this category do not vary much from the overall average for the entire 1980 survey. Responses to the 1984 survey suggest just the opposite pattern. The average categorical ratio of manager expertise varied substantially in 1984 from its overall survey average, and the ratios grew larger as the length of the workweek increased. That is, managers were reporting a greater imbalance between years of education and years of experience when classified by the number of hours worked per week.

By the time of the 1984 survey, years of academic training were—for whatever reasons (and across all categories of hours worked per week)—consistently reported as proportionately higher than years of CAO experience. This was at a time when managers were also reporting that they had gotten more pre-CAO government experience before obtaining their first full-time CAO position (recall that prior non-CAO experience was not calculated into ratio of expertise), and also that they were staying at each CAO appointment—as well as sustaining their careers as managers—for longer periods of time. While this may help to explain why the 1984 ratios of expertise are considerably higher than those

# Table 3.1
## Average Ratio of CAO Expertise and Selected Individual Factors Associated with Career Development

| SALARY GROUP | 1973-74 Avg | No. | 1980 N.A. | | 1984 Avg | No. | 1986-87 N.A. | |
|---|---|---|---|---|---|---|---|---|
| 0-24,999 | 4.0177 | 2241 | | | 6.7558 | 184 | | |
| 25K-34,999 | 3.4141 | 341 | | | 5.1985 | 515 | | |
| 35K-44,999 | 3.1019 | 67 | | | 3.8916 | 529 | | |
| 45K-54,999 | 0.9024 | 5 | | | 3.2279 | 391 | | |
| 55K-64,999 | 1.3846 | 1 | | | 3.3480 | 193 | | |
| over 65K | -- | -- | | | 2.6359 | 140 | | |
| Average Ratio Per Survey | 3.9102 | | | | 4.2296 | | | |
| Survey Response, Total No. | 2655 | | | | 1952 | | | |

| AVG. HOURS WORKED PER WEEK | 1973-74 N.A. | | 1980 Avg | No. | 1984 Avg | No. | 1986-87 N.A. | |
|---|---|---|---|---|---|---|---|---|
| 0-40 | | | 1.6122 | 94 | 2.7194 | 75 | | |
| 41-50 | | | 1.5330 | 1238 | 3.8159 | 1234 | | |
| 51-60 | | | 1.4786 | 1143 | 4.5201 | 889 | | |
| 61 and over | | | 1.5226 | 222 | 5.1681 | 167 | | |
| Average Ratio Per Survey | | | 1.5119 | | 4.1413 | | | |
| Survey Response, Total No. | | | 2697 | | 2365 | | | |

| EDUCATION LEVEL | 1973-74 Avg | No. | 1980 Avg | No. | 1984 Avg | No. | 1986-87 Avg | No. |
|---|---|---|---|---|---|---|---|---|
| Some High School | 0.00 | 14 | 0.00 | 3 | 0.00 | 5 | 0.00 | 2 |
| High School Diploma | 2.6937 | 119 | 1.1368 | 90 | 3.1275 | 57 | 3.9606 | 34 |
| Some College | 3.4218 | 355 | 0.8448 | 261 | 2.4782 | 185 | 2.6770 | 65 |
| Associate Degree | 4.9372 | 44 | 1.4174 | 78 | 3.3263 | 62 | 4.0708 | 26 |
| BA/BS | 5.5997 | 405 | 1.5388 | 405 | 3.5481 | 309 | 3.8805 | 163 |
| Some Graduate | 5.2748 | 334 | 1.3452 | 470 | 3.4440 | 407 | 3.4697 | 160 |

| Degree | Avg | No. | Avg | No. | Avg | No. | Avg | No. |
|---|---|---|---|---|---|---|---|---|
| MA | 6.5309 | 666 | 1.8394 | 28 | 4.8335 | 25 | 3.8827 | 524 |
| JD | 8.2245 | 23 | 1.4591 | 1269 | 5.0928 | 1303 | 5.9608 | 17 |
| PhD | 8.6657 | 7 | 1.2131 | 40 | 5.3766 | 25 | 3.1240 | 12 |
| Technical Certificate | -- | -- | -- | -- | -- | -- | 4.1284 | 18 |
| Average Ratio Per Survey | 5.2779 | | 1.5554 | | 4.1635 | | 3.7707 | |
| Survey Response, Total No. | | 1967 | | 2644 | | 2378 | | 1021 |

## AGE

| | Avg | No. | Avg | No. | Avg | No. | Avg | No. |
|---|---|---|---|---|---|---|---|---|
| 20-30 | 11.5245 | 238 | 3.4097 | 360 | 8.2347 | 189 | 5.3633 | 81 |
| 31-40 | 6.2443 | 552 | 1.6651 | 1028 | 5.4552 | 995 | 3.9985 | 484 |
| 41-50 | 3.9958 | 587 | 0.9731 | 702 | 2.8863 | 624 | 2.8669 | 311 |
| 51-60 | 3.0552 | 452 | 0.7465 | 508 | 1.9843 | 477 | 2.2501 | 222 |
| 61 and over | 0.5634 | 826 | 0.8873 | 125 | 1.5221 | 111 | 1.5896 | 56 |
| Average Ratio Per Survey | 3.9102 | | 1.5102 | | 4.1322 | | 3.3361 | |
| Survey Response, Total No. | | 2655 | | 2723 | | 2396 | | 1154 |

## YEARS OF SERVICE

| | Avg | No. | Avg | No. | Avg | No. | Avg | No. |
|---|---|---|---|---|---|---|---|---|
| 0-4 | 9.8578 | 867 | 7.1363 | 126 | 9.3927 | 749 | 8.5754 | 304 |
| 5-14 | 1.9306 | 759 | 1.8958 | 1024 | 2.1548 | 1142 | 1.8339 | 567 |
| 15-24 | 0.8429 | 278 | 0.8523 | 703 | 0.8938 | 367 | 0.8221 | 204 |
| 25-34 | 1.7853 | 66 | 0.8975 | 528 | 0.5896 | 121 | 0.5298 | 60 |
| 35-High | 0.3184 | 2 | 0.3619 | 190 | 0.4191 | 13 | 0.1915 | 19 |
| Average Ratio Per Survey | 5.2560 | | 1.5489 | | 4.1391 | | 3.3361 | |
| Survey Response, Total No. | | 1972 | | 2571 | | 2392 | | 1154 |

## NUMBER OF POSITIONS

| | Avg | No. | Avg | No. | Avg | No. | |
|---|---|---|---|---|---|---|---|
| 1 | 7.2750 | 1126 | 2.5771 | 290 | 6.2660 | 1175 | N.A. |
| 2, 3 | 2.7006 | 618 | 1.6863 | 1116 | 2.2565 | 985 | |
| 4, 5, 6 | 1.2692 | 180 | 1.1783 | 1126 | 1.0934 | 191 | |
| 7-HI | 0.3694 | 729 | 0.6820 | 169 | 1.5414 | 25 | |
| Average Ratio Per Survey | 3.9044 | | 1.5073 | | 4.1383 | | |
| Survey Response, Total No. | | 2653 | | 2701 | | 2376 | |

Table 3.1 (continued)

| YEARS IN CURRENT POSITION | 1973-74 Avg | No. | 1980 Avg | No. | 1984 Avg | No. | 1986-87 Avg | No. |
|---|---|---|---|---|---|---|---|---|
| up to 2 | 8.3521 | 615 | 2.0912 | 1066 | 7.6188 | 837 | 5.3208 | 440 |
| 3-6 | 3.1691 | 537 | 1.5881 | 500 | 2.9894 | 910 | 2.4840 | 361 |
| 7-10 | 1.6319 | 241 | 1.0352 | 471 | 1.5818 | 290 | 1.5336 | 151 |
| 11-15 | 1.2073 | 152 | 0.9571 | 270 | 1.0378 | 203 | 0.9865 | 88 |
| 16 and over | 0.8394 | 91 | 0.4857 | 128 | 0.7139 | 145 | 2.5754 | 114 |
| Average Ratio Per Survey | 4.5792 | | 1.5735 | | 4.1385 | | 3.3361 | |
| Survey Response, Total No. | | 1636 | | 2435 | | 2385 | | 1154 |

| SEX | Avg | No. | Avg | No. | Avg | No. | Avg | No. |
|---|---|---|---|---|---|---|---|---|
| male | 5.2072 | 1971 | 1.4969 | 2608 | 4.0213 | 2276 | 3.2276 | 1085 |
| female | 5.0637 | 19 | 1.9075 | 106 | 6.5011 | 115 | 5.6116 | 62 |
| Average Ratio Per Survey | 5.2058 | | 1.5129 | | 4.1406 | | 3.3565 | |
| Survey Response, Total No. | | 1990 | | 2714 | | 2391 | | 1147 |

Note: For each career development factor, an average ratio of expertise was calculated by dividing the number of academic years typically credited for the manager's highest achieved educational diploma or degree by the number of calendar years of full-time CAO local-government experience. Certain career information items were not collected on three of the four survey instruments and are designated as N.A. (not available).

Source: Compiled by the author from responses to the 1973–74 and the 1984 ICMA/CAO surveys introduced in Chapter 2, from responses to "A Profile of the Local Government City Manager/Chief Administrative Officer/Executive Director—1980" (the survey instrument administered by the ICMA in that year), and from responses to a 50-percent random sample survey of ICMA's recognized communities by the author with B. J. Reed, entitled "Local Government Manager Stress and Mobility Questionnaire: 1986."

# Table 3.2
## Importance of Local Public Management Skills, 1980 and Projected for the Year 2000

| SKILLS | TODAY Total # Reporting | TODAY Ranking | YEAR 2000* Total # Reporting | YEAR 2000* Ranking | Perceived Skill Stability and Change — Total Respondents (A) If Skill One of Top 3 Choices | 1980-2000 %(A) Reporting Same Choices | Ranking by Least % of Change |
|---|---|---|---|---|---|---|---|
| Budgeting and Finance | 1435 | 1 | 1039 | 1 | 2033 | 71.4 | 3 |
| Management & Control Programs | 737 | 2 | 624 | 2 | 1040 | 59.6 | 7 |
| Personnel/Labor Relations | 686 | 3 | 536 | 3 | 921 | 54.7 | 8 |
| Planning/Evaluation | 460 | 4 | 525 | 4 | 693 | 68.8 | 4 |
| Public Relations | 459 | 5 | 359 | 7 | 665 | 61.8 | 6 |
| Human Relations | 415 | 6 | 512 | 5 | 587 | 79.2 | 1 |
| Assisting Elected Officials | 384 | 7 | 349 | 8 | 583 | 65.2 | 5 |
| Brokering/Negotiating | 304 | 8 | 475 | 6 | 364 | 76.6 | 2 |
| Building Community Support | 289 | 9 | 337 | 9 | 377 | 52.3 | 10 |
| Economic Development | 241 | 10 | 247 | 10 | 322 | 41.0 | 13 |
| Grantsmanship | 125 | 11 | 65 | 14 | 191 | 20.4 | 15 |
| Maintenance/Development of Physical Infrastructure | 104 | 12 | 120 | 13 | 137 | 43.8 | 11 |
| Development of New Programs | 92 | 13 | 204 | 12 | 134 | 42.5 | 12 |
| Data Processing | 43 | 14 | 225 | 11 | 71 | 53.5 | 9 |
| Other | NA | NA | NA | NA | NA | NA | NA |
| Emergency (Disaster) Management | 12 | 15 | 33 | 15 | 15 | 26.7 | 14 |

*Note:* The "skill stability and change" columns were compiled by the author after computing the percentage of respondents who had indicated that a particular skill was among the three most important to them individually in 1980, and who also thought that it would be as important to them (in the top three) in the year 2000.

*Source:* On the 1980 ICMA/CAO survey, the question was asked: "Please indicate which three of the following skills you believe are most important to a local government manager/CAO/ED today and which three will be most important in the year 2000." The totals for the year 2000 were first reported by Richard J. Stillman, "Local Public Management in Transition: A Report on the Current State of the Profession," in *The Municipal Year Book 1982* (Washington, D.C.: ICMA, 1982), p. 172.

Table 3.3
Average Ratio of CAO Expertise in Relation to Selected Community Characteristics

| | 1973-74 | | 1980 | | 1984 | | 1986-87 | |
|---|---|---|---|---|---|---|---|---|
| | Avg. | No. | Avg. | No. | Avg. | No. | Avg. | No. |
| CITY SIZE | | | | | | | | |
| 1000K+ | 2.1111 | 3 | 0.9460 | 22 | 1.9138 | 20 | 1.5000 | 1 |
| 500K-1000K | 3.1919 | 110 | 1.1440 | 46 | 3.3918 | 28 | 1.6000 | 1 |
| 250K-499,999 | 4.5931 | 20 | 1.0758 | 73 | 3.1127 | 53 | 1.9850 | 6 |
| 100K-249,999 | 3.2662 | 73 | 1.2424 | 171 | 3.6261 | 112 | 2.8792 | 24 |
| 50K-99,999 | 2.7289 | 162 | 1.1144 | 216 | 3.3433 | 168 | 1.7953 | 72 |
| 25K-49,999 | 3.8207 | 328 | 1.1885 | 333 | 3.5365 | 303 | 2.5773 | 135 |
| 10K-24,999 | 3.8623 | 691 | 1.4855 | 671 | 3.8809 | 603 | 2.7800 | 323 |
| 5K-9,999 | 4.5082 | 661 | 1.7058 | 538 | 4.3904 | 503 | 3.3507 | 245 |
| 2500-4,999 | 3.6202 | 570 | 1.8196 | 446 | 5.0139 | 353 | 4.0092 | 221 |
| 2,499 and less | 5.2979 | 106 | 2.2051 | 144 | 5.4123 | 186 | 5.5696 | 110 |
| Avg. Ratio Per Survey | 3.9397 | | 1.5205 | | 4.1489 | | 3.3206 | |
| Survey Response, Total No. | 2624 | | 2660 | | 2329 | | 1138 | |
| | | | | | | | | |
| METRO STATUS | | | | | | | | |
| City/SMSA | 3.2986 | 291 | 1.0757 | 339 | 3.1129 | 291 | 1.9760 | 107 |
| Suburb/part SMSA | 3.9900 | 1341 | 1.5386 | 1246 | 4.0636 | 1139 | 3.1267 | 600 |
| City/more than SMSA | 4.0597 | 992 | 1.6445 | 978 | 4.6175 | 867 | 3.9244 | 431 |
| Non SMSA | 0 | 0 | 1.7551 | 40 | 2.4336 | 10 | 0 | 0 |
| Avg. Ratio Per Survey | 3.9397 | | 1.5214 | | 4.1448 | | 3.3206 | |
| Survey Response, Total No. | 2624 | | 2603 | | 2307 | | 1138 | |

| RECORD TYPE | Avg. | No. | Avg. | No. | Avg. | No. | Avg. | No. |
|---|---|---|---|---|---|---|---|---|
| US over 2500 | 3.9397 | 2624 | 1.5302 | 2204 | 4.1855 | 2106 | 3.3206 | 1138 |
| US Counties | 0 | 0 | 1.5272 | 299 | 4.0828 | 140 | 0 | 0 |
| COGS | 0 | 0 | 1.3710 | 157 | 3.3306 | 83 | 0 | 0 |
| Avg. Ratio Per Survey | 3.9397 | | 1.5205 | | 4.1489 | | 3.3206 | |
| Survey Response, Total No. | 2624 | | 2660 | | 2329 | | 1138 | |

| FORM OF GOVERNMENT | Avg. | No. | Avg. | No. | Avg. | No. | Avg. | No. |
|---|---|---|---|---|---|---|---|---|
| Mayor/Cty Bd | 2.7188 | 928 | 1.8359 | 627 | 5.1036 | 448 | 4.0099 | 252 |
| Manager | 4.7947 | 1524 | 1.3550 | 1601 | 3.8956 | 1652 | 3.1192 | 835 |
| Commission/App't A O | 2.1870 | 53 | 1.6423 | 147 | 4.5629 | 57 | 2.0500 | 6 |
| Town Mtg/City Exec | 3.3124 | 108 | 2.2355 | 106 | 4.3891 | 75 | 3.0278 | 37 |
| T.M./Cty Exec & Mgr | 3.0795 | 11 | 1.3785 | 22 | 5.3639 | 14 | 4.9374 | 8 |
| Avg. Ratio Per Survey | 3.9397 | | 1.5298 | | 4.1791 | | 3.3206 | |
| Survey Response, Total No. | 2624 | | 2503 | | 2246 | | 1138 | |

| GEOGRAPHIC REGION | Avg. | No. | Avg. | No. | Avg. | No. | Avg. | No. |
|---|---|---|---|---|---|---|---|---|
| Northeast | 3.6445 | 610 | 1.6757 | 553 | 3.9347 | 446 | 3.1195 | 241 |
| North Central | 3.4150 | 769 | 1.6101 | 729 | 4.3367 | 626 | 3.6305 | 315 |
| South | 4.2072 | 739 | 1.5069 | 828 | 4.2010 | 722 | 3.3316 | 327 |
| West | 4.7021 | 506 | 1.2660 | 550 | 4.0372 | 535 | 3.1137 | 255 |
| Avg. Ratio Per Survey | 3.9397 | | 1.5205 | | 4.1489 | | 3.3206 | |
| Survey Response, Total No. | 2624 | | 2660 | | 2329 | | 1138 | |

*Source:* Compiled by the author from responses to the 1973–74, 1980, and 1984 ICMA/CAO surveys, and from the 1986–87 Green–Reed survey.

83

computed for 1980 (that is, it takes time to get more education as well as more government experience), it does not suggest any particular rationale for why in 1984 the average number of hours worked per week increased, along with the size of the ratio (becoming larger than 1.00).

Further insight can be garnered by considering a number of other factors often associated with differences among individuals who are at different stages in their careers: total years of (CAO) experience, number of (CAO) positions held, years in current position, and age. For each of these career factors, there are again two basic patterns. The first trend is similar to that seen earlier in the relationship between increasing levels of salary and decreasing ratios of expertise. Table 3.1 indicates that—when there is an increase in years of CAO service, number of CAO positions held, years in the current position, and age of the manager— there is also (with a couple of modest exceptions) a consistent reduction in the ratio of expertise (closer to 1.00). This seems logical: As the managers gained in experience, they would have a greater opportunity to change positions or to stay longer in their current posts (and maybe even to live longer!), and there would be an increase in the balance between their years of academic training and years of CAO experience.

However, the second trend evident in these other career factors suggests at least one plausible explanation for the conflict in trends cited in our discussion of the hours-worked category. There is a crosscutting pattern here that could not be seen earlier because of missing information (in both the salary and the hours-worked categories). It is what may be described as a "surge and subside" trend. The average ratio of expertise for the 1973–74 respondents is substantially higher than that computed for the 1980 respondents. Except for a lack of 1986–87 data regarding number of CAO positions held, this surge-and-subside pattern is seen again between the overall average ratios of expertise for the 1984 and the 1986–87 survey responses. It seems potentially quite significant that the average ratio calculated for these career factors in 1986–87 did not drop back to the previous average recorded for the 1980 survey. This twice-recurring pattern does seem to suggest that managers as a whole occupational group are responding to some uniform array of career factors.

A closer inspection of these two contrasting trends—coupled with some reflection on the national and professional developments identified in our earlier review of the literature (described in Chapters 2 and 3)—suggests at least one explanation. By the time of the 1980 survey of ICMA-recognized communities, the managers and their communities were confronting new (and perhaps recurring) stages, or conditions for transition. These stages of community transition may be conceived of as (and also reflected in manager reactions to): (1) changes in the emphasis on—or in the need for—certain types of CAO expertise; (2) an altering of the basic power arrangements within each community, and then the resulting changes in the balance of authority represented among and shared by government officials and institutions; and (3) the time that it takes managers to adjust to all these changes. It seems at least possible that the actual number of hours worked by managers is directly related to the basic balancing act of aligning their evolving professional expertise (at least our measure of it) with changes within and without the community.

For another perspective, consider the relationship between the pursuit of higher levels of formal education and the ratio of expertise. Table 3.1 offers a hint as to just how sustained, simultaneous, and perhaps significant is the demand on managers to be pursuing and securing more expertise through increased education, as well as through work experience. The data in their raw state (even more so than in the ratio-of-expertise calculations arrayed in Table 3.1) display a relatively consistent and interlocking pattern of education with work, and work with education. This increasing commitment by career CAOs to advanced and continuing education matches one of the most basic characteristics of all other acknowledged professions. It certainly seems to be the case for the CAOs officers serving in ICMA-recognized communities. For the field of local government management as a whole, there seems to be an ongoing gravitational pull toward a balanced ratio of expertise between educational achievement and years of CAO experience—creating a pattern (at least as indicated by the data from these four surveys) of an increasingly interdependent need for more education and more experience. While the educational credential of choice has become the M.P.A.—as noted in Chapter 2—a small but growing proportion of managers are working on post-master's degrees. It will be interesting to see whether this trend continues, and—if so—which degree specializations will be emphasized.

Perhaps as a final illustration of the measure, and of the pivotal role played by professional expertise among local government managers, Table 3.1 shows the current imbalance of years of education to years of experience for the still relatively small—but growing—proportion of CAOs who are women. The current imbalance is demonstrated by the higher (greater than 1.00) ratio of expertise for women in comparison to men for each of the surveys. This seems due in part to the later entry of women into the profession, and is occurring at a time when longer periods of pre-CAO government experience are being experienced and expected of all professional local government managers. However, in the general survey population, the proportion of women with advanced college degrees is much higher than men, and this is represented in differences between the ratios of expertise among women and men in the ICMA and Green–Reed surveys. Nevertheless, the same surge-and-subside pattern is present for the women as for the men; they are—both in common—adjusting forces requiring changes in managerial expertise.

It seems clear from this comparison of the surveys that a substantial majority of the managers were reporting a rather uniform, composite view of the expertise required by their career choice. As arrayed in Table 3.2, responses from the 1980 ICMA survey also indicate that, when individual managers were asked to compare skills most important to them at the time with those they predicted would be most important to them in the future, the traditional skill areas remained primary. Managers ranked the traditional skills of budgeting and finance, management and control of programs, personnel and labor relations, and planning and evaluation as first through fourth—respectively—for the year 2000 as well as for the year 1980. The more topical or specialized skills of grantsmanship, maintenance and development of physical infrastructure, development of new programs, data processing, and emergency (disaster) management were not indicated very often as being of predominant importance, then or in the future.

The "skill stability and change" columns in Table 3.2 take the analysis one step further, by displaying the percentage of responding managers who had indicated that a particular skill was among the three most important to them individually in 1980, and who also thought that it would be equally as important to them in the year 2000. Six skill areas were indicated by managers as having the greatest continuity of importance, or stability of value; these six retained at least 60 percent of their previous adherents. Ranked in order, they were in areas of human relations, brokering and negotiating, budgeting and finance, planning and evaluation, assisting elected officials, and public relations. While these six were ranked by the managers in the aggregate as being among the top one-half of all the skills listed on the survey (there were 16) both currently and in the future, the managers were also cognizant of changing career and community needs, demands, and circumstances.

Richard Stillman appears to support this interpretation. In an analysis of other data derived from the same 1980 ICMA survey, Stillman reported,

[managers] saw their influence growing in four categories in particular during the years ahead: planning and evalution (56%), labor relations (55%), policy recommendations and formulation of policies (47%), and public opinion leadership (44%). It was their general belief, however, that their influence over the "bread and butter" concerns of city management would remain about what it has been: 63% saw their influence remaining the same over administration; 60% saw their influence remaining the same over purchasing/procurement; 59% saw it remaining the same over budgeting; and 56% saw it staying about the same in personnel policies.[32]

A new age of increased local government responsibility, along with a pattern of greater public sector fiscal conservatism, has been requiring that local CAOs meet their traditional obligations with a new professional creativity. In order to successfully meet the traditional responsibilities of budgeting and finance, organization management, personnel, and public relations, managers are discovering the need to acquire new proficiencies and competencies in such areas as general human relations, brokering and negotiating, and planning and evaluation.

As a method of situating the reference points for this interpretation of trends, we turn briefly to consideration of a number of community and governmental variables that are frequently used to characterize the national marketplace for professional local government managers and their expertise. These factors include: population size of the community, relationship of the community to the standard metropolitan statistical areas (SMSAs), type of government, and geographic region. These important community and governmental factors are often described and thought of as regulating the flow and distribution of expertise among local government managers across the nation. On Table 3.3, the ratios of expertise for each of the three ICMA surveys and the Green–Reed survey are displayed for comparison with these community and governmental variables.

Table 3.3 leads us to two additional observations regarding the argument that changing community environments are expanding the nature and scope of professional expertise required of local government managers. The first item of interest is that the recurring surge-and-subside pattern of rising educational requirements followed by a balancing increase in CAO experience—at least among our surveyed communities—is again clearly recognizable at each point in time. The second observation, however, is in counterpoint to the evolving personal career factors that had displayed a rather consistent pattern of variation between 1973–74 and 1986–87, but had also been tied to point of entry and stage of career among the different categories of managers. That is, when the community factors of population size, metropolitan status, form of government, and geographic location are considered, there is little variation separating the managers' ratios of expertise from the individual overall survey average ratios of expertise—regardless of where the CAOs were reporting from or which type of government they were serving. This suggests that the forces of community change reflected in the changing career path (expertise) factors of these local government managers were truly time related and nationwide in scope.

## PROFESSIONALISM AS LEADERSHIP STYLE

There are probably as many who have disagreed as have agreed with Murray Edelman's overriding thesis that

[in an era of] organizations the decisions of officials about the allocation of tangible resources to groups of the population are controlled far more than in simpler polities by the factual and value premises assembled through organization. . . . Individuals may differ in the quickness with which they recognize what is required, but maneuverability is severely limited, even for the highest officials, by the information the organization supplies and screens. In short, the difference between two political leaders in the same position today rests relatively little on differences in policy direction and very largely on other behaviors which we can label "leadership styles." Leaders rely increasingly on style differences to create and emphasize an impression of maneuverability, and the impression remains an important political fact even if the maneuverability is not.[33]

It is important to appreciate that Edelman's central point was not that government leaders are impotent, but rather that—on most important public policy issues—they are as constrained by the areas of community consensus as they are by the areas of competition and conflict dividing their constituencies. It is by working out policies of reconciliation and by establishing balanced priorities—

rather than by establishing independently defined community agendas—that maneuverability can be created by managers using a variety of leadership styles. Managerial strategies must be considered and implemented under the increasing glare of greater standards of public accountability, responsibility, and constraint. In the aftermath of the national scandals of Watergate and—more recently—"Iran-gate" plus a variety of federal, state, and local investigations into more local scandals, new formal and informal accountability standards have caused important changes in the working conditions of public officials. And these expectations for public officials are much more pronounced than the comparatively modest changes that have been mandated for nonprofit entities and private sector firms.

Perhaps—after the turmoil of the 1960s, 1970s, and early 1980s—there are many more now who would find Edelman's thesis to be not such an extreme nor provocative interpretation or explanation of community affairs. The public-policy research wars continue to investigate and debate this maneuverability issue. Much of the warring has to do with determining who loses by gaining only the symbolic policy victory and who wins by receiving the actual and material program benefits, and how long a period of time and how many channels of government decision making must be considered before being able—if ever—to make a determination.

My concern is to focus on the occupational maneuverability associated with the adoption of various managerial styles—on what Howard Vollmer and Donald Mills refer to as "professionalism" and define as the "ideology and associated activities that can be found in . . . occupational groups where members aspire to professional status."[34] I will focus on questions of role value and performance that are exhibited in the reports of professional local government managers while inservice—that is, their attitudes toward and activities within the general value scheme attributed by George Strauss to all professionals: expertise, autonomy, responsibility, and commitment. In the following sections, we will analyze the ideology and reported activities of those who serve within the legally based authority ascribed to the professional local government manager and recognized by the ICMA. We examine these perceptions and activities within the contexts that we have outlined from general research conducted on the administrative constituencies. We will reserve for the next chapter a more complete discussion of the occupationally induced processes, forces, and pressures that are felt by local government managers as they try to perform as professionals within their occupational and overall personal contexts.

## CAREER MOBILITY PATTERNS

As we move to address these important issues, we begin by recognizing that professional local government managers demonstrate a pronounced pattern of career mobility. In this field, career mobility is frequently associated with major geographic moves, as well. That is to say, by definition, there can be only one professional CAO per community; and when a manager changes position, he or she also generally changes location (the exceptions being when the manager changes positions within an extended metropolitan area or between levels of government within an area). When I speak of "a pronounced pattern of career mobility," I do not mean to suggest that the frequency of positional change is an occupational by-product chosen solely by the managers due to their particular professional style, but rather that the managers' "choice" or "change" of style is an important factor in their (market) value to governments, as community needs vary at different points in time.

This regular mobility feature in the profession of local government management makes it somewhat distinctive compared with the general impression of the more traditional professions (of medicine, law, accountancy; and perhaps in education, as well), where building up a stable clientele (reputation) is the most desired path. But this pattern of occupational mobility among local government managers is not so totally unique as it first appears—even compared to the traditional professions. For example, the U.S. military services and the U.S. Forest Service regularly rotate their personnel. And there is a complete array of professionals—including many from the traditionally acknowledged professions—who are employed by consulting firms and whose business is premised on taking the service to the client's location.

Take, for example, the study done on the U.S. Forest Service by Herbert Kaufman. Kaufman found that rangers are regularly rotated among geographically separated parks to further the service's federal policy goals. The agency does not want its personnel to be co-opted by local constituencies with vested interests in particular parks, programs, or projects. However, in complete contrast, the mobility pattern among CAOs is inevitably tied to and driven by local dynamics.[35]

However, there is an interesting counteranalogy to be drawn between the Forest Service and the mobility pattern of local government managers. The service's purpose in rotating their rangers from park to park is to promote the standardization of national policy objectives, in an organizational situation where the rangers operate in relative isolation. CAOs—on the other hand—are not only required to be the instruments of policy, but also to be participants in the processes for developing and managing implementation of policies, programs, and projects. In light of the U.S. Forest Service's rotation policy for its rangers, a series of important questions can be raised. Are the local government managers' professional values being altered or co-opted by local administrative constituencies—specifically, the government that they work for? Do the professional values of managers change over time? Do the expectations of communities for those professional values and roles change with varying local conditions? Or does the national marketplace for managerial expertise work to balance the local dynamic forces?

Before discussing these questions, we must first address a more basic issue:

What are the main attributes of a professional that would be subject to co-optation and change? Most students interested in the evolution and standing of professions make three basic assumptions about common characteristics:

1. Members of a profession have similar—if not identical—perceptions, values, and experiences.
2. The job requirements at one site for any member of a profession are very similar to the job requirements for another member of the profession at a different site.
3. The members of the profession govern themselves according to their own standards and ethics.[36]

However, in a recent study on professional bureaucracies, Mary Guy found her evidence to be at odds with these assumptions. Guy found that "managing professionals [are] not too different from managing nonprofessionals, with the exception that professionals typically place heavy emphasis on academic degrees and articulate their expectation to play an influential role in organization decision making."[37] Her study is of particular interest because it was based on an analysis of "firms which rely on [the most respected] professionals to perform the mission of the organization. Included in this genre are schools, hospitals, universities, research and development laboratories, technical laboratories, social welfare agencies, and a plethora of others, in the private, public, and not-for-profit sectors."[38]

Guy then raises a particularly pertinent question for this study, by asking, "Is professionalism a control mechanism within an organization, or is it a structural variable, or is it neither?" Which set of values (personal, professional, or organizational), then, predominate when there are conflicts caused between organizationally or politically established values and the occupational values associated with particular professionals represented within that organization—for example, between city attorneys and city managers?

While Guy did not study local government, her argument is of interest to us here because she concluded that neither set of values predominates.

Professionalism is a label useful for categorizing groups of staff members who have similar training and similar work responsibilities. . . . As we look at the decisions resulting from trade-offs among personal goals, organizational goals, and professional goals, that different groups of professionals are about as likely to agree with members of other professions, as they are to agree with a professional peer. This does not take away from the status roles of professionals, but it does tell us that we as administrators should not put too much credence in generalizing that "all doctors are alike," "all teachers are alike," "all social workers are alike" and so on. Rather, we should realize that it is how we structure work teams and units and work tasks that determines which members of an organization are more likely to reach a consensus among themselves in accord with the goals of the organization.[39]

There has been a great deal of discussion and writing focused on the professional value implications of CAO career mobility patterns—particularly as an-

primary reasons—from among 14 possibilities listed (eight may be characterized as career based; six as community based)—were what may be described as career rationales. This basic pattern held true regardless of manager age group, sex, educational level, years as a manager, number of previous local governments served, years in current position, community population size, geographic region, or metropolitan status. Career-based rationales—it would seem—are overwhelmingly behind the most recent change in position.

The next step in this analysis was to classify each manager responding to the 1984 ICMA survey into one of three categories of professional mobility (community based, mixed, or career based) depending on the combination of reasons indicated for leaving the previous position. A manager's most recent experience with professional mobility was characterized as being community based if all the reasons cited for leaving were associated with conditions external to the manager's career development (personal stress, family, electoral or other political factors), career based if all the reasons cited were linked directly to career motivations for advancement (salary, retirement plan, prestige, larger government, desire for new experience, climate or scene), or mixed if there was any combination between the two basic sets of rationales.[45]

The reader will notice that this approach limits our analysis to only those managers who have held at least one previous position. We cannot, then, use this *scale of professional mobility* to study the reasons managers have chosen to stay with only one position—regardless of how long or short their career has been to date. And to put the scale in its proper context, we note that 49 percent of all respondents to the 1984 survey indicated that their current CAO position was also their first full-time position, and that 31 percent reported having been a local government manager for less than the average five-year period.[46] Another battery of survey questions was used to address some of this scale's (time) limitations, as discussed later.

In the final analysis, 974 managers (41.2 percent) were included in the scale of professional mobility, from among the 2,360 responding to the overall 1984 survey instrument. The balance between this and the percentage reported above for managers in their first positions is accounted for by item nonresponses about previous positions held. Of those in the scale, 565 managers (58.1 percent) were classified as having given purely career-based reasons for changing positions; 155 (15.9 percent) could be identified by the purely community-based items selected to explain their leaving; and 253 (26.0 percent) indicated a mixed array of reasons. When the ratio of expertise was computed for each of these categories, there was a clear pattern of reduced ratio size when the career-based rationale (2.1372) was compared with the mixed (2.0759) and the community-based (1.5482) reasons for position change.

To the extent that 1984 represents a typical year (as it does on many other dimensions when compared with the 1973–74, 1980, and 1986–87 surveys), the scale shows that a clear majority of managers identify purely career-based reasons for making position changes. But on the other hand, nearly 42 percent of the managers described their most recent change as being for either purely community-based reasons or a more complicated mixture of reasons. The computations also indicate that, when managers leave for primarily career-based reasons, their average ratio of expertise is higher than those leaving for mixed reasons—and even higher than those leaving for community-based reasons. As discussed below, this classification of professional local-government managers according to their reasons for changing positions must be examined within the context of a variety of other occupational factors.

While this scale represents only one point in time, it seems to suggest that professional mobility patterns may not be driven exclusively by a singular or fixed view held by managers toward their CAO careers. More specifically, the pattern for ratios of expertise within the scale of professional mobility may be indicating that, when there is an individually felt or fieldwide persistency in the overbalancing of education to experience among managers, this may mark a substantial buildup of desire and pressure for position exchanges (both individually and across the field). This would seem to be particularly likely when a manager or a (newer) class of managers have been in the process for some time of serially or simultaneously earning higher educational credentials and securing preparatory government and CAO experience.

It does seem that the ability for significant numbers of position moves to take place depends importantly on the proportion of managers in various stages of professional transition (marked by their reaching or exceeding the ratio-of-expertise balance point of 1.00 through an imbalancing trend of greater CAO experience to years of education; and by the rationales that they associate with position changes in the field, as traced through the scale of professional mobility). Some of these managers can be described as being in professional transition because they are essentially meeting their career goal expectations (represented by a shifting from the mixed to the community-based categories or directly from the career-based to the community-based categories of professional mobility), even when they find it necessary or are forced to make a position change. And these senior managers are characterized by having longer tenures in their most recent job postings—which suggests that they like what they are doing and the type of place that they are doing it in.

A second significant group of managers in professional transition (possessing essentially the same career mobility and ratio-of-expertise markings are those about to make a decision to leave the profession itself. This second group of managers represents those who are growing in frustration—either in regard to what they do for a living or else with their inability to make a change into the type of community situation that they desire, even when they have advanced educations and substantial years of general government and CAO experience.

This interpretation of the patterns revealed through the scale professional mobility is symmetrical with the surge-and-subside wave action found in the levels of CAO expertise for the field as a whole. We have already noted that, at least for local government managers serving in ICMA-recognized communities, there has been an aggregate increase in the proportion of managers who have and are working to secure advanced degrees, with the M.P.A. degree being the credential of choice. We also noted that most managers are reporting an increasing amount of pre-CAO government experience before their initial appointment as local government manager. Further, the numbers of new positions for professional local-government management are increasing, but at a modest rate.

At this point, we have identified two potentially important occupational dynamics that can be linked to the surge-and-subside pattern for this sample of CAOs. First, there is a stepwise increase in the overall levels of expertise in the field represented by our sample of managers. This is generally consistent with the fact that more managers report that they have been sustaining their career interest for longer periods of time. The near-term prognosis seems to be an increased demand for education and experience—components associated with professionalism.

Second, there appears to be a relationship between the increasing levels of expertise reported by managers in the field over the past decade and a half, and the nature of change in the types of managers who will make up the field if present trends continue. The linkage has to do with maturing occupational expectations, which seem to be influenced by the differing processes of professionalization that managers as individuals and as professional generations experience during the course of their careers. These dynamics may help to explain the surge-and-subside trend in the ratios of expertise. The surge-and-subside trend may be associated with why and when different managers choose to exchange positions or to leave the profession. We will examine these processes of professionalization more closely in Chapter 4.

We should note that the single item frequencies observed above for the managers' most recent changes of position do not directly conflict with Timothy Almy's central theme: Indeed, some managers do change positions because of a desire for new professional challenges. However, now we have additional evidence indicating that a substantial portion of these managers (only 8 percent less than one-half) report changing positions not for reasons associated with career, but for personal or community reasons. Further, the evidence suggests that a fixed view of managers' career motivations is not likely to take into account the experience impacts of professionalization and the maturation of managers' career expectations. Neither—in a fixed view—would the possible linkages be noticed between a manager's decision to change position and his or her independent anticipation of certain community-based developments (political, economic, social, technological, and so forth) that "require" a change in the manager's position sooner rather than later. These may be perceived by the managers themselves or else by their councils and the other administrators as a need for change in the particular form of CAO expertise or for a different management style, in general.

## PERCEIVED COUNCIL EXPECTATIONS

The perceptions that local government managers have of their councils' primary expectations for them are significant in terms of the potential role and authority conflicts that may be revealed. Being potential sources of conflict, the CAOs' perceptions (and the councils' expectations) may also be linked to the profession's mobility patterns. As displayed in Table 3.4, when respondents to the 1984 ICMA survey were asked which of the listed roles best described their councils' overall expectations for them, the answers were ranked—not surprisingly—thus: exercise administrative leadership (61.1 percent), provide issue formulation guidelines (25.3 percent), advise council with factual data (7.9 percent), recommend strategies and development plans (4.6 percent), and exercise political leadership (0.8 percent).

There was a similar inquiry made by ICMA in the 1973–74 survey; but that questionnaire was directed solely toward municipal managers, and involved a somewhat different scaling approach. Nevertheless, these municipal managers, too, overwhelmingly voted the exercise of administrative leadership as the primary role expectation of their councils. Interestingly, when contrasting the perceived councils' expectations solely among "municipal managers" in 1973–74 with those reported by "city managers" in 1984, "the most substantial change in perception of the council's expectations of their city managers was the increased incidence of obligation to participate in the formulation of issues, objectives, and plans (a 17.5% increase)."[47]

This comparison also reveals a countervailing 22.2 percent reduction in 1984 from the 1973–74 survey high of 83.2 percent of councils who were reported as expecting the manager's primary role to be the exercise of administrative leadership. In 1984, council-of-government (COG) directors reported an even more strongly felt (31.1 percent) board expectation that they were to participate in issue formulation than did city managers (25.5 percent) with regard to their councils. However, the increase in this perceived expectation for CAO participation in issue formulation was less emphatically replicated in county manager perceptions (18.5 percent) of their commissions' expectations. On balance, there were at least some managers who felt that they were being asked to delegate part of their administrative responsibilities and authorities to other staff members in order to take on additional commitments and functions. By contrast, less than 1 percent of all the reporting CAOs chose the exercise of political leadership as their councils' primary expectation.[48]

The responses reproduced in Table 3.4 also indicate that the one area where there is an asymmetrical pattern among the three types of managers is in the proportion of COG directors who perceive their boards as primarily expecting them to recommend or develop objectives and planning strategies. As a group, COG directors reported a 13.4 percent greater perception in this category than municipal managers, and a 16.0 percent greater perception than county managers. These survey results suggest that there is some variation in the emphasis—if not

**Table 3.4**
**Summary of Council Expectations regarding Manager/CAO as Perceived by Respondents, 1984**

| Respondents | No. of Respondents (A) | Exercise Political Leadership | | Exercise Administrative Leadership | | Advise Council | | Participate in Issue Formulation | | Develop Objective Strategies | | Other Expectations | |
|---|---|---|---|---|---|---|---|---|---|---|---|---|---|
| | | No. | % (A) | No. | % (A) | No. | % (A) | No. | % (A) | No. | % (A) | No. | % (A) |
| Total | 2065 | 17 | 0.8 | 1262 | 61.1 | 163 | 7.9 | 522 | 25.3 | 94 | 4.6 | 7 | 0.3 |
| Managers of cities over 2,500 | 1867 | 15 | 0.8 | 1138 | 61.0 | 152 | 8.1 | 476 | 25.5 | 79 | 4.2 | 7 | 0.4 |
| County managers | 124 | 0 | 0.0 | 92 | 74.2 | 7 | 5.6 | 23 | 18.5 | 2 | 1.6 | 0 | 0.0 |
| Councils of government directors | 74 | 2 | 2.7 | 32 | 43.2 | 4 | 5.4 | 23 | 31.1 | 13 | 17.6 | 0 | 0.0 |

*Note:* Respondents were asked which of the listed roles best described their councils' expectations. Percentages for each row may not add up to 100% due to rounding.

*Source:* First reported by the author in "Local Government Managers: Styles and Challenges," *Baseline Data Report* 19, no. 2 (Washington, D.C.: ICMA, March/April 1987), p. 6.

the general pattern—in the perceived primary expectations of councils/commissions/boards, according to type of government managed.

And when the councils' perceived primary role expectation for the managers is compared with the professional mobility scale (data not displayed), the managers who indicated that their rationales for changing jobs were career based represent a clear majority of all who reported primary role expectations for managers. But in fact, in all three categories, managers were close to being proportionately represented within the professional mobility scale (career based, mixed, and community based). This portion of the analysis seems to suggest that, for those managers who have held at least one previous position as CAO, the decision to change positions (whether made on their own, or by others) was not due to any uniform pattern of misunderstanding or confusion on the part of the managers about what their primary role ought to be—at least according to their reported perceptions of council expectations.

## ALLOCATION OF WORK TIME AS A DESCRIPTOR OF PROFESSIONAL STYLE

In the 1984 ICMA survey, local government managers were asked how they allocated their work time. From among the wide-ranging types of activities offered for their consideration—and listed in Table 3.5—it is perhaps not surprising that managers reported spending nearly half (a total of 49.9 percent) of their time on the most spontaneous, pressing, and immediate types of responsibilities. When ranked by the average proportion of time that the activity consumed, these pressing responsibilities include: responding to crises (14.6 percent); the continuous—but often crisis-related—need to act as a negotiator of problems, conflicts, and compromises (12.9 percent); the ongoing—but crisis-altering—allocation of governmental resources such as money, time, and attention (12.1 percent); and the general and ongoing management responsibilities (hiring, scheduling, training, motivation) regarding government personnel (10.3 percent).

It seems, then, that most CAOs are required to commit substantial portions of their time responding to the most immediate types of governmental responsibilities. Long-term community or governmental scanning is the activity that received the smallest proportion of the reporting managers' time—an average of only 6.2 percent. The assessment of what and how environmental forces might affect the long-term needs of the community and government is an activity that is understandably difficult to practice while responding to crises.

While an assessment of the largest demands on CAOs' time is revealing, the responses displayed in Table 3.5 also demonstrate why local government managers are most often described—by themselves as well as by others—as being generalists (thus the title: chief administrative officer). Including the activities listed above, managers reported spending an average of not less than 6.0 percent nor more than 14.6 percent of their time on any one of the ten types of activity

# Table 3.5
## Current Allocation of CAO Work Time in Relation to the Scale of Professional Mobility, 1984

| ACTIVITIES | No. of Managers Reporting | Mean % of Time Spent Per Week | Scale of Professional Mobility | | | | | | Row Totals |
|---|---|---|---|---|---|---|---|---|---|
| | | | Career-Based Mean % | No. | Mixed Mean % | No. | Community-Based Mean % | No. | |
| Pct. Time as Figurehead | 2172 | 8.7 | 8.54 | 511 | 7.57 | 229 | 7.23 | 137 | 877 |
| Pct. Time on Personnel | 2172 | 10.3 | 10.31 | 511 | 10.18 | 229 | 11.00 | 137 | 877 |
| Pct. Time on Outside Liaison | 2172 | 9.6 | 9.54 | 511 | 10.23 | 229 | 10.96 | 137 | 877 |
| Pct. Time on Environmental Assessment | 2172 | 6.2 | 6.41 | 511 | 6.42 | 229 | 5.82 | 137 | 877 |
| Pct. Time on Sharing Info. in Org. | 2172 | 9.2 | 9.24 | 511 | 9.74 | 229 | 9.49 | 137 | 877 |
| Pct. Time as Org. Spokesman | 2171 | 7.3 | 7.78 | 511 | 7.27 | 229 | 7.63 | 137 | 877 |
| Pct. Time as Org. Entrepreneur | 2171 | 8.9 | 9.67 | 511 | 9.63 | 229 | 8.35 | 137 | 877 |
| Pct. Time in Crisis Mgm't | 2171 | 14.6 | 13.88 | 511 | 13.72 | 229 | 13.99 | 137 | 877 |
| Pct. Time Resource Allocation | 2172 | 12.1 | 11.62 | 511 | 12.10 | 229 | 13.18 | 137 | 877 |
| Pct. Time as Negotiator | 2172 | 12.9 | 13.08 | 511 | 13.11 | 229 | 12.35 | 137 | 877 |

*Note:* Each responding manager to the 1984 ICMA/CAO survey was classified into one of three categories of *professional mobility* if the position that they held immediately prior to their current position was also as a manager/CAO/ED, and if they indicated on the survey at least one or more of 14 possible reasons why they had left (they could check all that were applicable). A manager's professional mobility was characterized as being *community based* if all reasons cited for leaving were any combination of personal stress (two items), family concerns, desire for smaller local government, electoral or political factors (two items); *career-based* if all reasons cited had to do with career advancement, salary, retirement plan, prestige, desire for larger local government, desire for new experience, climate, or scene; or *mixed* if there was any combination of the two basic sets of rationales.

*Source:* An initial compilation from the question (columns 1 and 2) was first reported by the author in "Local Government Managers: Styles and Challenges," *Baseline Data Report* 19, no. 2 (Washington, D.C.: ICMA, March/April 1987), p. 7. Respondents to the 1984 ICMA/CAO survey had been asked to "Please indicate the approximate percentage of your time spent on the following types of activities. (Percentages should total 100% regardless of the number of hours you work per week.)

listed on the survey instrument. But a closer look suggests that the managers' apparently generalized pattern of roles is often a product of the integration of more specialized core functions. Serving their communities as public liaison officers; acting as gatherers of public policy, program, and project intelligence; being enterprising in how they assist their governments in adjusting to changing conditions; being promotional figureheads as well as governmental spokespersons—all these activities are often simultaneous and integrated functions.

In this vein, it is interesting to note how the substance of these specific occupational roles that are commonly and widely played by the CAOs of most local governments in our sample assume a knowledge—that is, a professional literacy—in the traditional areas of expertise: finance and budgeting, administration, personnel, and public relations. Our review of the research and anecdotal literature would imply that many of the listed manager activities are new. However, it now seems at least as plausible to submit that most—if not all—of them have always been part of the actual roles played by the local government manager. However, what does appear to be new is that they take increasing amounts of the managers' work time, and are more explicitly required as part of the managers' job description and their official roster of duties.[49]

One further point is suggested by analysis of Table 3.5. The pressures of competing time commitments are likely to seem a product of the pace and timing of changing regional, national, and international economic, social, political, and technological impacts on localities. We have already acknowledged that there is an increased economic and technological competitiveness and stress in the nation and the world. But the emphasis on many of the newer skills among managers reporting to the ICMA and Green–Reed surveys and included in this study also seems to be derivative of how their local governments are politically, professionally, and structurally organized. The fluidity of these governmental considerations becomes ever more important as managers respond to altering community circumstances. As local governments recognize and move to address the individual interdependencies of their communities with these external changes and developments, the new skills may easily become more visible and necessary. But our analysis of manager perceptions implies that these issues and trends be considered as extensions of the profession's historical core areas of expertise and responsibility, not as replacements to them.

One illustration of this point is found in the skill area of local government manager as negotiator and broker. We can see how much negotiating and brokering of public interest conflicts, responsibilities, and compromises might need to be done between the local government's departmental personnel, professional management team (city attorneys, auditors, comptrollers, treasurers, and so forth), and elected council, as well as with individual private-sector administrative constituencies and with the larger array of community interest groups. Delegation of combinations of some of the newer as well as some of the core CAO responsibilities is often necessary, but primary public accountability for the quality of their administration remains with the chief administrative officer.

Recalling Murray Edelman's description of roles and expectations, we can appreciate why the manager is called upon to undertake these responsibilities (by virtue of being in a strategic, pivotal government position, and being the one expected to possess the requisite expertise); we can also see why there would be a great sensitivity to the nature of the manager's professional values and commitments, on the part of various political, administrative, and public constituencies.

The observation that there has been increasing pressure to delegate varying combinations of managerial responsibilities receives some additional support from an analysis of manager work loads as reported in the 1984 ICMA survey. It is clear that local government managers continue to maintain a demanding work schedule. The hours that managers reported working per week (including evenings and weekends) ranged from 54.2 hours for county managers, to 52.4 hours for municipal managers, and to 50.4 hours for COG directors (data not displayed). It should be noted that a good portion of their work time outside the conventional workday is spent at meetings and other obligatory functions not scheduled during the day. The most common evening work activities are council meetings (averaging 4.0 hours of evening time per week) and paperwork (averaging 3.8 hours of evening time per week); and the most common weekend activities are paperwork (2.7 hours per weekend) and attending social events (1.8 hours per weekend).

However, when a comparison is made between the reported average number of hours worked in 1980 and those reported for 1984 (these data were not collected in the 1973–74 and 1986–87 surveys), the overall length of the managers' workweek was slightly reduced from a high in 1980. The difference was a modest reduction of 1.3 average weekly hours for municipal managers, and 1.5 average weekly hours for county managers. While the reduction is not large, the reported decline does represent a marked interruption of past trends. All the evidence suggests that this stabilization—or even slight reduction—in the managers' average workweek is not due to a reduction in the demand for their time and energies! Rather, such a trend can be reasonably explained by increased delegation of authority—secured as a result of an increase in the training and experience of administrative staff, and also by necessity.[50] In the next section, I offer additional support for the plausibility of my explanation that professional role expansion is linked to increasing delegation of authority and responsibility, but not necessarily through an abdication by managers of their historical core of CAO expertise responsibilities.

## PROFESSIONALISM AMIDST MULTIPLE FUNCTION RESPONSIBILITIES

Table 3.6 displays the range of functions performed by managers in addition to being the local government's CAO. It is clear from the 1984 questionnaire that managers do frequently perform multiple functions. The data in Table 3.6

**Table 3.6**
**CAO Functions in Addition to Serving as Manager, 1984**

| Function | Cities | | Counties | | COGs | |
|---|---|---|---|---|---|---|
| | No. Reporting (A) | % of Total Cities | No. Reporting (B) | % of Total Counties | No. Reporting (C) | % of Total COGs |
| Total, all cities/counties/ COGs | 2131 | | 238 | | 144 | |
| Perform no other functions | 529 | 24.8 | 53 | 22.3 | 33 | 22.9 |
| Also Finance Director | 624 | 29.3 | 30 | 12.6 | 16 | 11.1 |
| Also Personnel Director | 1175 | 55.1 | 55 | 23.1 | 35 | 24.3 |
| Also Public Works Director | 276 | 13.0 | 9 | 3.8 | 1 | 0.01 |
| Also Engineer | 69 | 3.2 | 3 | 1.3 | -- | -- |
| Also Municipal/County Clerk | 298 | 14.0 | 27 | 11.3 | -- | -- |
| Also Planning Director | 489 | 22.9 | 15 | 6.3 | 18 | 12.5 |
| Also Purchasing Director | 911 | 42.7 | 38 | 16.0 | 14 | 9.7 |
| Also Other | 459 | 21.5 | 31 | 13.0 | 9 | 6.3 |

*Note:* Respondents could check as many functions as were individually applicable.

*Source:* First reported by the author in ''Local Government Managers: Styles and Challenges,'' *Baseline Data Report* 19, no. 2 (Washington, D.C.: ICMA, March/April 1987), p. 8.

indicate that less than one-quarter of the city, county, and COG managers reported performing no other functions (other than being the chief administrative officer). That is, more than three-quarters of each of the three government types of managers reported performing multiple functions in 1984—with only city managers reporting a proportion nearly as high in 1980 (73.2 percent).

But as occurred in our review of other data from this survey, a pattern emerges—this time relating the size of the community's population to the number of functions performed. Managers in smaller communities generally spread their time over a more varied range of functions (data not displayed). Nevertheless, the responses presented in Table 3.6 indicate that—on the average—municipal administrators most frequently doubled as personnel director (55.1 percent), purchasing director (42.7 percent), and finance director (29.3 percent). Similar to responses given in 1980, the 1984 data show that city managers in communities with populations ranging between 25,000 and 50,000 say they varied from this pattern by serving as municipal clerk and planning director more frequently than as finance director.

Table 3.6 also reveals which additional functions the county managers and COG directors report that they most frequently perform. While the 1980 survey data indicate that "over half of the managers in counties and COGs (53.6 percent and 54.5 percent, respectively) reported they perform the duties that usually are delegated to persons in other positions," the 1984 data indicate that an even higher proportion of county and COG managers (77.7 percent and 77.1 percent, respectively) reported performing additional functions—a higher proportion than city managers, as well.[51]

The ranking of these extra functions remains basically the same in 1980 and in 1984 for all three types of professional managers. The one change of note is that, in the 1984 survey, COG directors reported the role of planning director as having replaced finance director as the second most often performed additional function; and finance director ranked third. However, again comparing 1980 with 1984, a significant change appears in the overall proportion of managers who indicated additional functions. There is a decreased proportion of managers who reported in every category, except for a slight increase in county managers serving as county clerk (up 0.5 percent from 1980). When municipal and county managers did report an increase in functional responsibilities, a noticeable proportion of the increase took place within responses characterized as "other" or "unspecified" functions (up 12.7 percent and 5.0 percent, respectively, over the four-year period). COG directors reported a slight decrease in unspecified functions (down 1.3 percent).

Using Table 3.7, we can compare these additional functions of managers against variations in their professional role perceptions as measured in the scale of professional mobility (that is, community based, mixed, or career based—depending on the combination of reasons that managers indicated for leaving their previous position). Once again, the most significant finding is that (at least based on this scale of professional mobility) the types of functions performed by managers in addition to being CAO do not seem to be predicated on any

**Table 3.7**
**Current CAO Multiple Functions in Relation to the Scale of Professional Mobility, 1984**

| Function | Respondent Total (A) | Scale of Professional Mobility | | | | | | | |
|---|---|---|---|---|---|---|---|---|---|
| | | Career-Based | | Mixed | | Community-Based | | | |
| | | No. | % of (A) | No. | % of (A) | No. | % of (A) | | |
| Perform no other functions | 296 | 189 | 63.9 | 67 | 22.6 | 40 | 13.5 | | |
| Also Finance Director | 219 | 130 | 59.4 | 53 | 24.2 | 36 | 16.4 | | |
| Also Personnel Director | 480 | 257 | 53.5 | 135 | 28.1 | 88 | 18.3 | | |
| Also Public Works Director | 85 | 53 | 62.4 | 14 | 16.5 | 18 | 21.2 | | |
| Also Engineer | 18 | 9 | 50.0 | 3 | 16.7 | 6 | 33.3 | | |
| Also Municipal/County Clerk | 121 | 78 | 64.5 | 25 | 20.7 | 18 | 14.9 | | |
| Also Planning Director | 159 | 81 | 50.9 | 47 | 29.6 | 31 | 19.5 | | |
| Also Purchasing Director | 341 | 181 | 53.1 | 94 | 27.6 | 66 | 19.4 | | |
| Also Other | 195 | 97 | 49.7 | 58 | 29.7 | 40 | 20.5 | | |

*Note:* Respondents could check as many functions as were individually applicable.

*Source:* On the 1984 ICMA/CAO survey, the question was asked: "What functions do you perform within your local government in addition to serving as manager/CAO/ED?"

particular pattern of orientations toward career or community. That is to say—regardless of their career motivations or level of personal commitment to the individual communities being served—managers demonstrate a substantial professional commitment to accommodate the particular management deficiencies of the community's governing capacity. Of particular note is the fact that the most frequently performed of these additional functions are essentially from among the historical core areas of managerial expertise: personnel, purchasing, finance, clerk, and planning.

Thus, we have additional support for the plausibility of the explanation that professional role expansion is linked to increasing delegation of authority and responsibility. While there was a reported decrease in the proportion of managers performing in almost every listed category of dual responsibility, municipal and county managers indicated some increase in functional responsibilities that were described as "other" or "unspecified" functions for the four-year period 1980–84. COG directors reported a slight decrease in unspecified functions (down 1.3 percent). More than three-quarters of the responding managers reported that they had taken on additional responsibilities—a trend that represents an overall increase from the 1980 responses (tabulated by subtracting from the total the proportion of managers reporting that they performed no other function). Nevertheless, the primary dual or multiple functions were most often still reported to be from among the traditional core areas of managerial expertise. And all this was occurring when managers were reporting a stabilization in or a slight decrease in the hours worked per week!

## THE PROFESSIONAL VALUE SYSTEM

We now consider more directly how the managers' career and community orientations (the scale of professional mobility) and management styles are represented within a variety of professionally discriminated role-playing activities. This section focuses on identifying and comparing how managers see their responsibilities for setting the council's agenda, the conditions under which managers report participating in policy formulation, what their specific expectations are for ongoing consultations with the council, as well as what their perceptions are toward the general nature of council–manager relations—and finally, how managers delineate themselves over the age-old professional issue of political involvement with incumbent council members.

I will complete my comparison of managers' career and community orientations—having examined their perceived council expectations for the primary CAO role, how managers have reported allocating their work time, and the multiple functions officially performed by them—with a concluding assessment of the concentrations and variations in their professional role perceptions. I will then have the opportunity to draw some conclusions about what the outline of a professional value system may look like, at least as it exists among this sample of local government managers. In this context, the question of determining whether or not there is a professional ideology becomes a basic question about how widely shared and how consistent a body of concepts there are that actually describe operating occupational activities, roles, and values.

Table 3.8 arrays the frequencies with which managers in 1984 indicated that they were involved in each of 16 different occupational role situations. According to the responses, activities that the managers engaged in most often included setting the council's agenda; sharing their professional opinion on major issues with new council members; participating in the council's policy formulation; consulting with the council before drafting the budget proposal; and resisting council involvement in administration.

A similar inquiry was made by the ICMA in the 1973–74 survey; but—as noted earlier in the chapter—that questionnaire was directed only toward municipal managers, and a somewhat different scaling technique was used. Any attempt to make direct statistical comparisons between the two surveys would be invalid and misleading. However, it is worth observing that, when comparing only the rank ordering of the four items in which managers were most often engaged, they remained the same for both the 1973–74 and the 1984 respondents. Likewise, when comparing the rank ordering of the 1973–74 and 1984 responses on the activities in which managers were least likely to be engaged, we find that the same two items were cited: assisting council members up for reelection, least likely; and encouraging the council to participate in management decision, second. These response patterns are quite consistent with James Svara's earlier model in which councils and managers shared authority in the areas of policy formulation and administration.

In 1984, responding managers indicated that nearly nine out of ten (86.6 percent) local government administrators always set their council's agenda. And nearly three-quarters of the managers reported always participating in policy formulation; but in the latter role, they also indicated that their level of involvement varies substantially. Managers appear to feel less involved as leading players in the policymaking process (only 40.3 percent indicating "always"), and appear to be even less involved in initiating policy (33.1 percent, always). By contrast, a mere 2.2 percent felt that they never initiate policy, and only 6.4 percent felt that they never play a leading role in the policymaking process. Nevertheless, only 19.0 percent indicated that they always act as administrators, leaving policy matters to the council; while 15.4 percent said that they never act solely as administrators.

These results suggest that city, county, and COG managers see their involvement in policymaking from the perspective of their core administration responsibilities. In general, while the professional scope of the 1984 survey was substantially broader than the municipal management focus of the 1973–74 survey, the authors of a report on the earlier survey found essentially the same pattern of involvement: "Managers who perceive themselves as administrators feel that they can only engage in municipal policy issues while maintaining a predominately administrative role."[52]

**Table 3.8**
**CAO Management Styles, 1984**

| ACTIVITY | No. of Mgrs. Reporting (A) | Always | | Sometimes | | Never | |
|---|---|---|---|---|---|---|---|
| | | No. | % of (A) | No. | % of (A) | No. | % of (A) |
| Initiate Policies | 2371 | 785 | 33.1 | 1533 | 64.7 | 53 | 2.2 |
| Formulate Policies | 2384 | 1731 | 72.6 | 645 | 27.1 | 8 | 0.3 |
| Consult BD Before Budget | 2386 | 1341 | 56.2 | 795 | 33.3 | 250 | 10.5 |
| Consult BD Before App't of Dep't Heads | 2366 | 1087 | 45.9 | 825 | 34.9 | 454 | 19.2 |
| Consult BD Before Removal of Dep't Heads | 2362 | 1265 | 53.6 | 752 | 31.8 | 345 | 14.6 |
| Orient New BD on Issues | 2374 | 1863 | 78.5 | 487 | 20.5 | 24 | 1.0 |
| Ass't BD Members on Re-election | 2352 | 165 | 7.0 | 663 | 28.2 | 1524 | 64.8 |
| Work w/BD on Policy Proposals | 2376 | 638 | 26.9 | 1647 | 69.3 | 91 | 3.8 |
| Leading Policy Making Role | 2380 | 958 | 40.3 | 1269 | 53.3 | 153 | 6.4 |
| Resist BD Involvement in Admin | 2372 | 1288 | 54.3 | 938 | 39.5 | 146 | 6.2 |
| Speak Publicly on Issues | 2374 | 210 | 8.8 | 1802 | 75.9 | 362 | 15.2 |
| Work through Committee Members | 2375 | 275 | 11.6 | 1735 | 73.1 | 365 | 15.4 |
| Maintain Neutral Issue Stand | 2361 | 490 | 20.8 | 1609 | 68.1 | 262 | 11.1 |
| Act Solely as Admin | 2360 | 448 | 19.0 | 1549 | 65.6 | 363 | 15.4 |
| Set BD Agenda | 2381 | 2071 | 86.6 | 260 | 10.9 | 60 | 2.5 |
| Encourage BD Involvement in Mgm't | 2378 | 174 | 7.3 | 955 | 40.2 | 1248 | 52.5 |

*Note*: Percentages for each method may not add up to 100, due to rounding.

*Source*: First reported by the author in "Local Government Managers: Styles and Challenges," *Baseline Data Report* 19, no. 2 (Washington, D.C.: ICMA, March/April 1987), p. 3.

The responses arrayed in Table 3.8 also demonstrate that managers generally consult with their council, commission, or board prior to drafting the budget and appointing or removing department heads. However, while more than half of these local managers indicated that they always consult with the council before drafting the budget (56.2 percent) and before removing department heads (53.6 percent), noticeably fewer indicate such absolute commitment to always consulting with the council before hiring department heads (45.9 percent). The analysts of the 1973–74 survey of municipal managers also found that "for each of these three issues over half of the managers always or nearly always consult with [their] council prior to taking action."[53]

Finally, let us consider manager perceptions on the general nature of council–manager relations, and look at variations in their concern for delineating the proper political involvement with incumbent council members. More than three-fourths (78.5 percent) reporting in 1984 indicated that they always orient new council members to their position on major issues. There appears to be little variation on this responsibility when it comes to population size of the community, type of government, or geographic region. Responses to survey items regarding the role of the council in management issues show a reinforcing pattern. More than half of the managers (54.3 percent) reported that they always resist council involvement in management issues, and nearly an equal proportion (52.5 percent) indicated that they never encourage council involvement in management decisions. Conversely, only 6.2 percent reported that they never resist council involvement in management issues, and only 7.3 percent indicated that they always encourage council involvement in management decisions. These patterns hold true regardless of local population size, type of government, or geographic region.

And with regard to direct involvement in the electoral processes of council members, nearly two-thirds (64.8 percent) of all local government managers responding to the 1984 survey indicated that they never provide assistance to council members coming up for reelection. There were 28 percent who indicated that they sometimes give assistance; and only 7 percent reported that they always give help to incumbent candidates. Again, these patterns hold true regardless of population size, type of government, or geographic region.

Finally, Table 3.9 compares variations in these professional role issues along the scale of professional mobility (community based, mixed, or career based— depending on the combination of reasons indicated for leaving previous position). Two patterns of significance are worth noting. Not too surprisingly, the first pattern is that the overall averages for each role activity closely parallel (although not exactly) the ranking of the activities found in Table 3.8. Of the top five most frequent activities and the two least frequent, only consulting with the board before preparation of the budget and resisting board involvement in administration are altered in Table 3.9.

Of potentially greater significance is the observed pattern that there was only one switch in the rankings of these varied activities from the overall averages

Table 3.9

Current CAO Management Styles in Relation to the Scale of Professional Mobility, 1984

| Activities | Total No. | Scale of Professional Mobility | | | Average for Activity |
|---|---|---|---|---|---|
| | | Career-Based no.=553-566 | Mixed no.=248-252 | Community-Based no.=154-155 | |
| Initiate Policies | 967 | 1.70 | 1.69 | 1.74 | 1.70 |
| Formulate Policies | 974 | 1.28 | 1.25 | 1.31 | 1.28 |
| Consult BD Before Budget | 970 | 1.60 | 1.60 | 1.59 | 1.60 |
| Consult BD Before App't of Dep't Heads | 968 | 1.79 | 1.80 | 1.65 | 1.77 |
| Consult BD Before Removing Dep't Heads | 967 | 1.66 | 1.62 | 1.60 | 1.64 |
| Orient New BD on Issues | 970 | 1.19 | 1.23 | 1.29 | 1.22 |
| Ass't BD Members on Re-election | 956 | 2.58 | 2.63 | 2.61 | 2.59 |
| Work w/BD on Policy Proposals | 968 | 1.78 | 1.80 | 1.81 | 1.79 |
| Leading Policy Making Role | 967 | 1.67 | 1.64 | 1.69 | 1.67 |
| Resist BD Involvement in Admin | 968 | 1.49 | 1.44 | 1.47 | 1.48 |
| Speak Publicly on Issues | 967 | 2.03 | 2.01 | 2.02 | 2.02 |
| Work through Committee Members | 967 | 2.02 | 2.06 | 2.00 | 2.02 |
| Maintain Neutral Issue Stand | 968 | 1.90 | 1.96 | 1.90 | 1.91 |
| Act Solely as Admin | 964 | 2.01 | 1.96 | 1.97 | 1.99 |
| Set BD Agenda | 969 | 1.15 | 1.15 | 1.15 | 1.15 |
| Encourage BD Involvement in Mgm't | 968 | 2.49 | 2.49 | 2.46 | 2.49 |

Note: The mean score was derived from the respondents' indications of managerial styles on a three-point scale: 1.0 = always; and 3.0 = never.

Source: Compiled by the author from responses to the 1984 ICMA/CAO survey, on the question, "Please indicate the frequency of your involvement in each of the following activities."

computed for Table 3.8. One can argue that, at least based on this scale of professional mobility, position changes among professional local government managers are apparently not predicated on any particular pattern of orientations toward career or community. That is to say—regardless of their career motivations or levels of commitment to the communities served—managers demonstrate great consistency among themselves in how they view their varied professional roles. And these patterns bear up despite variations in the population sizes of the communities served, type of government, and geographic region.

The first conclusion to be drawn from the analysis undertaken in this chapter, then, is not that there are variations among practitioners in the field of professional local government management. As we have seen, there are indeed variations, and they have in fact changed over the decade and a half for which we have survey data. This finding should not disqualify CAOs—at least those serving in ICMA-recognized communities—from being considered legitimate professionals, and members of an identifiable profession. But rather, these variations in professional style mostly serve to confirm the patterns of activity, role, and value variation that Mary Guy had witnessed in her studies of other professionals and professions. All professionals are not alike—even those who are members of the most traditionally acknowledged fields of medicine, law, education, and so on!

I have essentially argued that professional local government managers—like professionals in other fields—have adapted their repertoire of expertise for meeting the changing needs of the time. These adaptations are being attempted—and, it seems, increasingly accomplished—in order to improve the CAOs' professional utility as defined by their traditional responsibilities and commitments to the communities in which they serve. This is not being done—to any marked extent—through substitution of the traditional core of expertise associated with the field, but rather through skill expansion. This expansion is based on mastery of the changing substance of the core areas of expertise. The diversification of CAO skill seems to be coupled with necessary delegations of some authorities and responsibilities to ever better trained and experienced administrative staffs.

The concept of occupational or professional setting has greater ramifications for the field of local government management than are suggested from a narrow focus on variations in the specific characteristics of the government organization and community location that managers inherit and are then charged with administering. The other end of the occupational/professional-setting dimension—that is, the career mobility factor—also has an impact on the uniformity of managers' perceptions, values, and experiences. What I have suggested from an analysis of the responses to these surveys is that professional local-government managers show a great stability and coherency in their range of managerial styles over at least the past 14 years.

It is clear from Guy's analysis and from my analysis of the ICMA and Green–Reed survey data that community and personal variables (values) can be an important consideration in explaining why particular individuals within a particular profession differ or deviate from the dominate professional style (values, roles, and activities). Using a facsimile of the Thomas Dye–Timothy Almy scale of localism–cosmopolitanism to develop a scale of professional mobility for the data at hand, I have shown that manager role orientations do indeed represent differences in career and community attachments. It seems reasonable to consider these differences as measures of professional style, stage of career, and differences in community and market need—rather than as final measures of professionalism itself. And when there does occur a shift in the career or community role orientation of managers, it appears to have more to do with the individual career stage (transition) that a manager has reached, which in turn seems to be a by-product of professional expertise and style factors, along with community and market needs.

This, in fact, is the most remarkable finding to come from these analyses. The evolution of professions and their professionals need to be considered along a newly conceptualized fourth dimension of the professional model. Chapter 1 described three dimensions to the model for measuring and comparing change among professionals: values, sources, and time. The fourth dimensional test is whether style variations of the individual managers are changed or remain stable when different stages of professional expectation are obtained or are frustrated. These issues are examined more closely in the next chapter.

## NOTES

1. See in particular ch. 5, "The Public Administrator: Professional or Entrepreneur?" in James A. Stever's *The End of Public Administration: Problems of the Profession in the Post-Progressive Era* (Dobbs Ferry, N.Y.: Transnational Publishers, 1988).

2. An interesting cross section of reports on the theme of professional ethics in government would include Joseph F. Zimmerman, *Ethics in Local Government*, Management Information Service Report 8, no. 8 (Washington, D.C.: International City Management Association, August 1976); "Honesty and Ethical Standards," *Gallup Report*, no. 239 (August 1985), pp. 2–28; and Dennis F. Thompson, "The Possibility of Administrative Ethics," *Public Administration Review* 45, no. 5 (September/October 1985), pp. 555–61.

3. O. P. Dwivedi, "Ethics and Values of Public Responsibility and Accountability," *International Review of Administrative Sciences* 51, no. 1 (1985), p. 61.

4. Ibid., p. 62.

5. Ibid., p. 61.

6. See H. George Frederickson's review essay, "The Lineage of New Public Administration," *Administration and Society* 8, no. 2 (August 1976), pp. 149–74.

7. James H. Svara, "Dichotomy and Duality: Reconceptualizing the Relationship between Policy and Administration in Council–Manager Cities," *Public Administration Review* 45, no. 1 (January/February 1985), p. 221.

8. Richard J. Stillman II, "The City Manager: Professional Helping Hand, or Political Hired Hand?" *Public Administration Review* 37, no. 6 (November/December 1977), pp. 659 and 666.

9. Samuel Bowles, "Relations of State to Municipal Government and the Reform of the Latter," *Journal of Social Science* 9 (January 1878), p. 263.

10. Doyle W. Buckwalter and J. Ivan Legler, "City Managers and City Attorneys: Associates or Adversaries?" *Public Administration Review* 47, no. 5 (September/October 1987), p. 393.

11. Ibid., p. 394.

12. Ibid., p. 395.

13. Svara, "Dichotomy and Duality," p. 221.

14. See, for example, Wayne F. Anderson, Chester A. Newland, and Richard J. Stillman II, *The Effective Local Government Manager*, Municipal Management Series (Washington, D.C.: International City Management Association, 1983); Laurence Rutter, *The Essential Community: Local Government in the Year 2000*, Municipal Management Series (Washington, D.C.: International City Management Association, 1980); and Brian W. Rapp and Frank M. Patitucci, *Managing Local Government for Improved Performance: A Practical Approach* (Boulder, Colo.: Westview Press, 1977).

15. Svara, "Dichotomy and Duality," p. 221.

16. Murray Edelman, *The Symbolic Uses of Politics* (Chicago: University of Illinois Press, 1964).

17. Ibid., p. 176.

18. Alan L. Saltzstein, "City Managers and City Councils: Perceptions of the Division of Authority," *Western Political Quarterly* 27, no. 2 (June 1974), pp. 276 and 288.

19. John Nalbandian, "Local Government Professionals under Stress: In Pursuit of Economic Development, Efficiency, and Equity," *Public Administration Review* 48, no. 1 (January/February 1988), p. 591.

20. Edelman, *Symbolic Uses*.

21. Glenn Abney and Thomas P. Lauth, "Councilmanic Intervention in Municipal Administration," *Administration and Society* 13, no. 4 (February 1982), pp. 435 and 449.

22. Kenneth R. Greene, "Municipal Administrators' Receptivity to Citizens' and Elected Officials' Contacts," *Public Administration Review* 42, no. 4 (July/August 1982), pp. 351–52.

23. Edelman, *Symbolic Uses*, pp. 188 and 73.

24. Buckwalter and Legler, "City Managers and City Attorneys," pp. 401–2, 400, and 394.

25. Edelman, *Symbolic Uses*, pp. 108–10.

26. Nalbandian, "Local Government Professionals under Stress," p. 591.

27. Edelman, *Symbolic Uses*, pp. 103–4.

28. Ibid., p. 173.

29. Ibid., pp. 132–33.

30. Ibid., pp. 145–46.

31. For a variety of insightful and current treatments of these issues for the professions, see the edited volume by Thomas L. Haskell, *The Authority of Experts: Studies in History and Theory* (Bloomington: Indiana University Press, 1984).

32. Richard J. Stillman II, "Local Public Management in Transition: A Report on the Current State of the Profession," in the *Municipal Year Book 1982* (Washington, D.C.: International City Management Association, 1982), p. 171.

33. Edelman, *Symbolic Uses*, p. 74.

34. Howard M. Vollmer and Donald L. Mills, eds., *Professionalization* (Englewood Cliffs, N.J.: Prentice-Hall, 1966), pp. vii–viii.

35. Herbert Kaufman, *The Forest Ranger: A Study in Administrative Behavior* (Baltimore: Johns Hopkins University Press, 1960).

36. In structuring her own study, Mary Guy summarized the work of most of the major schools in the field—including March and Simon—and developed this listing of the three most commonly shared assumptions about professions. See the introduction to Guy's *Professionals in Organizations: Debunking a Myth* (New York: Praeger Publishers, 1985), p. 7.

37. Ibid., p. 15.

38. Ibid., p. 5.

39. Ibid., p. 19.

40. For example, two of the most recent survey studies published by the ICMA have focused on different aspects of mobility: the reduced frequency of CAO changes of position over time, and the nature of the professional and family stress impacts associated with a change of position. See Roy E. Green, "Local Government Managers: Styles and Challenges," *Baseline Data Report* 19, no. 2 (Washington, D.C.: International City Management Association, 1987); and Roy E. Green and B. J. Reed, "Occupational Stress and Mobility among Professional Local Government Managers: A Decade of Change," in the *Municipal Year Book 1988* (Washington, D.C.: International City Management Association, 1988), pp. 35–42.

41. Timothy A. Almy, "Local–Cosmopolitanism and U.S. City Managers," *Urban Affairs Quarterly* 10, no. 3 (March 1975), p. 244.

42. Ibid., p. 244.

43. Ibid., pp. 269 and 267.

44. Green, "Local Government Managers," p. 9.

45. In his 1975 study, Timothy Almy used the following statements (drawn from Thomas Dye's earlier study) to categorize his responses:

(a) The most rewarding organizations a person can belong to are local clubs and associations rather than large nationwide organizations; (b) Despite all of the media coverage, national and international events do not seem as interesting as events that occur in this community; (c) No doubt many newcomers to the community are competent people, but when it comes to choosing a person for a responsible position, I prefer a man whose family is well established in the community; (d) Big cities have their place but the local community is the backbone of America; (e) I have greater respect for a man who is well established in his local community than a man who is widely known in his field but has no local roots.

See fn. 2 in Almy, "Local–Cosmopolitanism," p. 272.

46. Mary A. Schellinger, "Local Government Managers: Profile of the Professionals in a Maturing Profession," in the *Municipal Year Book 1985* (Washington, D.C.: International City Management Association, 1985), p. 186.

47. Green, "Local Government Managers," pp. 4–5.

48. Ibid.

49. This latter observation is based in part on impressions derived from a nonscientific review of the past ten years of position descriptions and personal (talent-for-hire) advertisements published by the American Society for Public Administration, the International City Management Association, and a variety of newspapers.

50. Green, "Local Government Managers," pp. 6–7.

51. Amy Cohen Paul, "Local Government Managers: On the Job and Off," *Urban Data Service Reports* 13, no. 9 (Washington, D.C.: International City Management Association, September 1981), p. 7.

52. Robert J. Huntley and Robert J. Macdonald, "Urban Managers: Organizational Preferences, Managerial Styles, and Social Roles," in the *Municipal Year Book 1975* (Washington, D.C.: International City Management Association, 1975), p. 151.

53. Ibid., p. 154.

# 4

## ... TO THE INWARD IMPACTS OF PROFESSIONALIZATION ON PRACTITIONERS

It may be worthwhile to step back for just a moment to refresh our perspective. The frame of reference used in this study is derived from Howard Vollmer and Donald Mills's distinctive description of *professionalization*. Vollmer and Mills refer to professionalization as an essentially "dynamic process whereby many occupations can be observed to change certain crucial characteristics in the direction of a 'profession' "—meaning the perpetual striving toward achievement of a professional model.[1] In their estimation, this process of professionalization can be differentiated from the individual characteristics keyed to particular stages of *professionalism*, described earlier as an established "ideology and associated activities that can be found in many and diverse occupational groups where members aspire to professional status."[2]

At first blush, there appears to be little difference between the two concepts. But on closer inspection, we see that analysts have used them to structure and separate two different dimensions critical to an evaluation of professional standing. The term "professionalism" has been used mostly to focus attention on the benchmarks of career standards, stages, types, and styles. By contrast, a focus on the processes of professionalization most often emphasizes change and change agents, and a concern for variations in the scope, dynamics, and direction of occupational characteristics. Both dimensions are linked to the professional model as a unifying and comparative point of reference.

We begin our discussion on the impacts of professionalization by asking a very direct and important question: Are the CAOs in ICMA-recognized communities (as a role model group) becoming professionalized through a process of conscious choice and rational goal-setting and achievement; or are there other independent forces at work here, as well? And in which professional direction are the CAOs going? We have found from our analyses of this sample of managers that there seem to be important standards of professionalism present, and that they possess certain professionally essential characteristics that have remained identifiable and relatively stable over an extended period of time. It is important to consider, then, the possibility that environmental factors may also be influencing the near-term occupational setting of local government CAOs, as well as the long-term dynamics of their professional development.

Traditional wisdom says that no person can live long as an island. If this principle be sound, then so is the corollary that professionals cannot long be immune to the broader demographic, political, social, economic, and technological changes occurring in their environment. Which aspects of the environmental changes will become relevant to a profession's course of development— and at what points in time any of them may become salient—is not always all that obvious. Much of the analysis and the research literature assessed so far in this study has focused narrowly on the internal perspectives and unique dimensions of professional local government management. In this chapter, I will add some environmental texture to the occupational setting of the CAO.

Our focus here is on the linkages between the environmental forces that seem to be nationalizing the development and use of professional managers in local government. Specifically, we must consider how nationwide changes in the managers' occupational settings and working conditions may be standardizing capacity and performance expectations, and altering career mobility choices. Of particular interest will be the influence of the Baby Boom generation on public-service career longevity and plateauing, as well as on the growth in numbers of dual-earner/career couples. Occupational stress and the increasing numbers of dual-career couples are two of the most contemporary and historically novel career considerations taking place within the nation's work force—in both professional and nonprofessional occupations—and may become particularly important to the future of professional local-government management.

After determining the relevant (external) environmental factors, we will turn in Chapter 5 to a consideration of what Vollmer and Mills have referred to as the "intended (institutionalizing) processes of professionalization." These are the processes that seek "to clothe a given area [groups of individuals] with standards of excellence, to establish rules of conduct, to develop a sense of responsibility, to set criteria for recruitment and training, to ensure a measure of protection for members, to establish collective control over the area, and elevate it to a position of dignity and social standing in the society."[3] Frederick Wirt recently validated this institutionalizing process when he recommended that "another way to understand the professional influence in local decision making is to view professionals as national institutions designed to transmit accepted knowledge and values into the local scene."[4] However, the first step is to establish some benchmarks for measuring occupational working conditions.

## REWARDS AND FRUSTRATIONS OF THE JOB

Over the past three decades, a number of important national trends have developed that may explain why factors such as job characteristics, satisfaction levels, and aspirations for intrinsic fulfillment through work have created such a growing interest among researchers studying the public sector. First, there has been "a steady increase in the number of workers who regard themselves as professional and also an increase in the number of professional occupations"; second, "as society increasingly has turned to government for the provision of important services, the public sector has grown from 10% of the total, civilian work force in 1948 to 17.6% in 1983"; and third, "the public sector has become the largest employer of professionals."[5]

In fact, an important field of study has evolved in the past quarter of a century to monitor and measure various trends toward occupational professionalization within the U.S. workplace and economy. Most recently, the interrelated specializations of human resource management and organizational behavior and development have taken particular interest in what has been called "designed jobs."[6] Research in the field has been attempting to isolate organizational and personal characteristics and how they may be linked with positions created to accomplish specific goals in prescribed manners. The purpose of most of this investigation has been to relate conditions of the workplace to occupational performance and to impacts on and well-being of the individuals holding the positions.

It does not take much to appreciate the relevance of this body of research to our investigation of an occupation specifically designed by the government reform movement for the purpose of providing professional-quality management to municipal administration. What students of organizational development might call an "enriched job" has been the major focus of the reform movement's attempt to increase the management capacity of local government.[7] With this purpose in mind, levels of job satisfaction and frustration represent important measures by which to assess the effects of job conditions on the individuals who are today's local government CAOs.

To date, most research associating levels of job satisfaction and frustration with different types of occupational settings and conditions has attempted "to measure the degree to which particular jobs possess the conceptually independent task characteristics of skill variety, task identity, task significance, autonomy, and feedback-from-the-job." Implicit to most of the research being conducted is the presumption that these dimensions "coincide with certain psychological states which, according to the developing theory, are critical for achieving and sustaining high employee motivation, satisfacton, and commitment."[8] In this sense, professionalization is a particular type of occupational socialization, which is part of a more general process that goes on—whether purposely or not—in all workplaces.

One scholar in the field—Ralph Katz—argued that

previous survey results suggest that, in general, these job characteristics, especially autonomy and skill variety, correlate strongly with overall job satisfaction and relate only slightly, though at times significantly, to absenteeism, overall effectiveness, and the quality of performance when examined across respondents from a wide range of heterogeneous jobs.[9]

Reviewing the literature, Katz also found that

individuals with high growth need . . . tend to react more positively, in terms of job satisfaction, to enriched tasks than do employees with low growth need. . . . In addition, . . . the degree of employee satisfaction with the contextual features of their work environment, such as peers, supervisors, and organizational policies, affects the extent to which job satisfaction will be linked positively with challenging tasks.[10]

Katz's own research was a survey of the full range of jobs and employees (administrative, professional, technical, protected service, paraprofessional, clerical, skilled craft, and maintenance) in one state, one county, and two municipal governments—each one representing a different region of the United States. Katz reported,

Basically, the analysis shows that the strength of the relationships between job satisfaction and each of the task dimensions depends on both the job longevity and organizational longevity of the sampled individuals. . . . Indeed, it appears that newcomers are concerned most with becoming a helpful, necessary, and important part of the overall operation, while veterans are concerned most with establishing and demonstrating their competence.[11]

His research appears to provide additional credibility to our earlier argument that managers' professional relationships in the workplace depend on their tenure and career status.

More recently, researchers have discovered that "none of the previous research on professional work experiences and satisfactions has *focused* on professionals working in the public sector" (emphasis added).[12] And among those analysts who have discussed the issue, there is no consensus about what performance expectations there should be from this growing public sector use of professionals. One school of analysts seem to view public sector professionals as "initially [approaching] work with higher expectations concerning autonomy and intrinsic fulfillment. But . . . [they then] usually find themselves in highly routinized jobs, constrained by close supervision and rigid bureaucratic controls."[13] This line of thinking is in contrast to the views of a second school of social researchers who argue that "professional work, even in the public sector, is less frustrating and more fulfilling than work encountered by lower status occupations."[14] However, most research literature has focused on the employment of the traditional professions in the public sector, in contrast to those professions that have evolved as unique aspects of the turn-of-the-century government reform movement and the post–World War II growth in the public sector's mandate and influence.

After conducting a survey of these traditionally recognized professional groups (excluding "officials and administrators") and of blue-collar workers in a Northeastern state government, Cary Cherniss and Jeffrey S. Kane wrote,

[Their] results suggested that there was no difference between the two groups in job satisfaction. However, professionals rated their jobs as significantly lower in skill variety, task identity, task significance, autonomy, and knowledge of results [than did blue-collar workers]. Professionals also believed that their jobs should provide less intrinsic fulfillment than did the blue-collar workers. [These researchers] . . . speculated that professionals employed in government maintain minimal levels of job satisfaction despite less fulfilling jobs by reducing their aspirations for fulfillment in work.[15]

The analyses undertaken in the following sections have been constructed to make comparisons with these previous research findings. However, preceding research has largely been concerned with the experiences either of all employees in the public sector, or else of the traditionally recognized professionals employed by the public sector. The levels of job satisfaction of the managers serving in ICMA-recognized communities may prove to be of particular interest and significance. The essential features of the CAO's job description were codified as part of a model for government reform that was initiated before the advent of Franklin Roosevelt's New Deal administration and World War II. Therefore, it represents the experience base of one of the earliest "designed" professional positions developed specifically for the nonelected civil service. In this way, the views of CAOs can serve as a useful reference point for the public sector occupations that have evolved from the post–World War II governmental merit systems.

We now turn to an analysis of the survey data at hand. The 1984 ICMA survey gave managers the option of indicating their level of frustration and/or satisfaction from a listing of 18 different job-related factors. Let us first assess which general conditions associated with their work responsibilities may have the greatest potential for impact on the level of their performances and the course of their careers. Manager evaluations of these job-related factors are displayed in Table 4.1. Results have been aggregated to include all three types of managers (city, county, and council-of-government).

Five job factors were rated by at least 20 percent of the responding local government managers as being the cause of the highest levels of job frustration. In rank order, they are: available public resources (30.5 percent), time for family and self (30.2 percent), citizens' feelings about local government (29.9 percent), pressure (27.1 percent), and local government's level of ability to take advantage of opportunities and to solve problems (23.3 percent). Three of the factors rated as causing the highest levels of frustration were also rated by at least 20 percent of the managers as offering the lowest levels of job satisfaction: time for family and self (26.1 percent), pressure (21.9 percent), and citizens' feelings about local government (21.0 percent).

When a weighted-average score is computed for each job factor by multiplying the number of managers who indicated each of the three levels of frustration by their scalar values (1 being high, and 3 being low) and then dividing each set of totals by the total number of responses to that survey item, the same five

## Table 4.1
## Levels of CAO Job Frustration and Satisfaction, 1984

| Job Factor | Frustration Total (A) | High (%A) | Mid-Range (%A) | Low (%A) | Weighted Average Score | Rank | Satisfaction Total (B) | High (%B) | Mid-Range (%B) | Low (%B) | Weighted Average Score | Rank | Frustration/Satisfaction Difference per Factor Weighted Average Score | Rank |
|---|---|---|---|---|---|---|---|---|---|---|---|---|---|---|
| Policy Formulation | 1380 | 12.5 | 43.3 | 44.1 | 2.32 | (13,14) | 2099 | 45.2 | 48.1 | 6.7 | 1.62 | (5) | +0.70 | 5,6,7 |
| Policy Implementation | 1284 | 10.9 | 47.4 | 42.1 | 2.31 | (11,12) | 2174 | 49.7 | 44.9 | 5.4 | 1.56 | (3) | +0.75 | 4 |
| Relationship to Council/ Board | 1461 | 19.0 | 39.8 | 41.1 | 2.22 | (7,8) | 2070 | 44.1 | 48.1 | 7.8 | 1.64 | (6,7) | +0.58 | 8 |
| Relationship with Citizens | 1359 | 10.7 | 44.9 | 44.4 | 2.34 | (15) | 2151 | 43.4 | 48.7 | 7.9 | 1.64 | (6,7) | +0.70 | 5,6,7 |
| Relationship with Department Heads | 1208 | 6.4 | 38.2 | 55.4 | 2.49 | (17) | 2267 | 58.7 | 37.6 | 3.7 | 1.45 | (1,2) | +1.04 | 1 |
| Quality of Staff | 1350 | 13.9 | 41.1 | 45.0 | 2.31 | (11,12) | 2117 | 47.1 | 45.1 | 7.8 | 1.61 | (4) | +0.70 | 5,6,7 |
| Size of Staff | 1540 | 19.0 | 40.1 | 40.9 | 2.22 | (7,8) | 1877 | 27.9 | 52.1 | 20.0 | 1.92 | (12,13) | +0.30 | 12 |
| Resources | 1725 | 30.5 | 43.8 | 25.7 | 1.95 | (2) | 1691 | 24.2 | 53.2 | 22.1 | 1.98 | (14,15) | -0.03 | 16,17 |
| Govt Ability to Take Advantage of Opportunities | 1673 | 23.3 | 50.7 | 26.0 | 2.03 | (6) | 1769 | 31.1 | 52.5 | 16.4 | 1.85 | (9) | +0.18 | 13 |
| Seeing Results | 1233 | 11.3 | 42.6 | 46.1 | 2.35 | (16) | 2166 | 60.9 | 32.9 | 6.2 | 1.45 | (1,2) | +0.90 | 2 |
| Citizens' Feeling About Government | 1772 | 29.9 | 43.3 | 26.9 | 1.97 | (3) | 1677 | 23.0 | 56.0 | 21.0 | 1.98 | (14,15) | -0.01 | 14 |
| Public Exposure | 1391 | 14.1 | 39.4 | 46.5 | 2.32 | (13,14) | 1988 | 26.9 | 54.2 | 19.0 | 1.92 | (12,13) | +0.40 | 10 |
| Amount of Travel | 1281 | 5.0 | 23.2 | 71.8 | 2.67 | (18) | 2090 | 31.6 | 47.7 | 20.7 | 1.89 | (10,11) | +0.78 | 3 |
| Job Security | 1510 | 19.0 | 35.9 | 45.1 | 2.26 | (10) | 1897 | 34.9 | 46.9 | 18.2 | 1.83 | (8) | +0.43 | 9 |
| Pressure | 1828 | 27.1 | 45.9 | 27.0 | 2.00 | (4,5) | 1581 | 20.0 | 58.1 | 21.9 | 2.02 | (16) | -0.02 | 15 |
| Work Hours | 1672 | 17.8 | 41.4 | 40.8 | 2.23 | (9) | 1732 | 28.0 | 55.3 | 16.7 | 1.89 | (10,11) | +0.34 | 11 |
| Time for Family/Self | 1737 | 30.2 | 39.6 | 30.2 | 2.00 | (4,5) | 1657 | 23.1 | 50.8 | 26.1 | 2.03 | (17) | -0.03 | 16,17 |
| Other | 103 | 60.2 | 26.2 | 13.6 | 1.53 | (1) | 892 | 4.7 | 28.1 | 47.2 | 2.22 | (18) | -0.69 | 18 |

*Note:* A weighted-average score was calculated for each job factor by multiplying the number of managers who indicated each level of frustration and/or satisfaction separately by their scalar value (1 = high; 3 = low), and then dividing each set of totals by the appropriate total numbers of respondents. Percentage totals may not equal 100, due to rounding.

*Source:* An initial compilation (columns 1–4 and 7–10) was reported by the author in "Local Government Managers: Styles and Challenges," *Baseline Data Report* 19, no. 2 (Washington, D.C.: ICMA, March/April 1987), p. 9. Respondents had been presented with this request: "What one manager/CAO/ED finds frustrating may be a source of satisfaction to another. Use the following scale to indicate your level of frustration and/or satisfaction with each of the following."

factors emerge—but in a slightly different rank order. And while the ranking did vary slightly for municipal, county, and COG managers, four of these same issues were identified by managers responding to the 1980 ICMA survey as being among the five most frustrating concerns.[16]

Table 4.1 also reveals that three job factors were rated in 1984 as giving nearly one-half of all responding managers their highest levels of satisfaction: seeing results (60.9 percent), relationship with department heads (58.7 percent), and policy implementation (49.7 percent). However, among the three, only the relationship with department heads was rated by at least one-half of the managers as causing a low level of frustration (55.4 percent). When a weighted-average score is again computed for each job factor, the same three factors emerge, and in essentially the same rank order.

Although ranked differently in 1980 than in 1984, these three items were rated by municipal and county managers as the most satisfying in both ICMA surveys. However, COG directors did not include seeing the results or policy implementation as ranking in the top three. The primary responsibility of a council-of-government is to plan and coordinate among legally separate jurisdictions in pursuit of regionally shared objectives. Nevertheless, this objective seems to be a primary source of COG director frustration—rather than satisfaction.

When the levels of frustration and satisfaction are compared within each job factor a revealing set of patterns is discovered. First, some managers chose to indicate that job factors simultaneously cause them both frustration and satisfaction, while other managers seemed to suggest more intensity in their reactions by identifying only a frustration or only a satisfaction level. Second, the range of weighted-average scores reported for levels of frustration is substantially wider (1.14) than for levels of job satisfaction (0.77). This seems to indicate a greater consensus on the job factors that provide these managers with satisfaction, but substantial variation over the factors causing them frustration. Third, when the job factors are ranked by their individual frustration/satisfaction differences and the direction of the differences (+ for satisfaction; − for frustration), an interesting field profile of professional working conditions emerges.

When the weighted-average scores for all 18 job factors are compared, five result in a group level of frustration that is marginally higher than the group level of satisfaction. These five can be ranked as follows: the miscellaneous "other" category; time for family/self and resources (which were tied in the ranking); pressure; and citizens' feelings about government. However, 13 of the job factors reveal totals where the group level of satisfaction is higher—ranked as follows: relationship with department heads; seeing results; amount of travel; policy implementation; policy formulation, relationship with citizens, and quality of staff (which were tied in the ranking); relationship to council/board; job security; public exposure; work hours; size of staff; and government ability to take advantage of opportunities. By nearly 3:1, managers rated this wide variety of job factors as most often being a source of greater satisfaction than frustration. (Direct comparisons of weighted-average scores from the 1980 survey were not possible because of substantial differences in the nature and range of scale values offered on that questionnaire.)

Overall, it seems clear that CAOs consider most of the job factors associated with their profession to be—on balance—satisfying. However, there is substantial variation in the range of managers' reactions: That is, these CAOs also seem to be reporting that they are continually stretched to cope with a demanding and diverse set of work conditions. The survey responses suggest that many of the occupational cross-pressures occur because professional responsibilities often come into direct conflict with personal needs and family responsibilities.

The investigation so far suggests more questions and additional analysis: Do differences in each individual's professional development and motivation make a difference in how managers react to their demanding occupational conditions? Are changes occurring in the occupational setting influencing how managers currently evaluate their professional responsibilities and purpose?

## LOCAL GOVERNMENT AS WORKPLACE

To gain some further and comparative insights into how CAOs in the field today assess their occupational setting in terms of their individual well-being, let us examine Table 4.2, which displays how managers responding to the 1986–87 Green–Reed survey rated the general effects that current job responsibilities were having on their careers and personal lives. The responses indicate that, in contrast to the 1978 Green–Reed survey results, there was an across-the-board reduction in the proportion of respondents who evaluated the effects of being a local government manager as markedly positive for themselves as careerists and professionals. This is a drop-off—from a high of nearly two out of every three who in 1978 reported such a markedly positive effect—to less than one out of two in 1986–87.[17]

Interestingly, however, managers responding to the 1986–87 questionnaire indicated a 10 percent increase in the positive effects that their professional responsibilities were having on their families—that is, from the levels reported by city managers in 1978. In this instance, the markedly positive and the slightly positive ratings in both surveys were aggregated for comparison. Managers also readjusted upward (an increase of more than 13 percent) the positive effects that they felt their colleagues' responsibilities were having on their respective families. And, when a weighted-average effect score is computed for the career and personal factors listed in Table 4.2, the managers did report—on balance—that their responsibilities were yielding more positive rewards for themselves professionally and personally than for their families. Therefore, it does not appear that these managers feel exactly trapped by their career choices.

Yet this does not negate the recent and somewhat puzzling reduction in manager self-assessments of professional well-being—which we must explore further. The managers were also asked in the 1986–87 survey to evaluate how major workplace conditions had changed since they began their careers as full-

**Table 4.2**
**Perceived Effect of Managerial Responsibilities on Career and Personal Life, 1986–87**

| Classification | Total | Markedly Positive no. | Markedly Positive % | Slightly Positive no. | Slightly Positive % | Slightly Negative no. | Slightly Negative % | Markedly Negative no. | Markedly Negative % | Average Score | Rank |
|---|---|---|---|---|---|---|---|---|---|---|---|
| CAREER FACTORS | | | | | | | | | | | |
| Utilization of personal abilities | 1101 | 521 | 47.3 | 475 | 43.1 | 89 | 8.1 | 16 | 1.5 | 1.64 | (3-4) |
| Openness/honesty of professional relationships | 1125 | 538 | 47.8 | 507 | 45.1 | 71 | 6.3 | 9 | 0.8 | 1.60 | (1) |
| CAREER/PERSONAL FACTORS | | | | | | | | | | | |
| On you generally | 1138 | 592 | 52.0 | 417 | 36.6 | 110 | 9.7 | 19 | 1.7 | 1.61 | (2) |
| Achieve life's goals | 1126 | 518 | 46.0 | 510 | 45.3 | 78 | 6.9 | 20 | 1.8 | 1.64 | (3-4) |
| PERSONAL FACTORS | | | | | | | | | | | |
| On your family | 1095 | 247 | 22.6 | 512 | 46.8 | 297 | 27.1 | 39 | 3.6 | 2.12 | (5) |
| On other managers' families | 868 | 59 | 6.8 | 520 | 59.9 | 267 | 30.8 | 22 | 2.5 | 2.29 | (6) |

*Note:* An average score was calculated for each factor based on a four-point scale (with 1 being markedly positive, and 4 being markedly negative). Percentage totals may not equal 100, due to rounding.

*Source:* An initial compilation from the question—but without the average scores and ranking—was reported by the author with B. J. Reed in "Occupational Stress and Mobility among Professional Local Government Managers: A Decade of Change," in the *Municipal Year Book 1988* (Washington, D.C.: ICMA, 1988), p. 40. On the 1986–87 Green–Reed survey, the respondents had been asked: "How would you rate the effect of your current managerial responsibilities on each of the following?"

time CAOs of local government. Specifically, the managers were asked whether there had been an increase or decrease in their authority over subordinates, the public's confidence in governmental institutions, and their employees' dedication to work, and also whether their employees' involvement in decision making had changed. Responses from this inquiry are displayed in Table 4.3.

The managers' responses have been organized around three career factors that, according to previous research, may have a significant effect on their perceptions: age, years of service as a full-time manager, and geographic proximity of the local government to a central city. Responses were weighted to range from 1 (factor has increased) to 3 (factor has decreased). These tabulations reveal that, as a national sample, a majority of the managers had witnessed some increase in all four conditions during the course of their careers. Managers responding to the 1986–87 survey reported that employee involvement in decision making ranked first in magnitude of increase and change—followed by the managers' authority over subordinates, public confidence in local government institutions, and employee dedication to work.

The differences in age of the responding managers seem to correspond to a consistent pattern of variation in their views about changes that have taken place in the workplace. Apparently, as managers fall into progressively older age categories, they report proportionately less dramatic change as having taken place during the course of their careers. As a group, managers arrayed by their ages reported greatest variation in their views on changes in the manager's authority over subordinates (0.34) and employee dedication to work (0.30); and least variation and, hence, greater commonality of perception on the conditions of public confidence in local government (0.19) and employee involvement in decision making (0.05). Perhaps the older the managers become, the more they feel that even the most dramatic changes are part of a long-term cycle that they have seen before—in other careers, if not specifically in local government.

However, this contrasts with the much greater breadth of views held by the managers when years of full-time CAO experience is the variable used to rank change in the four workplace conditions. In fact, "years of CAO experience" yields the greatest variation of views on changes occurring across all three career factors and within all four workplace conditions. Here the greatest range of perceptions was held for public confidence in local government (0.73)—followed by a still wide range of views held for employee dedication to work (0.59) and managerial authority over subordinates (0.46), and showing the smallest range of views for the condition of employee involvement in decision making (0.39).

A relatively small subsample of responding managers with 25–34 years of full-time CAO experience indicated that employee involvement in decision making was the work condition where the greatest average increase had occurred—with a weighted-average score of 1.34. Further, it is only within this group of experienced managers where a decrease in the occupational workplace conditions was reported for all three of the other categories (as indicated by weighted-average scores over 2.00). Their responses suggest a modest decreasing shift in

## Table 4.3

## Perceived Changes in Workplace Environment in Relation to CAO's Age, Years in Profession, and Geographic Location, 1986–87

| | Manager's Authority Over Subordinates | | Public Confidence in Mun. Inst. | | Employee Dedication to Work | | Employee Decision Making | |
|---|---|---|---|---|---|---|---|---|
| | Avg. | No. | Avg. | No. | Avg. | No. | Avg. | No. |
| **GEOGRAPHIC LOCATION** | | | | | | | | |
| Rural Area | 1.75 | 290 | 1.69 | 329 | 1.74 | 328 | 1.75 | 326 |
| 50 Miles of Metro | 1.70 | 227 | 1.73 | 258 | 1.77 | 257 | 1.67 | 257 |
| Suburb/Metro Area | 1.84 | 376 | 1.89 | 424 | 1.88 | 424 | 1.61 | 425 |
| Central City | 1.84 | 100 | 1.82 | 108 | 1.88 | 108 | 1.49 | 108 |
| Avg. Ratio Per Survey | 1.78 | | 1.79 | | 1.82 | | 1.65 | |
| Survey Response, Total No. | | 993 | | 1119 | | 1117 | | 1115 |
| **YEARS HAVE BEEN FULL-TIME MGR.** | | | | | | | | |
| 0-4 | 1.65 | 259 | 1.55 | 295 | 1.58 | 294 | 1.73 | 294 |
| 5-14 | 1.78 | 494 | 1.80 | 559 | 1.84 | 558 | 1.64 | 556 |
| 15-24 | 1.87 | 180 | 1.96 | 202 | 2.00 | 202 | 1.64 | 202 |
| 25-34 | 2.11 | 54 | 2.28 | 58 | 2.17 | 58 | 1.34 | 58 |
| 35-up | 1.71 | 17 | 1.89 | 18 | 1.83 | 18 | 1.72 | 18 |
| Avg. Ratio Per Survey | 1.78 | | 1.79 | | 1.82 | | 1.65 | |
| Survey Response, Total No. | | 1004 | | 1132 | | 1130 | | 1128 |
| **RESPONDENTS AGE** | | | | | | | | |
| 30 and under | 1.54 | 63 | 1.61 | 74 | 1.66 | 74 | 1.68 | 74 |
| 31-40 | 1.77 | 424 | 1.73 | 480 | 1.78 | 479 | 1.65 | 479 |
| 41-50 | 1.80 | 273 | 1.87 | 302 | 1.84 | 302 | 1.65 | 302 |
| 51-60 | 1.81 | 196 | 1.86 | 221 | 1.87 | 221 | 1.66 | 219 |
| 61 and over | 1.88 | 48 | 1.80 | 55 | 1.96 | 54 | 1.63 | 54 |
| Avg. Ratio Per Survey | 1.78 | | 1.79 | | 1.82 | | 1.65 | |
| Survey Response, Total No. | | 1004 | | 1132 | | 1130 | | 1128 |

*Note*: An average ratio was calculated for each manager factor based on a three-point scale (with 1 indicating an increase; 2, the same; and 3, a decrease).

*Source*: Compiled by the author from the 1986–87 Green–Reed survey, where the respondents had been asked, "In your experience as manager, how have the following conditions in the workplace changed since your initial employment as a full-time professional?"

the manager's authority over subordinates (2.11) and employee dedication to work (2.17), with a somewhat more substantial decrease for public confidence in local government (2.28).

This group of experienced managers is followed by another numerically small group—the youngest age group (30 years of age and under)—in magnitude of reported changes occurring the workplace. In this instance, the work condition with the greatest reported increase is the managers' authority over subordinates (1.54). Perhaps this change perceived by the youngest managers represents their initial awareness of the step-up in occupational authority and responsibility that goes with becoming a CAO.

However, a third group of managers reporting an increase among the listed occupational conditions within the 1.00 to 1.59 range (using 1.59 as the continuum break point) is equal in importance—if not magnitude—to the first two groups because it represents a substantially larger proportion of the total sample (approximately one-third of all respondents). This group of managers is characterized by their relative lack of CAO seasoning, with each possessing something less than four years of full-time experience. A substantial proportion of this relatively new group of managers reported a weighted-average score increase both in public confidence in local government institutions (1.55) and in their employees' dedication to work (1.58). These reactions may in part be a product of their enthusiasm, and the deference shown to them in their new positions of authority and responsibility.

The career factor covering geographic proximity of the manager's job site to a central city reveals only a marginal (0.09 to 0.26) range of differences in views held for all four workplace conditions. The consistency of views held by managers across job site locations suggests the existence of a commonly felt set of occupational conditions that transcends place, but is affected by the interrelated factors of age and experience.

In general, then, the most commonly shared perception of change in the managers' workplace (at least for those responding to the 1986–87 survey) is the reported expansion of employee involvement in CAO decision-making processes. This pattern is accompanied by a less widely shared perception that there had been an increase in the level of managerial authority over subordinates—with a modest increase also perceived for public confidence in local government institutions, and an indication that employees' dedication to work had also marginally increased. But—as noted above—no other group besides the managers with extensive (25–34) years of experience reported a weighted-average score above 2.00 for any of the four conditions—which essentially means a decrease in their effect as a change in the workplace.

These reports of changes in the occupational setting seem to reflect a generally expanding environment of governmental as well as professional responsibilities. This conclusion is consistent with those reached in Chapter 3 after an assessment of the managers' work time and multiple functions. It is possible that another look at professional motivations (mobility and style) would provide some added insight into how changing conditions within the occupational setting are linked with the reduction in managers' positive feelings about the personal and professional effects of their current responsibilities?

Table 4.4 arrays the assessments of changes in occupational setting by managers who responded to both the 1984 and the 1986–87 surveys and who could therefore be classified in relation to the scale of the professional mobility and style. This makes the managers whose responses are represented in Table 4.4 a distinctive subsampling of the 1986–87 survey. By the time of that survey, this subgroup of managers had been serving in their current position for at least the three years between questionnaires, and had held at least one previous CAO position by the time of the 1984 survey. Yet this group of managers does represent a significant proportion of the total sample (slightly less than one-fourth of the 1986–87 survey).

The same weighted-average score system will allow us to see whether this more experienced group of managers assesses any differently the changes that they have witnessed over the course of their longer careers. Table 4.4 gives the reactions of these managers to the same set of four workplace conditions. And indeed, this subsample of CAOs did perceive less change to have occurred in the areas of managerial authority over subordinates, the public's confidence in local government, and employee dedication to work. Of most potential significance, though, is that the weighted subsample score measuring the perceived change in demands by employees to participate in decision making shows an even more commonly shared sense of increase for this factor (at 1.59) than was reported by the total sample. In general, this confirms the observation made earlier that managers with more experience see less overall change in their occupational settings than do managers with less extensive backgrounds—with, however, the important exception of increasing demands being placed on them by their subordinates for participation in decision making.

A further analysis of Table 4.4 reveals why professional motivations and style are important to consider here. Of these three groups (community based, career based, and mixed of more experienced CAOs, the managers whose primary rationales for changing positions were community based actually reported seeing smaller increases—and, in fact, some group decreases—in the areas of managerial authority, employee dedication, and the demand from employees to participate in decision-making processes. Their group weighted-average score was virtually the same modest increase in change reported by the motivationally mixed group of managers with regard to the public's confidence in local government. Professional motivations may represent different sets of sensitivities to changing conditions in the workplace. In this context, such differences could have important implications for managers when they are looking for new community environments and challenges, as well as for communities when they are seeking a specific type of manager at a critical point.

In any case, one can make a reasonably strong argument that managers do sense and see changes and challenges in the workplace differently depending on

**Table 4.4**

**Current Workplace Conditions in Relation to Rationales for Exchanging Previous Position, 1986–87**

| Workplace Conditions | Scale of Professional Mobility | | | | | | | |
|---|---|---|---|---|---|---|---|---|
| | Respondents | | Career Based | | Mixed | | Community Based | |
| | Total | Avg. | No. | Avg. | No. | Avg. | No. | Avg. |
| Manager's authority over subordinates | 240 | 1.90 | 127 | 1.86 | 70 | 1.89 | 43 | 2.05 |
| Public confidence in municipal institutions | 268 | 1.90 | 139 | 1.86 | 81 | 1.95 | 48 | 1.94 |
| Employee dedication to their work | 268 | 1.97 | 139 | 1.90 | 81 | 1.98 | 48 | 2.15 |
| Employee demand for participation in decision-making | 268 | 1.59 | 139 | 1.60 | 81 | 1.53 | 48 | 1.65 |

*Note:* An average was calculated for each category of professional mobility based on a three-point scale (with 1 indicating increase; and 3 decrease).

*Source:* Responses concerning the workplace conditions were compiled by the author from the 1986–87 Green–Reed survey. The scale of professional mobility was constructed from items on the 1984 ICMA/CAO survey (see the footnote to Table 3.5); therefore, the responses displayed in this table are from only those managers who responded to both questionnaires.

their ages and on their levels of professional experience. They are also affected by their own career motivations and expectations for professional mobility. The timing and variation in career development of managers, and their abilities to match professional expectations with job assignments, can result in side effects that lead to unequal professional, personal, and family benefits (albeit, in the most recent surveys, this has been reported to be generally positive for most parties). But if age, professional experience, and motivations are all so important, then how will the future be affected by changes in the occupational mobility of these managers? Will increased levels of competition for CAO positions and the rising professional expectations of the managers who hold them alter the longevity and direction of career development?

## OCCUPATIONAL MOBILITY RECONSIDERED

One of the most distinctive features ascribed here to a professional career as chief administrative officer of local government is the increasingly pronounced mixture of advanced educational training, pre-CAO local government work experience, and occupational mobility—a mixture that has come to characterize the course of current professional development. Most often, a manager's first appointment as CAO occurs as a result of promotion from a subordinate local government position. This may take the form of promotion within the same local government, but it also often involves a geographic move to a CAO position in another local government. There has been very little research conducted on the factors affecting this initial decision to exchange positions.

However, Chris Argyris and D. A. Schon did undertake one of the few assessments of the impact that the initial step-up to a CAO position has on a career. The researchers argued in their 1974 study that education and early experiences are extremely powerful in shaping managers' subsequent perceptions, and their organizational and personal performances. As we too have found, Argyris and Schon suggested that managers' perceptions of professional effectiveness are slow to change after the initial CAO appointment and experience, and often shape their behavior throughout their careers.[18]

More recently, William R. Fannin and Don C. Moore examined the importance of these initial CAO appointments through a random sample of personal interviews and mailed questionnaires among Texas city managers. They found that

the data on career moves on all managers confirm the importance of early training, professional education, and initial work experiences. City managers remain very much on their initial paths in terms of size of city managed. Managers of large cities reach prominence in their profession through specific preparation of city management in college and generally enter municipal service soon after school. These results also hint that not only are city managers shaped by their professional preparation and initial jobs, but they may even be "trapped" by their early experiences. . . . Managers of larger cities generally progress up a series of increasingly responsible positions in large cities, not smaller cities.[19]

The pertinence of this pattern—"as the twig is bent, so grows the tree"—must also be considered within the long-term career pathways of all CAOs. The same pattern of occupational mobility remains clearly evident in all the surveys analyzed here regardless of whether the move is within similarly sized communities, or involves a change in size. Indeed, if the Texas study conclusions be proven true in the national marketplace and for an extended period of time (that is, initial appointments preempt long-term career mobility options), it could well have important and largely unappreciated implications for university-based professional programs and placement efforts. Nevertheless, CAO occupational mobility continues to be characterized by a national—rather than a local—marketplace. Since there can be only one CAO per municipality, county, or council-of-government, occupational mobility nearly always involves consideration of a geographic move for the individual and their family. The conditions that establish professional opportunity, and the circumstances under which occupational mobility is considered, appear to be importantly interrelated issues.

Analysis of the most current survey information available indicates that differences in past career development patterns may be linked partly to important changes now occurring in the demographic profile of the nation. After reviewing the post–World War II editions of the *U.S. Census of Governments*, James F. Wolf reports,

It is no secret to demographers that the effect of the baby boom generation of the late 1940s through the mid–1960s on the labor market has been profound. . . . From 1955 until approximately 1980, there was nearly a three-fold increase in public sector jobs. . . . In the late seventies and early eighties, several facts combined to drastically change the public sector labor market future. First was the arrival of the post-war baby boom generation on the employment scene. . . . In 1975, there were 40 million workers between the ages of 25 and 45. By 1999, this work group will total 60 million. . . . In addition to their numbers, members of the boom generation have unique characteristics which represent the best striving of an upwardly mobile middle class, i.e., a better education and a greater level of expectation about their work life. In 1950, only 6 percent of 25-year-olds had four-year degrees. By 1977, this percentage increased to 15.[20]

As a consequence, there is now a much larger group of graduates with advanced credentials available in the work force generally—and specifically, within the public sector.

However, until the decade of the 1980s, occupations and careers within the public sector were largely exempted from recessions and other private-sector restrictions on job opportunities. No doubt, current circumstances in the field of local government management have been exacerbated by the recent federal cutbacks in intergovernmental aid programs. While this was not the main purpose of Wolf's analysis, he nevertheless identified in the Baby Boom a major environmental force animating progress toward the primary goal of the local government reform movement—that is, to promote the professionalization of its management. It is clear, however, that census numbers by themselves cannot describe the broader significance of the issue. Wolf was depicting "a group of highly educated public employees at the early and middle career stages . . . that is larger than any comparable age group [and that will be intensely] bidding for top professional management positions during the next two decades."[21]

In line with Wolf's study of public sector employment, analysis of the 1978 Green–Reed survey indicates that the typical tenure for these professional city managers in ICMA-recognized communities was 30–35 years, with another 10–15 years spent working in an alternative occupation. The span of a full-length working career is estimated to be 45 (post–high school) years. And even when a six-year period of full-time academic preparation is subtracted for responding managers who had secured a master's degree (well over 50 percent of the sample)—and frequently managers worked toward their graduate degrees with an occupationally accommodating part-time course load—there still remains a minimum (average) period of 4–9 years, depending on the age group, during which alternative vocations were being pursued. The older the age of the manager, the more likely was he or she to have had a longer average non–local government career before entering the field.

While the proportion of all local government managers with a master's degree had increased substantially by the time of the 1986–87 Green–Reed survey, the proportion of local government managers with extended alternative careers (more than four years) outside local government management had decreased. CAOs now seem to be securing an advanced degree earlier in their careers and are gaining experience in subordinate local government positions—rather than in other occupations—before securing their initial CAO positions. As noted in previous chapters, analysts disagree about whether this is leading to greater or less breadth of preparation for local government management. Some argue that a wide array of preparations on the part of management candidates offers localities a wider choice in matching the manager with the community's needs and current capacities. Abstaining from this particular debate for the moment, I would only suggest that the apparent trend away from extragovernmental experience directly corresponds to the processes and characteristics of professionalization described by Vollmer and Mills.

Other researchers such as Frederick Wirt have insisted that the penetrating effects of this evolution toward professionalism in areas of local decision making are clearly part of a greater "meshing of American cities with nationalizing forces[, which] raises the possibility that local control may be either depleted . . . or enhanced."[22] The type of impact would depend on how one views and measures the effects of professionalized managers on local government policy development and implementations. For Wirt, the issue is not whether professionalism in local government is occurring—but what its scope, nature, and consequences are likely to be. As he observes,

The decisions that professionals make about their service–their quantity, their quality, the personnel qualified to tender them, and the evaluation of their work—are the source of their power. . . . This general phenomenon is linked to American cities and their decisional spaces through a set of special professionals who are chief administrators of major urban services. . . . They possess an expertise in public service delivery derived from professional training programs in universities. These are the thousands of school superintendents, city managers or chief administrative officers, planning directors, city attorneys, and heads of police, fire, engineering, medical, and welfare services in our cities.[23]

A growing body of research has been reporting an increase in the numbers of professions and professionals at all levels of government since World War II.[24] Frederick Mosher and Richard Stillman put it thus:

A great many professions are almost exclusively governmental; some of the others exist by virtue of governmental authorization and operate within the constraints and delegations of government; and many exert vigorous and sometimes monopolistic influence upon those powers and constraints.[25]

The competition among a local government's different professionals, the overall channels of influence in the government, and the actual comparative levels of influence among professions and between professionals and the elected leadership were all part of our discussion on professionalism in Chapter 3, where the focus was on professional expertise and role-playing (as derived from the ICMA and Green–Reed surveys). It is worth noting yet again (but from another independent and recent national survey) that these professional executive officers report "experiencing greater pressure, greater direct involvement in policymaking, and greater acceptance of their policy judgments—all independent of community and career differences." However, community context does make a difference, "as judged by comparative case studies of superintendents, city managers, and planners."[26]

In addition to demographic forces, though, other factors have also been important in creating an environment conducive to the increasing pace and widening scope for professionalization among CAOs in local government. The reform movement and community experiments with a variety of governmental structures have—over time—provided a basic ideology and framework for a wide cross section of U.S. localities. Evolving social, political, economic, and technological developments have maintained—if not increased—the need for professional skills, as perceived by managers and apparently by communities as well. But a manager's individual desirability and a community's perceived need for his or her professional skills may not be simultaneously—nor equally—extended or maintained by all of the involved parties!

Our analysis of the most recent 1986–87 cross section of CAOs has revealed a wide variation among the career pathways leading managers to their current careers. But longitudinal analysis indicates that a professional generation gap may be starting to appear between managers with long tenure in the field and extensive alternative occupational experience, and a younger generation of managers who have committeed themselves to local public service at earlier points in their work careers. This trend may be due to greater opportunities on the part of younger managers to pursue their educational and professional choices more immediately and directly. But there is now increasing evidence to suggest that another aspect of this trend toward professionalization is a result of changes in the marketplace for management expertise. Localities can now expect to find— and, in fact, are securing—local government managers with more advanced training and experience. The push–pull combination of both factors interacting— which was initially identified in Chapter 3—is only part of the change in career pathways. We can now appreciate some of the occupational impacts that Baby Boom demographics may be having on the processes of professionalization.

Nonetheless, these important changes must be considered in light of yet another enduring occupational feature. The typical career pathway reported by managers in the ICMA and Green–Reed surveys right into the late 1980s is characterized by the managers ultimately holding several positions as CAO during the course of their professional lives, with the average tenure for the first position being shorter than for subsequent appointments. Overall, the average tenure for managers reporting from ICMA-recognized communities is still about five years. The CAOs who have been responding to this battery of surveys during the past decade and a half have in recent years been reporting somewhat greater longevity in their careers, higher levels of advanced training, and subordinate-level local government experience. But perhaps more importantly, they have been reporting only very modest increases in the average length of time spent at each CAO appointment.

We can now address the basic questions raised at the beginning of this chapter. Are there unique facets within this changing work environment and occupational configuration of expectations that may be enhancing professionalization? What type of occupational stress does professionalization bring to individuals pursuing this type of career? Explanations about the rationales (career based) for previous position exchanges have shed some light on the differences among managers with regard to professional style. And, as already noted, there may be further changes brewing in the balance of environmental factors and forces that managers must cope with as they contemplate career development and direction. In particular, subordinates on the management team have been pressing CAOs for greater participation in the decision-making process.

It does seem somewhat ironic that occupational mobility may be such a significant factor animating professionalization of the occupation. A career commitment to serving as professional CAO for a local government ultimately seems to require a recognition and willingness to be occupationally and geographically mobile. This is the case whether occupational mobility be viewed from the perspective of individuals trying to enter or maintain themselves as practitioners in the field, or from the perspective of managers' efforts to pursue a particular self-definition for being upwardly mobile or successful. In the 1986–87 survey, CAOs were asked how they would rate (decisive, important, or not significant)

12 factors thought to represent a composite community profile that managers would consider when assessing the prospects for a new position. Table 4.5 displays their aggregated responses. Also displayed in the table is a weighted and ranked average score for each community factor—ranging in possible value from 1.00 (decisive) to 3.00 (not significant).

Managers rated geographic location as the most decisive community factor (1.58). Tied for second and third most-decisive factors were the community's political reputation and salary (1.63)—trailed by (in decreasing order of importance): compensation package, stress on family, interview experience, staff capacity, professional prestige associated with the position, predecessor's experience in the job, spouse's potential for employment in the new community, marital status, and spouse's current employment status. This array of factors represents an interesting prioritization of criteria—given the range of choices offered. "Wholistic" may be an apt term. Yet one finding of particular interest concerns the relative importance of the spouse's employment status—since nine out of ten reporting managers indicated being married, and two-thirds of the married managers reported their spouses to be currently in salaried positions. It is somewhat surprising, then, that two of the three community-related selection factors with the highest weighted scores (indicating least comparative significance) pertains to the employment status of a spouse.

How might managers representing different professional styles (career motivations for occupational mobility) vary in their evaluations of this composite of community selection factors? Again, the reader must remember that the scale of professional mobility and style was developed from manager responses made on the 1984 ICMA questionnaire, and therefore applies to only about one-quarter of the total 1986–87 survey respondents. Nonetheless, it is worth noting that the weighted-average scores of the community selection factors were ranked by the subsample in the same sequence as they were by the complete 1986–87 sample, with a slightly wider range of scores. There has been only one switch between factors (compensation package ahead of salary). We can conclude that, at least for this list of factors, the subsample is not measurably different from all the others who responded to the 1986–87 questionnaire.

Based on this subsample, then, further analysis reveals that there is no consistent pattern of differences among managers when they are classified by their rationales for making the most recent position exchange. This finding should not be viewed as too surprising. The composite of community selection factors offered to the surveyed managers cuts across a broad and complex range of personal, contractual, and uniquely local (circumstantial) issues that—without knowing more about the managers' specific characteristics—may well be of varying and fluid categorical interest to managers of all professional styles.

One might speculate that, if managers were indeed being indoctrinated over the course of their careers into holding a well-defined set of professional values, then this would be revealed by presenting them with a survey that measured certain managerial and organizational factors associated directly with their local

Table 4.5
Factors That CAOs Consider in Selecting a New Community, 1986–87

| Community Factors | No. Reporting | Ratings | | | | | | Weighted Average | |
|---|---|---|---|---|---|---|---|---|---|
| | | Decisive No. | % | Important No. | % | Not Significant No. | % | Score | Rank |
| Stress on your family | 1118 | (453) | 40.5 | (569) | 50.9 | (96) | 8.6 | 1.68 | (5) |
| Spouse's current employment status | 1084 | (123) | 11.3 | (352) | 32.5 | (609) | 56.2 | 2.45 | (12) |
| Spouse's potential for employment in new community | 1088 | (176) | 16.2 | (419) | 38.5 | (493) | 45.3 | 2.29 | (10) |
| Geographic location | 1144 | (527) | 46.1 | (572) | 50.0 | (45) | 3.9 | 1.58 | (1) |
| Professional prestige associated w/position | 1136 | (165) | 14.5 | (681) | 59.9 | (290) | 25.5 | 2.11 | (8) |
| Community's political reputation | 1141 | (531) | 46.5 | (500) | 43.8 | (110) | 9.6 | 1.63 | (2-3) |
| Salary | 1142 | (439) | 38.4 | (686) | 60.1 | (17) | 1.5 | 1.63 | (2-3) |
| Staff capacity | 1141 | (245) | 21.5 | (792) | 69.4 | (104) | 9.1 | 1.88 | (7) |
| Compensation package | 1143 | (427) | 37.4 | (691) | 60.5 | (25) | 2.2 | 1.65 | (4) |
| Predecessor's experience in that job | 1140 | (149) | 13.1 | (690) | 60.5 | (301) | 26.4 | 2.13 | (9) |
| Interview experience | 1134 | (325) | 28.7 | (628) | 55.4 | (181) | 16.0 | 1.87 | (6) |
| Marital status | 1090 | (159) | 14.6 | (326) | 29.9 | (605) | 55.5 | 2.41 | (11) |

*Note:* A weighted-average score was calculated for each community factor based on a three-point scale (with 1 indicating decisive; and 3, not significant). Percentage totals may not equal 100, due to rounding.

*Source:* Compiled by the author from the 1986–87 Green-Reed survey, where the question was asked: "How would you rate the following factors in selecting a new community in which to serve as manager?"

government responsibilities. Table 4.6 arrays the reactions of the ICMA managers to just such a composite listing of ten job evaluation factors that managers often consider when deciding whether to apply for and to accept a new local management job offer.

As it turns out, in the 1986–87 survey responses, a relatively distinct criterion for assessing the professional merits of a CAO position was uncovered. An analysis of Table 4.6 suggests a clear differentiation and prioritization of job factors. In this rather narrow, occupationally defined context, the range of weighted scores for the ten-item list of specific professional factors ranged more widely—from 1.34 to 2.65—than when the managers were rating characteristics of the community (see Table 4.5, where the weighted scores ranged from 1.58 to 2.45). Specifically, ranking the job factors by their weighted-average scores, the managers identified the lines of authority between mayor, council, and manager as the most decisive factor (1.34) in their decision-making matrix. Next came the "history of city divisions and conflicts" factor—and then: administrative structure; norms, values, and motivations of the staff, and professional qualifications of the staff (tied for fourth and fifth places); followed closely by past career experience; the reputation of local management among nonresident professional colleagues; the state and regional professional network; the office arrangements and conditions; and ending with the predecessor's relationships with the media.

These findings contrast with how the managers considered the relative importance of the 12-item community composite profile (again, see Table 4.5). Most community factors were seen as relatively equal in their importance (proximate to the 2.00 value); and past career motivations for position change offered little additional insight to the weighted-average score ranking. Perhaps we should not be too surprised to learn that a manager's decisional matrix about the relevancy of various community selection factors often gives equal weight to complex personal and family dimensions in addition to a strict concern over the professional merits of the position involved.

Some standardization of the professional prerogatives and values associated with applying for and accepting a CAO position does seem to be apparent from the survey responses. There is a quite widely shared sense of order among the job factors that are considered most salient, as seen in their weighted score rankings. And underlying these professional prerogatives, there exists an associated set of normative expectations about what the proper rules of the game should be.

Also revealed by this ranking of managerial and organizational job factors is the relatively clear view held by managers about the occupational requirements of their profession. As it turns out, this composite view of the managers is quite similar to the framework offered by James Svara in his dichotomy–duality model (see the discussion in Chapter 3).[27] Managers—it seems—are quite aware of and sensitive to the issues associated with their professional prerogatives in areas relating to the management of programs by administrative staff—while still

**Table 4.6**
**Factors Important to CAOs When Applying for and Accepting a New Management Job Offer, 1986–87**

| Job Factors | No. Reporting | Ratings | | | | | | Weighted Average Score | Rank |
|---|---|---|---|---|---|---|---|---|---|
| | | Decisive No. | % | Important No. | % | Not Significant No. | % | | |
| Norms, values & motivation of staff | 1136 | (145) | 12.8 | (839) | 73.9 | (152) | 13.4 | 2.01 | (4-5) |
| Professional qualifications of staff | 1137 | (133) | 11.7 | (865) | 76.1 | (139) | 12.2 | 2.01 | (4-5) |
| Reputation of local management among non-resident professional colleagues | 1123 | (87) | 7.7 | (693) | 61.7 | (343) | 30.5 | 2.23 | (7) |
| History of city divisions/conflicts | 1137 | (440) | 38.7 | (616) | 54.2 | (81) | 7.1 | 1.68 | (2) |
| Administrative structure | 1136 | (259) | 22.8 | (726) | 63.9 | (151) | 13.3 | 1.90 | (3) |
| Office arrangements/conditions | 1137 | (36) | 3.2 | (518) | 45.6 | (583) | 51.3 | 2.48 | (9) |
| Predecessor relationships w/media | 1136 | (23) | 2.0 | (346) | 30.5 | (767) | 67.5 | 2.65 | (10) |
| Lines of authority between mayor, council and manager | 1140 | (774) | 67.9 | (345) | 30.3 | (21) | 1.8 | 1.34 | (1) |
| State and regional professional network | 1137 | (40) | 3.5 | (648) | 57.0 | (449) | 39.5 | 2.36 | (8) |
| Past career experience | 1128 | (149) | 13.2 | (796) | 70.6 | (183) | 16.2 | 2.03 | (6) |

Total Survey n = 1165

*Note*: A weighted average was calculated for each job factor based on a three-point scale (with 1 indicating decisive; and 3, not significant). Percentage totals may not equal 100, due to rounding.

*Source*: Compiled by the author from the 1986–87 Green–Reed survey, where the question had been asked: "In your decision to apply for or accept a new local management job offer, how important are the following factors in making that decision?"

showing a deference to elected officials, whose responsibility it is to establish and define the governments' overall mission. We can also see the professional sensitivity of managers in their judging a potential position primarily on the merits of its character in the shared areas of policy development and administration, which fall in between mission and management.

One additional issue to be considered is whether classifying managers according to their career rationalizations for changing positions might reveal any important differences or continuities in how they will consider future positions. Do the managers' professional styles seem to be associated with how they assess the relevancy of job-related factors when considering a new position? The survey responses have been analyzed along these lines, cross-tabulated, and displayed in Table 4.7.

Once again, the weighted-average scores for the 1984/1986–87 subsample are arrayed similarly to those of the total 1986–87 sample: That is, the subsample rated the job selection factors in the same sequence and with a similar range of scores. And again, there has been only one slight switch in factor positioning (tying past career experience up with norms, values, and motivations of the staff—just ahead of professional qualifications of the staff). We can therefore assume that this subset of responses to the job-related factors—like those to the community-related factors—are not on these criteria measurably different from the total sample.

With one important exception—community-based managers gave the highest average priority to the factor that "lines of authority between mayor, council, and manager" should be clearly established—community-motivated managers consistently rated every other job-selection factor as being comparatively less important than did their career—and mixed—motivation colleagues. This is in contrast to the lack of differentiation found when their responses were compared with respect to the community selection factors. Interestingly, the three job factors representing the greatest variation in score between the community-motivated managers and the mixed and career-based groups are: (1) norms, values, and motivation of staff; (2) professional qualifications of staff; and (3) reputation of local management. However, there is no similarly consistent pattern of responses separating career-based managers from managers with mixed motivations.

These findings are quite a contrast to what Ralph Katz contends to be the important situational factors related to job satisfaction:

Employees who have recently entered an organization [or are considering such a move] tend to be more preoccupied than other employees with job safety and security and with establishing their own identities within the organization. . . . More specifically, it would seem that only after grappling with the problem of establishing a somewhat stable situational identity can the individual in the midst of a new job comfortably direct his attention to task features involving high achievement, challenge, and autonomy.[28]

**Table 4.7**

**Important Job Factors in Relation to Rationales for Exchanging Previous Position, 1986–87**

| | Scale of Professional Mobility | | | | | | | |
| | Respondents | | Career Based | | Mixed | | Community Based | |
| Job Factors | Total | Avg. | No. | Avg. | No. | Avg. | No. | Avg. |
|---|---|---|---|---|---|---|---|---|
| Norms, values & motivation of staff | 272 | 2.03 | 142 | 2.01 | 82 | 1.96 | 48 | 2.17 |
| Professional qualifications of staff | 272 | 2.05 | 142 | 2.01 | 82 | 2.04 | 48 | 2.17 |
| Reputation of local management | 267 | 2.25 | 141 | 2.25 | 80 | 2.16 | 46 | 2.41 |
| History of City divisions/conflicts | 272 | 1.62 | 142 | 1.60 | 82 | 1.61 | 48 | 1.69 |
| Administrative structure | 271 | 1.92 | 142 | 1.87 | 82 | 1.98 | 47 | 1.98 |
| Office arrangements/conditions | 272 | 2.54 | 142 | 2.52 | 82 | 2.55 | 48 | 2.60 |
| Predecessor relationships with media | 272 | 2.64 | 142 | 2.61 | 82 | 2.66 | 48 | 2.67 |
| Lines of authority between mayor, council & manager | 272 | 1.32 | 142 | 1.34 | 82 | 1.30 | 48 | 1.29 |
| State & regional professional network | 270 | 2.40 | 141 | 2.40 | 81 | 2.33 | 48 | 2.52 |
| Past career experience | 269 | 2.03 | 141 | 2.04 | 81 | 2.11 | 47 | 1.89 |

*Note:* An average score was calculated for each job-factor category of professional mobility, as based on a three-point scale (with 1 indicating decisive; and 3 not significant).

*Source:* Job-factor responses were compiled by the author from the 1986–87 Green–Reed survey. The scale of professional mobility was constructed from items on the 1984 ICMA/CAO survey (see the footnote to Table 3.5); therefore, the responses displayed in the table are from only those managers who responded to both questionnaires.

The Katz characterization seems most like our community-based managers' weighted scores, which demonstrate the most immediate concern over occupational security.

However, the proportionately larger group of managers who report being most directly career motivated (representing approximately one-fifth of all managers responding in 1984, and more than half of the 1984/1986–87 subsample used in Table 4.7) indicate a somewhat greater comparative concern and preoccupation with staff factors than with other political and organizational factors. One plausible explanation—although these differences are not categorical, but rather only a matter of degree—is that career-motivated managers may perceive themselves as (and perhaps are sought after as) "agents for change."[29] In that case, the conditions characterizing staff norms, values, motivations, qualifications, and reputation would be less important when deciding to apply for or to accept a new CAO appointment, since these are likely to be the very targets of change.

Occupational mobility has shown itself to be a significant characteristic of—and requirement for—having a long-term career as a local government CAO. It has revealed a number of important dimensions to the scope and direction of the CAOs' professionalization. That is to say, for proportionately fewer available positions, local government managers are now facing greater competition among more highly educated and experienced colleagues. The frequency and conditions associated with occupational mobility, then—as well as the expectations and responsibilities involved in actually being a professional local government manager—constitute a number of different and potentially very stressful, complex influences on the managers' professional capacities, career choices, and longevity. It is to a discussion and assessment of occupationally induced stress factors that we now turn.

### OCCUPATIONAL STRESS

Occupational stress research has been conducted by numerous students of physiology, psychology, and sociology.[30] But stress researchers have reached no consensus on the meaning of the term "stress"—much less, formulated behavioral prescriptions for alleviating its deleterious effects. For our purposes, perhaps the most useful description of stress is that it "occurs where there are demands on the person which tax or exceed his adjustive resources."[31] But researchers generally agree that stress is not entirely bad. It can be necessary and even useful for accomplishing tasks, and—if managed properly—will not necessarily lead to health problems. Nevertheless, stress can—and does—contribute to specific maladies (heart problems, hypertension, ulcers, and so forth) and can produce reactions that result in family, work, and other personal problems.[32]

In the 1970s, researchers shifted their focus from how people behave under stress, to its sources and consequences. The costs associated with the stress-induced dysfunctions and illnesses that result in lost work surprised many of the researchers.[33] Others found it difficult to accept that the organizational structure of the workplace can adversely affect the mental and physical health of Americans.[34]

In the 1980s, a new concern has been linking occupational stress–associated disabilities to organizational responsibility. Writing in a 1985 issue of the *Insurance Counsel Journal*, Donald T. DeCarlo—general counsel of the National Council on Compensation Insurance—observed,

All jurisdictions have now recognized the compensability of a physical injury resulting in mental disability traumatic neurosis. In addition, there is an increasing tendency to recognize the compensability of a mental stress causing a physical injury, particularly when the mental stimulus is sudden and unusual in magnitude, for example, a stress related heart attack. . . . [However,] in the last few years, there has been an unprecedented increase in claims in which neither the mental stimulus nor the resulting mental disability is associated with any physical event. And, in the eighties, there is a growing, and perhaps now a majority, trend which recognizes the compensability of such claims.[35]

According to the National Council on Compensation Insurance, claims involving mental disorders arising from psychological pressures now account for 10 percent of all occupational disease claims. Younger workers and female employees file more stress claims than they do other occupational disease claims. In the 1980s—for the first time—the average cost of a stress claim, as well as the average medical expenditures associated with these cases, surpassed the average costs for other occupational disease claims.[36] This growth in employee recognition that a stressful work environment can cause symptoms such as depression raises fundamental medical, legal, and insurance issues for occupations of higher risk. Managers—it now appears—may not only be subjected to a considerable amount of occupational stress themselves, but may also be the legally responsible official for stress-related claims filed against local governments. Here—however—the discussion will focus on stress levels among the managers themselves, as individuals.

Change can be stressful—regardless of the benefits gained in the bargain. Completing a graduate degree program, entering a new job position, or moving to a new home are viewed as exciting stages or opportunities; yet each requires relinquishing some familiar patterns and adjusting to different surroundings. Occupational stress researchers have attempted to identify the most stressful jobs, the nature of job stress, and the effect of job-related stress on job performance. Members of certain occupational groups exhibit higher levels of stress-related problems (such as ulcers, hypertension, alcoholism, suicide) and report experiencing more anxiety than others.[37] Because the nature of their positions may leave them vulnerable to sudden job loss and because their families' visibility in the community can be stressful for their marriages, local government managers can certainly be included in the high-risk category.

The local government manager's job represents a convergence of several stress factors. First, job mobility among local managers is high when compared to most other occupations. As mentioned above, the average tenure for a local government manager in a given position averages between 4.5 and 5.5 years. The manager is thus likely to face job changes—highly stressful events—more often than most people.[38]

Occupational mobility remains a fact of the local government manager's life. And when CAOs change jobs, they nearly always change their residences. Relocation is also highly stressful, and distant moves—the type that local government managers are likely to make—may be most stressful of all. The manager faces a completely new physical, social, political, and employment environment. The cast of characters and the surroundings are different with each move. The manager's family encounters similar disruptions. They enter new schools, try to make new friends, perhaps find new jobs, and learn to adapt to a new environment. Most local government managers must deal with such stress on themselves and their families with atypical frequency.

Second, the local government manager's job comes fraught with conflicts and ambiguities that are likely to produce stress—particularly when a new manager is trying to be flexible, yet retain his or her professional standards and integrity. The manager is a professional hired by elected officials. At one and the same time, CAOs must be politically sensitive and remote. They operate in an environment imbued with disparate policy directions. They are responsible for the administration of service departments, for enforcement of laws and ordinances, for providing pertinent information to the council, commission, or board, and for the operations and financial conditions of their units of government. Furthermore, when local government managers take a job, they know that they can be fired at any time. The longer managers remain in a position, the more opportunities exist for their decisions to alienate council members and result in dismissal. Insightful managers often try to stay one step ahead of their adversaries, and resign before they are fired.

And third, the local government manager contends with public scrutiny similar to that faced by elected officials. While committed to standards of professional and personal integrity, managers are often subjected to intense public pressure. The constant monitoring of public officials introduces another level of stress. The conduct of managers is measured by the public and their own colleagues in government. CAOs are accountable under the pertinent mandates of federal and state constitutions and statutes, as well as locally prescribed charter and ordinance responsibilities and commitments. And those managers who are members of the International City Management Association, the American Society for Public Administration, or any of a number of other associations may also be required to follow certain codes or principles of ethics that provide a framework for their professional conduct. Alleged violations of the ICMA code, for example, are investigated by a special committee, and sanctions may be imposed. Frequently, the perception of unethical behavior on the part of a manager is as detrimental as an actually unethical act: The ambiguities and doubt can be as stressful for the manager and his or her family as outright accusation.

Curiously, local government managers are not often selected as a discrete target population for stress-related research. City, county or council-of-government managers rarely appear in the job-burnout literature, and local government management has not been included in lists of high-stress occupations. The omission may be due to a perceived lack of drama in the nature of managers' crises. Local government managers do not deal with life-and-death situations daily. They usually confront such situations more indirectly—when deciding on the location of a hazardous waste site—for instance—or authorizing dangerous police activities. Also, they do not face threats to their lives every time they go to work—as do police officers, firemen, and emergency medical teams (all of whom are frequently employed by the local government where our professional manager is the chief administrative officer).

In summary, managers face a combination of job stressors: relatively high occupational mobility, ambiguous policy direction, and great responsibility. Furthermore, they must juggle expectations as they are pressured to keep government expenditures low and services adequate. They do not report to one supervisor; they are accountable to all citizens, to their councils, and to the various administrative constituencies and interest groups. Their effectiveness is not measured by increased profits or productivity. Most often their professional worth is determined by an ability to negotiate with conflicting interests and to operate in complex political environments.

According to my own survey research conducted in 1978, managers consider their jobs as stressful as those of medical doctors and more stressful than those of attorneys or other state, federal, and private-sector managers.[39] This may correspond in part to a transition thought to be occurring in the primary roles of managers, with the professionalization of the CAO position. ICMA's Committee on Future Horizons has observed,

In the past the focus [of local government management] has been on the technology of service delivery, the analytical skills of administration, and the strategies of direction from the top down. In the future [these leaders will be called on] . . . to direct an organization or group of people without dominating it. It will call on the ability to help people see their own desires and goals more clearly and (unobtrusively) to help them satisfy those desires and goals.[40]

Political scientists, public administrationists, and organizational theorists view the local government manager's occupational environment as a crucial factor in estimating the capacity of the locality to respond to citizen and intergovernmental demands. It is of some significance, then, that much of the stress experienced by professional local government managers is derived from the position's political and democratic environment (its setting and expectations), and that—as confirmed by the reports of managers—the antecedents of their occupational stress include role ambiguity (at least initially), substantial variation in the quality of elected officials, fiscal stringency, and ever-rising constituent demands.[41]

The Green–Reed 1986–87 survey instrument contained a number of important questions about the occupational dimensions that reflect on managerial experience and stress, including: career path history, professional choice and occupational mobility factors, spouse occupational status, and other family characteristics. Analysis of these survey responses is now in order for an assessment of the humanware factors and costs associated with professionalization of the CAO occupation.

### Occupational Mobility and Career Stress

There are two issues given special attention in the following sections of this chapter because of their potential significance in the 1990s and beyond. These issues are, first, that there is an increasing level of occupationally induced stress being placed on managers from a whole variety of external and extenuating factors that now face the governments and communities being served. Occupational stressors from this source are thought to have a direct impact on managers' health and their capacity to perform at expected professional levels, on their personal lives, and on the risk liability of their employing jurisdictions. The second issue involves the rise in occupationally induced stress that may be related to increasing numbers of managers—particularly among the newer and younger local-government CAOs—who have spouses pursuing independent careers. In this instance, the concern is over the personal stress caused whenever occupational mobility decisions are confronted and the decision to exchange CAO positions affects more than one career pathway.

The dynamics associated with these two sources of occupational stress raise a number of important concerns. How do their forces interact; and what types of impact do they have on individual practitioners and—in the aggregate—on the entire profession? Three questions regarding the consequences of these two potentially important sources of occupational stress will be pursued here. First, is there evidence that evolving professional expectations for the manager's role and performance in local government may be influencing their own expectations about occupationally induced levels of stress, and affecting the duration of their careers in the field? Of special interest are the reportedly increased levels of community- and career-based occupational stress.

Second, what would a continuing trend toward increasing numbers of dual-earner/career couples portend for the overall sense of well-being felt by the local government managers? And third—related to the second—does there seem to be any association between variations in the managers' perceptions of occupational stress and the family, educational, employment, and career status of their spouses? This third question has the potential for being doubly important, insofar as the increasing proportion of managers with spouses pursuing independent careers may serve to alter the supply dynamics of the marketplace for local government managers (that is, the potential pool of applicants as well as the characteristics of those actually selected).

Therefore, occupational stress—as a by-product of the forces influencing the scope and rate of professionalization in the field—may have important individual, family, organizational, community, and professional meanings. In the 1986–87 Green–Reed survey, managers were asked to compare the stress levels in their positions with those thought to be felt by four other occupations of acknowledged and substantial responsibility. The results were similar to those reported from the 1978 Green–Reed survey of city managers. Less than one out of five managers responding to the 1986–87 survey indicated that they felt under more physical or psychological stress than medical doctors would feel. However, slightly more than 40 percent of the responding managers felt that they were under a stress level similar to that experienced by doctors. Significant as these comparatively high levels of self-assessed physical and psychological stress seem, the 1986–87 responses actually represent a reduction in the level and extensiveness of self-perceived stress from those reported in 1978. Over 10 percent more of the 1986–87 respondents rated themselves as being under less stress than doctors.

This high self-assessment of perceived occupational stress is internally consistent with the managers' reports that they suffered from even higher levels of stress compared to lawyers, business executives, and state and federal government executives. Nonetheless, local government managers again reported in 1986–87 a proportionately lower level of stress per comparative occupational category than the city managers reported in 1978. Nevertheless—and consistent with the 1978 patterns—approximately half of the managers felt under more stress than lawyers, and almost two-thirds felt under more stress than state and federal government executives. Interestingly—since business was the alternative occupational preference most frequently mentioned by managers when asked to speculate about leaving their careers as CAOs—only about one-third of the managers perceived themselves to be under greater physical and psychological stress than business executives.

Having managers compare their previous non-CAO positions to their alternative occupational preferences should provide an even more valid approach to assessing perceived levels of stress. The former relates to the individuals' actual experience. The latter refers to the managers' estimate of the stress that comes with their alternative vocational preferences. Regardless of whether or not any particular alternative was also previously experienced, we can reasonably assume that the respondents had to some extent either observed or inquired about their preference as a potential work environment.

Similar to the response patterns from the 1978 Green–Reed survey, a majority of the 1986–87 respondents (59.0 percent) indicated that they were laboring under more stress currently than they had at their previous positions, with another 20.5 percent indicating that they were under similar stress levels. However, more than three-quarters (75.5 percent) of the local government managers also indicated that their alternative vocational preference would be more or about the same in stress level to what they perceived themselves to be functioning under currently. An overview of these comparisons made by local government managers in 1986–87 and a cautious further comparison with the responses of city managers in 1978 seem to suggest that these respondents did not perceive their relative (or our compared) stress levels to have been reduced significantly or changed. Instead, the overall perceived levels of stress among executives of all four other career categories were thought by managers to have increased. This initial conclusion can be drawn with regard to managers' comparisons of stress in their previous occupations as well as in their alternative career preferences.

Thus, a majority of the managers responding to the 1986–87 survey do not seem to regard stress level as a determining occupational screening device. However, let it not go unnoticed that, similar to the 1978 survey responses, almost 25 percent of the managers did feel that their alternative occupational preference would result in reduced job stress—suggesting that, for many, the high level of CAO occupational stress may very well be a relevant consideration in evaluating career options and may therefore also be a factor in the profession's attrition rate. Table 4.8 reveals more specifically how local government managers compared their current occupational levels of stress with a self-defined list of previous positions, as well as with a list of four frequently mentioned alternative occupations.

Not a single occupational category shows a majority of responding managers to the 1986–87 questionnaire rating their previous occupation as more stressful than their current position. On the other hand, positions in which at least half of the managers indicated that their previous occupation was similar or more stressful than local government management included educator, position in the private/non-profit sector, city/county clerk, student intern, and previous position as a public manager. By contrast, categories in which a majority of managers thought that their current position was more stressful than those held previously include assistant manager, department head, assistant to the manager, position in the private/for-profit sector, administrative assistant, various other governmental positions, consulting, assistant department head, the military, elected official, and full-time student.

Table 4.8 also allows us to consider more specifically several categories of alternative preferences. Once again, there is a marked reduction from 1978 in the extent to which 1986–87 respondents viewed their current stress levels as being higher than the stress levels of their alternative occupation preference. Whereas in 1978 at least a majority of the responding city managers found their current positions to be more stressful than teaching, other types of government service, business, and consulting, in 1986–87 a majority of the local government managers described teaching as the only alternative occupational choice listed that would be less stressful than their current one. (Some of us in the teaching profession may beg to differ!) Consistent with the pattern of responses in 1978,

**Table 4.8**
**Managers' Perceived Stress in Previous Position Held and in Alternative Occupational Preference, 1986–87**

| Previous Position | No. Reporting | Manager Under Less Stress no. | Manager Under Less Stress % | Manager Under Similar Stress no. | Manager Under Similar Stress % | Manager Under More Stress no. | Manager Under More Stress % |
|---|---|---|---|---|---|---|---|
| Total | 1010 | 207 | 20.5 | 207 | 20.5 | 596 | 59.0 |
| Assistant Manager | 205 | 44 | 21.5 | 35 | 17.1 | 126 | 61.5 |
| Local Public Manager | 28 | 10 | 35.7 | 7 | 25.0 | 11 | 39.3 |
| Department Head | 169 | 29 | 17.2 | 30 | 17.8 | 110 | 65.1 |
| Assistant to Manager | 50 | 12 | 24.0 | 8 | 16.0 | 30 | 60.0 |
| Private/For-Profit | 134 | 24 | 17.9 | 42 | 31.3 | 68 | 50.7 |
| Administrative Asst. | 89 | 14 | 15.7 | 14 | 15.7 | 61 | 68.5 |
| Other Govt. Position | 158 | 30 | 19.0 | 28 | 17.7 | 100 | 63.3 |
| Consultant | 7 | 3 | 42.9 | 0 | 0.0 | 4 | 57.0 |
| Asst. Department Head | 18 | 1 | 5.6 | 6 | 33.3 | 11 | 61.1 |
| City/County Clerk | 30 | 8 | 26.7 | 8 | 26.7 | 14 | 46.7 |
| Military | 49 | 10 | 20.4 | 13 | 26.5 | 26 | 53.1 |
| Intern | 7 | 3 | 42.9 | 2 | 28.6 | 2 | 28.6 |
| Elected Official | 8 | 2 | 25.0 | 1 | 12.5 | 5 | 62.5 |
| Private/Non-Profit | 17 | 7 | 41.2 | 2 | 11.8 | 8 | 47.1 |
| Educator | 22 | 6 | 27.3 | 7 | 31.8 | 9 | 40.9 |
| Full-Time Student | 5 | 1 | 20.0 | 0 | 0.0 | 4 | 80.0 |
| Other | 14 | 3 | 21.4 | 4 | 28.6 | 7 | 50.0 |

**Alternative Occupational Preference**

| | No. Reporting | no. | % | no. | % | no. | % |
|---|---|---|---|---|---|---|---|
| Total | 1117 | 273 | 24.4 | 361 | 32.3 | 483 | 43.2 |
| Teacher | 149 | 39 | 26.2 | 28 | 18.8 | 82 | 55.0 |
| Other Govt. Service | 192 | 44 | 22.9 | 55 | 28.6 | 93 | 48.4 |
| Politics | 40 | 7 | 17.5 | 20 | 50.0 | 13 | 32.5 |
| Business | 500 | 115 | 23.0 | 181 | 36.2 | 204 | 40.8 |
| Consulting | 156 | 42 | 26.9 | 50 | 32.1 | 62 | 41.0 |
| Other | 80 | 26 | 32.5 | 27 | 33.7 | 27 | 33.8 |

*Note*: Percentage totals may not equal 100, due to rounding.

*Source*: This table was adapted from Tables 4.4 and 4.5 in the article written by the author with B. J. Reed, "Occupational Stress and Mobility among Professional Local Government Managers: A Decade of Change," in the *Municipal Year Book 1988* (Washington, D.C.: ICMA, 1988), p. 38. On the 1986–87 Green-Reed survey, the respondents had been asked: "Other than being a student, please indicate the title of the last full-time position you held before becoming a local manager"; and "If you were to leave the local government management profession, what kind of job would you prefer?"

there are no categories in which more than one-third of the responding managers indicated their current position less stressful than any of the alternatives listed.

The relative weight that perceived occupational stress holds in personal career evaluation may have changed somewhat since 1978. Among the most interesting findings from the 1986–87 survey are those showing that local government managers were more likely to have had previous local government experience than was true a decade earlier, and also that business continued to beckon as the most popular alternative occupation. Still, local government managers appear to be staying in the field longer, while the tenure for individually held positions is about the same as it was in 1978. However, even while managers are likely to see themselves under more stress than lawyers as well as other state and federal executives (and almost one-half see their stress to be as great as that of business executives), managers have come to see most other professionals—indeed several of which could be considered logical alternatives to their own careers as CAOs in local government—as laboring under higher levels of stress than earlier. These perceptions may become increasingly important from the standpoint of managers extending their careers in local government.

### Stress: Education, Age, and Experience Factors

We have all seen the entry-level, modest-salary job description in the classified ads. Perhaps we even applied for it when first starting out, or considered it even more recently when we thought about changing directions. This is the one that advertises an exciting opportunity for those with youthful enthusiasm and a willingness to move and be adaptable to a fast-changing new environment—but that also requires the highest levels of professional training, and 7–10 years of similar experience elsewhere! This employer wish list—so distorted in its expectations—nevertheless highlights three personal factors often associated with a person's capacity to manage or control the dysfunctions caused by occupational stress: levels of training, personal maturity, and work experience.

What seems to connect these three factors is an underlying assumption that most occupational stress involves circumstances under which a person feels either no longer able to understand the causes of events taking place in the work environment, or no longer able to influence them meaningfully. Knowledge, maturity, and practice are often associated by the employer with the occupationally successful individual—and by the individual, with personal feelings of confidence and well-being. In fact, measures for two of these three factors were utilized as the key components in the definition and analysis of professional expertise, which was empirically introduced in chapter 3.

As noted earlier, survey respondents from ICMA-recognized communities are increasingly well educated (more than half of these managers now hold a master's degree or more, and another 14 percent have taken at least some graduate courses). Well over 80 percent of the managers have a bachelor's degree or higher. The data arrayed in Table 4.9 indicate that—regardless of level of ed-

**Table 4.9**
**Effect of Education on Perceived CAO Stress Level, 1986–1987**

| Education | Level of Stress Compared with Previous Position | | | | | | | | Level of Stress Compared with Alternative Occupational Preference | | | | | | | |
|---|---|---|---|---|---|---|---|---|---|---|---|---|---|---|---|---|
| | No. Reporting | More Stress no. | % | Similar Stress no. | % | Less Stress no. | % | Weighted Average Score | No. Reporting | More Stress no. | % | Similar Stress no. | % | Less Stress no. | % | Weighted Average Score |
| Total | 1109 | 232 | 20.9 | 220 | 19.8 | 657 | 59.2 | --- | 1117 | 273 | 24.4 | 361 | 32.3 | 483 | 43.2 | --- |
| Some High School | 2 | 0 | 0.0 | 0 | 0.0 | 2 | 100.0 | 3.00 | 2 | 0 | 0.0 | 1 | 50.0 | 1 | 50.0 | 2.50 |
| High School | 32 | 10 | 31.3 | 7 | 21.9 | 15 | 46.9 | 2.16 | 34 | 17 | 50.0 | 10 | 29.4 | 7 | 20.6 | 1.71 |
| Some College | 64 | 15 | 23.4 | 18 | 28.1 | 31 | 48.4 | 2.25 | 65 | 18 | 27.7 | 22 | 33.8 | 25 | 38.5 | 2.11 |
| Assoc. of Arts | 24 | 5 | 20.8 | 7 | 29.2 | 12 | 50.0 | 2.29 | 23 | 7 | 30.4 | 7 | 30.4 | 9 | 39.1 | 2.09 |
| B.A./B.S. + Some Grad Work | 307 | 64 | 20.8 | 62 | 20.2 | 181 | 59.0 | 2.38 | 309 | 73 | 23.6 | 109 | 35.3 | 127 | 41.1 | 2.17 |
| M.A./M.S./M.P.A. | 514 | 107 | 20.8 | 86 | 16.7 | 321 | 62.5 | 2.42 | 518 | 119 | 23.0 | 156 | 30.1 | 243 | 46.9 | 2.24 |
| Other | 166 | 31 | 18.6 | 40 | 24.1 | 95 | 57.2 | (NA) | 166 | 39 | 23.5 | 56 | 33.7 | 71 | 42.8 | (NA) |

*Note:* A weighted-average score was calculated based on a three-point scale (with 1 being more stressful, and 3 being less stressful). Percentage totals may not equal 100, due to rounding.

*Source:* An initial compilation from the questions, without the weighted-average scores, was reported by the author with B. J. Reed in "Occupational Stress and Mobility among Professional Local Government Managers: A Decade of Change," in the *Municipal Year Book 1988* (Washington, D.C.: ICMA, 1988), p. 39. On the 1986–87 Green–Reed survey, the respondents had been asked: "What is the highest level of education you have completed?"; "How would you rate the physical and psychological stress in your current position as manager, compared to your last position before becoming a manager?"; and "How would you rate the physical and psychological stress in your current position as manager, compared to your occupational preference outside local management?"

ucation—never more than one-third of the respondents thought that their current levels of stress were higher than the levels perceived for their previous occupations. And this basic pattern was also true when respondents were asked to juxtapose their current levels of occupational stress with that which they would expect from their alternative career choices (except for managers with high school diplomas). Still, two-thirds of the reporting managers felt that their current occupations were, in fact, as stressful if not more stressful than both their previous positions and alternative preferences. It appears that the responding managers did feel substantial levels of occupational stress—but not out of line with what they had experienced in their previous positions, nor would expect from their alternative career preferences.

However, education is also shown to be somewhat of a mitigating factor cutting across these comparative perceptions of occupational stress. That is— regardless of whether the managers were asked to compare their current stress level with their previous occupations or with their alternative career preferences— as the level of educational achievement increased, the relative proportion of local government managers who found their current positions more stressful decreased. The weighted-average stress scores indicate that higher levels of formal education are consistently associated with reductions in managers' comparative levels of perceived occupational stress. Once again, the scores could range between 1.00 for more comparative stress, to 3.00 for less comparative stress. Exempting the two managers who did not have a high school diploma, the actual range was from 2.16 to 2.42 (a narrow difference of 0.26) when comparisons where made with the CAOs' previous positions. The range was from 1.71 to 2.24 (a somewhat larger difference of 0.53) for comparisons made with the alternative career choices.

Another interesting finding can be identified when these patterns are contrasted with what the respondents to the 1978 survey indicated for the same set of comparisons. For all categories of educational obtainment, the city managers reported proportionately higher levels of stress in their current positions than did the cross-section of local government managers who responded in 1986–87. In summary, the higher the managers' level of education, the more likely were they to report that their current stress was lower—or, at least, not any higher— than in their previous occupations or alternative career choices. And this pattern was more pronounced in 1986–87 than it was in 1978.

The pursuit of a formal education takes—among other things—time. And time—whether expanded on education or other pursuits—is often thought of as part of a more generic maturation or aging process. In this context, moreover, maturation through the aging process is often linked with a greater capacity to handle various and varying levels of personal stress—whether the stress is occupationally induced or from some other source. However, in the responses to the 1986–87 questionnaire, age is not associated in any consistent manner with variations in perceived levels of stress—not in the aggregated survey totals, nor in comparisons with previous occupation and alternative career preference (data not displayed). When weighted-average stress scores are computed for each of ten discrete categories of age, they range much more widely than when education is the factor being considered—in this case: from 2.06 to 2.60 (a difference of 0.54) for the comparison made with the CAOs' previous positions; and from 1.75 to 2.50 (a difference of 0.75) for the comparison with their alternative career preferences. However, in contrast with the 1978 responses of city managers, there appears to have been a very modest but consistent decrease in the comparative perceptions of occupational stress—most noticeably among respondents over 50 years of age—than was revealed by the responses to the 1986–87 survey.[42]

Education may also be considered a form of experience—that is, as part of the managers' professional expertise on which they are expected to draw. This is circumstantially supported by the manager reports comparing education levels with perceptions of occupational stress, as discussed above. We may well extend this reasoning to expect reduced perceptions of occupational stress as seniority in the profession increases.

However, when manager responses are examined to determine what impact the number of years of local government management experience and the length of service in a given location might have, there is again little or no association. Increased experience in the profession does not seem to indicate any consistent or major differences among managers in regard to the comparative levels of occupational stress. When the weighted-average stress scores are computed for each of eight discrete categories of seniority, the scores range from 2.22 to 2.46 (a narrow difference of 0.24) for the comparison made with the CAOs' previous positions; and from 1.92 to 2.28 (an also narrow difference of 0.36) for the comparison with their alternative career preferences. This range of variation in the weighted scores is much less than when either age or education is the factor being considered, and is therefore even less discriminating as a factor to explain differences in the managers' views toward their occupational stress.

Thus, the analysis does not suggest any clear pattern of heightened or reduced perceptions of stress to be associated with years in the current location. However, in this instance, the data replicate the findings of the city managers responding to the 1978 survey, which also failed to reveal any significant degree of association between seniority factors and perceived occupational stress levels.[43]

Perhaps managers perceive the degree of occupationally induced stress under which they labor to be so intense that, even with increasing maturity and after increasing amounts of professional-level experience, they continue to burn out before being able to complete their work lives as CAOs. The findings here suggest that—at least for the purposes of research—any impact that age, years of professional experience, or length of residence may have on variations among manager perceptions of job-related stress is more likely to be identifiable and measurable as a component of actual professional expertise (a combination of education and experience) or uncontrollable/unpredictable exogenous personality factors, than as a component of maturation or an acquired and practiced tolerance for stress.

On the other hand, the timing of career choice and selected aspects of professional preparation do seem to be important factors affecting the comparative stress levels perceived by local government managers. Responses to both the 1978 and 1986–87 surveys reveal that a sizeable majority of these CAOs perceive themselves to be under considerable occupational stress. This may indicate that a relatively high level of perceived vocational stress is one of the most significant factors to examine when assessing the occupational mobility paths and longevity patterns of individuals in the profession, and when evaluating trends in the overall profession.

However—as noted earlier—the dilemma of occupational stress and its various associations with the processes of professionalization is not simply a by-product of individual work environment factors, but must also be considered in light of the broader changes occurring in U.S. society. One such fundamental change has been the growth in the proportion of family units where both spouses are committed to career pursuits, as well as to being basic economic partners engaged in salaried work.

### Dual-career Couples

Over the decades since World War II and the drafting of "Rosie the Riveter" into the national war effort, the number of women and dual-earner couples in the work force has become a significant feature of the U.S. labor market and economy. In fact, one analyst of the 1980 census reported that—of the 57,804,000 families identified—there were more than 46 million employed men and women who were part of dual-worker families, or 23 million families (40 percent) as of March 1979.[44]

Research on the implications of this important demographic phenomenon has increased substantially over the past 20 years. Its social, economic, political, and even technological implications for marriage and family life, the traditional career pathways pursued by men as well as women, and the advancement or constraint of occupational opportunities (that is, availability, mobility, and so forth) are just now being seriously examined.

A number of sobering consequences of this change in the U.S. labor market have been identified. One of the more recent assessments has been made by sociologist Nancy Gilliland:

Job scarcity makes both members of a dual career couple less competitive. That is, it may take a "two-person career," with one spouse serving a back-up function, to meet the higher standards of today's buyer's market. Job scarcity also reduces the number of possible job combinations in one geographic location, making coordination of two career paths more difficult.[45]

Gilliland also observes that

[the] viability of dual career marriages is primarily a matter of good will and willingness on the part of the partners. [But, she argues,] this may be the case with respect to all problems except . . . the career requirement that each spouse be geographically mobile. This problem, to a greater extent than any other, appears to be out of the individual couple's control.[46]

The impact of this emerging generation of managers with spouses who are salaried employees is of increasing importance to labor economics as well as to those of us with more specific interests. The extent to which spouses are pursuing independent careers—and not just supplementing their partners' incomes—may, in particular, have an impact on managers' professional mobility patterns, and therefore have an effect on the whole field of local government management. What should we expect for our population of highly mobile local government managers—where nearly 95 percent of the sample was male, nine out of ten reported being married, and more than two-thirds indicated that their spouses were engaged in work other than being a homemaker?

William T. Markham and Joseph H. Pleck examined the issue of sex and the willingness of men and women to move for occupational advancement; they were working with data collected from a national 1977–78 quality of employment survey conducted by the Institute for Social Research. What Markham and Pleck discovered was:

Based on relevant theory and past research, we have identified eleven variables likely to intervene between sex and willingness to move for advancement among employed persons: occupational level, self-employment, part-time employment, labor force continuity, seniority, job security, career commitment, perceived income adequacy, age, education, and marital status. For married workers only, spouse's employment status, spouse's education, marital satisfaction, and family involvement may also link sex to willingness to move. Finally, for members of dual-earner families, spouse's occupational level, spouse's self-employment, and spouse's part-time employment may also mediate the association.[47]

On further analysis, Markham and Pleck reported,

Sex proved to be a significant predictor of willingness to relocate, explaining 5% of the variance in the entire sample, 11% among married couples, and 14% among dual-earner couples. . . . Most of the factors suggested by past theory and research as links between sex and willingness to move were related to both variables as predicted, and many remained related to willingness to relocate when the others were controlled. . . . Age and income adequacy proved to be the best predictors of willingness to move across the three [groups], and marital status was an important factor in the equation for all respondents. . . . Sex continued to have considerable impact on willingness to move after the remaining variables were controlled.[48]

Table 4.10 displays how managers reported the effects of spousal employment on themselves and on their families. According to their responses, the managers generally believed that the spouse's career was having a comparatively positive effect on the spouse personally and professionally. And the spouse's current occupation was reported to have a relatively positive effect on the manager personally, as well. However, the managers reported much less of an overall influence of spouse's career on their own careers. Statutes of law and general public reaction against the practice of nepotism may partially ensure this separation of the spouse's occupational proximity and—hence—impact. The managers reported a similar drop in positivity from that felt by their own careers on themselves personally, when the various other effects were compared. Aside from the modest levels of either positive or negative effect that the spouse's career was reported to have on the manager's own professional life, managers perceived the spouse's career to be least positive in terms of its effect on their shared family life.

When a spouse is employed outside the household, the complications that can arise include perceived conflict of interest, lack of opportunity to attend community activities, and increased public scrutiny. The spouse is not always available to provide the emotional support sought by the manager in times of stress. The desires of a spouse who is also in public service may collide with those of the manager. When—for example—social workers' salary increases are limited by the manager who wants to channel those dollars in to another program, the home could become a forum for grievances—rather than a source of relief.

One would reasonably expect—then—that, whenever a change of location is being contemplated by the manager, the career interests of the spouse may generate an increase in family stress levels. In deciding to seek out new employment opportunities in other communities, managers overwhelmingly—and not too surprisingly—seem to consider the impact that this career change may have on their spouses. Fully 94 percent of the managers who were married when responding to the 1986–87 questionnaire ranked this factor as decisive or important in selecting a new community in which to serve. Of less importance to the managers, however, was the spouse's current employment status and potential for employment in the new community. In fact, more than 50 percent of the managers indicated that current employment status of the spouse was not a significant factor, and an almost equal proportion (45 percent) indicated that the spouse's potential for employment was not significant, when they were considering an occupational/geographic move.[49]

Looking at these apparently conflicting responses in more detail, we find a plausible explanation in the 1986–87 survey responses displayed in Table 4.11. Both the manager's age and the education level of the spouse appear to be significant factors affecting the manager's career decision-making process. Younger managers are likely to see their spouse's current careers as decisive or important to their own career decisions: That is, of the managers 49 years of age and younger, about one-half (51.4%) considered their spouses' current career status as not important to their own decision-making process. However, more

Table 4.10
Effect on CAOs of Spouse's Current Occupation, 1986–87

| Classification | No. Reporting (A) | Markedly positive % of (A) | slightly positive % of (A) | No Effect % of (A) | slightly negative % of (A) | Markedly negative % of (A) | Weighted Average Score | Rank |
|---|---|---|---|---|---|---|---|---|
| On manager('s): | | | | | | | | |
| Personally | 1003 | 47.9 | 32.0 | 12.7 | 6.0 | 0.6 | 1.85 | (1) |
| Professionally | 1002 | 37.3 | 35.3 | 22.2 | 4.9 | 0.3 | 2.00 | (3) |
| Spouse personally | 1000 | 51.3 | 27.2 | 5.7 | 13.9 | 1.9 | 1.92 | (2) |
| Spouse profession- ally | 977 | 43.7 | 23.4 | 17.9 | 10.5 | 4.4 | 2.12 | (5) |
| General family life | 1000 | 40.9 | 35.2 | 7.5 | 15.6 | 0.8 | 2.06 | (4) |

*Note*: A weighted-average score was calculated for each classification based on a five-point scale (with 1 being markedly positive; 3, no effect; and 5, markedly negative effect). Percentage totals may not equal 100, due to rounding.

*Source*: An initial compilation from the question—without the weighted-average scores and rankings—was reported by the author with B. J. Reed in "Occupational Stress and Mobility among Professional Local Government Managers: A Decade of Change," in the *Municipal Year Book 1988* (Washington, D.C.: ICMA, 1988), p. 40. On the 1986–87 Green–Reed survey, the respondents had been asked: "How would you rate the effect of your spouse's occupation?"

**Table 4.11**
**CAO's Assessment of Spouse's Current Employment Status**

| Importance of Spouse's Current Employment Status | Total | | Children | | | | Manager's Age | | | | | | | | Spouse's Education Level | | | |
|---|---|---|---|---|---|---|---|---|---|---|---|---|---|---|---|---|---|---|---|
| | | | Yes | | No | | Less Than 30 | | 30-39 | | 40-49 | | More Than 49 | | No College Degree | | College Degree | |
| | # | % | # | % | # | % | # | % | # | % | # | % | # | % | # | % | # | % |
| Decisive | 114 | 11.4 | 78 | 13.8 | 35 | 10.6 | 3 | 9.4 | 48 | 11.7 | 42 | 14.2 | 21 | 8.1 | 38 | 7.7 | 76 | 15.0 |
| Important | 334 | 33.4 | 239 | 35.4 | 90 | 32.5 | 17 | 53.1 | 148 | 36.0 | 110 | 37.2 | 59 | 22.7 | 130 | 26.2 | 204 | 40.4 |
| Not Important | 553 | 55.2 | 419 | 50.8 | 129 | 56.9 | 12 | 37.5 | 215 | 52.3 | 144 | 48.6 | 180 | 69.2 | 328 | 66.1 | 225 | 44.6 |

*Note:* Percentage totals may not equal 100, due to rounding.

*Source:* Compiled by the author from the 1986–87 Green–Reed survey, where the respondents had been asked: "How would you rate your spouse's current employment status as a factor in selecting a new community in which to serve as manager?" Excludes managers who were not married.

than two-thirds (69.2%) of the managers 50 years of age and older reported seeing their spouses' careers as not important when considering their own career moves.

Somewhat surprising, however, are the responses indicating that the presence of children in the household does not make much of a difference in how important the managers perceived their spouses' current employment status to be. Whether or not managers had children at home, slightly less than half of both age categories above reported that their spouses' employment was a decisive or important factor when considering their own career moves—while slightly more than half reported that it was not important. Another perspective from which to grasp this pattern is to report that, when managers felt that their spouses' positions were decisive or important in their own career choices (44.8 percent of the married respondents), there was little difference between the families with and without children at home (49.2 percent had children, and 43.1 percent did not).

Similarly, managers whose spouses had earned a four-year college degree or higher were much more likely to see their spouses' current careers as decisive or important. Less than half of the managers whose spouses had a bachelor's degree or more (44.6 percent) reported that their spouses' current employment status was not important to them when considering their own career moves. This pattern contrasts substantially with those managers whose spouses had not obtained a bachelor's degree, where two-thirds (66.1 percent) reported that their spouses' current employment status was not important to their own career moves. Thus, in the case of dual-career couples, managers of a relatively younger age, and with highly educated spouses—but regardless of whether there are children at home—are more likely to weigh their spouses' current careers as important or even decisive to their own career decision making.

Teaching and government service—specifically—were perceived by these managers to be the most mobile of their spouses' current careers, at least in terms of potential employment in a new community. Spouses who were currently pursuing business or consulting careers seemed to the managers to be less mobile and marketable. Perhaps the managers felt this way because most businesses and consulting firms operate with an established local clientele. The necessary conditions for a successful business or consulting practice may not be easily recreated in a different community without the individual's willingness to underwrite a major new investment in time, while at the same time often incurring a considerable loss of income. Of the four basic categories of occupations that were listed for spouses in the 1986–87 survey, 85.5 percent of the teachers (158 in all), 78.8 percent of all those in government service (80), 67.5 percent of those in business (200), and 66.6 percent of the consultants (12)—as well as the 68.0 percent of the managers themselves who listed a wide variety of other income-generating occupations (155)—were rated by managers as being decisive or important career-choice factors in their own decision to relocate.[50]

## TESTING THE MEASURES OF PROFESSIONALIZATION

So far we have considered a wide range of factors thought to be important to the processes of professionalization, and to be affecting the current careers of CAOs serving in local government. We have perused the research literature most thoroughly and have operationalized the available survey measures for each examined factor, according to the specifications (conceptual properties) of the professional model. I now pose an important summary question first raised by Markham and Pleck: How well do work environment and personal factors account for the various effects that managerial responsiblities are reported to be having on managers' careers and on their family lives (see again Table 4.2)?

I approached this question by performing a discriminant function analysis on the factors that we have been analyzing throughout this book. Discriminant analysis is a statistical test that can help to determine just how valid our measures have been in distinguishing among the reported levels of personal effects from the current burden of managerial responsibilities.[51] I will use it here to explore the differences among managers who classified themselves into one of four categories listed on the 1986–87 questionnaire: feeling (1) markedly or (2) slightly positive about the effects associated with the administration of their managerial responsibilities, or feeling (3) slightly or (4) markedly negative about these effects.

Under the first discriminant analysis—using 25 independent variables as effect descriptors—a single function (determined to be statistically reliable) accounted for more than 90 percent of the variation in managers' perceived personal effects from their responsibilities. The variables included indicators of sex, age, number of children, self-assessed conservatism/liberalism, proximity to a central city, years as a manager, years in current position, community population size, changes in managerial powers over career, effect of responsibilities on career and personal values, comparative rating of current physical/psychological stress to alternative career choice, and satisfaction with salary and compensation packages. Substantial discriminating power is clearly present from the use of these occupational and personal measures for three of the four manager categories above. The number of respondents who classified the effect of their managerial responsibilities as markedly negative was numerically too small to meet the tests of statistical reliability.[52]

The purpose of the second discriminant analysis was to focus as directly as possible on variations in the perceived effects that managers reported their responsibilities to be placing on their families. The second analysis utilized a subset of the previously used discriminating factors (variables)—while adding a number of new ones, including spousal level of education, rating of various spousal career impacts, two types of spousal and overall familial factors affecting managers' career choices, effect of managerial responsibilities on the CAO personally, and utilization of personal abilities on a variety of job satisfactions. Five variables from the first list were deleted for the second procedure—those that focused on the effects of the managers' responsibilities on their own careers: four, concerning managerial powers; and one, on the openness and honesty of the managers' own professional relationships. In total, there were 35 variables used in the second discriminant analysis—20 of which were shared with the first analysis.

In this instance, a smaller—but still impressive—80 percent of the perceived variance separating the perceived positive and negative effects of the managers' responsibilities could be explained with the construction of the initial function. Another 12 percent of the variation perceived for the affected families could be explained with the introduction of a second—and also statistically reliable—function. Again, the number of respondents who classified the effect of their managerial responsibilities as markedly negative on their families was numerically too small to meet the tests of statistical reliability.[53]

The variable composition of major functions in each analysis underscores the complex nature of the responsibilities that often must be shouldered by a professional local-government manager, as well as by his or her family. It seems clear from the previous sections' analyses that variations in perceived levels of occupationally induced stress are ultimately linked with personality types; professional expectations, requirements, and conditions; familial circumstances; and unique work environments. These are—as it turns out—important risk considerations for those charged with evaluating the potential of individuals as CAOs for various community types at different points in time. And these considerations are just as important to the individual manager who may be considering career options and strategies.

In summary, these discriminant function results are significant because they demonstrate the variety and interrelatedness of the personal and environmental factors that are indeed present and having an impact on how managers feel about the burdens of their professional responsibilities. But the results are also encouraging because—given such a rather concise array of relevant factors—examination and careful evaluations can now be more efficiently undertaken. However, the professionalization of the CAO is but one of the contemporary trends that are increasing the self-governing capacity of local communities. We conclude this chapter by placing our specific discussion of the environmental factors and forces that are influencing the professionalization of CAOs within the broader context of management capacity building.

## MANAGEMENT CAPACITY

Our analysis of the merits and limitations under which local government managers administer their duties is implicitly—but directly—linked to the broader issues of the need for and the practice of building management capacity in U.S. local governments. The desire for professional managers in local government has always been closely associated with an expectation that they would enhance the capabilities of government to meet its legitimate public responsibilities.

Beth Walter Honadle, recently completed a bibliographical review entitled "Capacity-Building (Management Improvement) for Local Governments," and defined *management capacity building* as "improving the ability of local communities and areas to deal with their problems. It means helping communities anticipate, influence, or direct change; attract and absorb resources; make decisions about policy; manage physical, human, financial, and information resources; and evaluate the results of such activities."[54]

But—as Leigh Grosenick has pointed out—during the growth era of intergovernmental grants-in-aid programs in the 1960s and 1970s, federal efforts to build the capacities of lower units of governments was premised on the critical assumption that "state and local governments are poorly managed and are therefore unable to meet their responsibilities for providing effective public service."[55] The issues went beyond the then current political and constitutional concerns for reapportionment and equality of representation, to a concern over the limited capacity and capacity-building efforts being made by all levels of government— federal, as well as state and local. As Philip Burgess explains, at least from the national government's perspective, capacity building came to mean that for "any federal activity (including grants, contracts and technical assistance) a primary purpose [was] to strengthen the capability of federal, state and/or local government officials to manage their programs, to provide services to their constituents or to manage their overall jurisdictional or inter-jurisdictional responsibilities."[56]

While the federal government had its reservations about the management capacities of state and local governments, William A. Jones and C. Bradley Doss offered confirmation via their survey of 258 local officials in eight Southeastern states that local governments had their own reservations about the necessity or desirability of receiving assistance from the federal government. As Jones and Doss determined,

Perhaps the most significant conclusion, is that less than fifty percent of the participants see a need in their communities for assistance in any of the categories [planning, training for local staff, management, assistance in goal setting, budget formulation, assistance with citizen groups, and other federally stipulated areas]. . . . It would appear that the respondents either consider themselves competent already or they are reluctant to become involved with this federal assistance program.[57]

And this was a view held not only by Southern officials. Like beauty and the beholder, the relevance of capacity building is importantly determined by the agenda of the goal setter![58]

Furthermore, respondents to the Jones and Doss survey indicated that money, which is so often the carrot used to drive home the capacity-building designs of federal programs, was not necessarily the answer to the problem. "Forty percent of the respondents . . . indicated that they either 'strongly agreed' or 'agreed' with the notion that 'more money' would solve their assistance problems. Very nearly the same percentage, . . . 38 percent, either 'strongly disagreed' or 'disagreed' with the idea that money would be such a panacea.'' As far as these local officials—at least—were concerned, ''it appears that the more localized assistance can be, the more likely it is that it will be accepted.''[59]

It is possible here only to summarize Anthony Brown's 1980 assessment of the particular demographic, social, economic, political, technological, and financial problems that governments in rural communities face—which are linked to a poverty cycle in management capacity. The traditional response that infuses technical assistance underwritten by various higher level government provider agencies is

primarily ad hoc and discontinuous, employing a narrow problem perspective in addressing local community needs. . . . Education and training activities are usually not a major component of the assistance given. . . . Management systems and procedures are developed by consultants on a project basis, often with little attention given to the problems of implementation and maintenance. . . . The most serious weakness [of currently available technical assistance] is a conceptual one. This ad hoc approach does not address the central need of small communities: the development of permanent management mechanisms.[60]

There have been a number of innovative proposals put forward to address such a poverty cycle in local government management capacity. Their common denominator has been the enhancement of management capacity as localities come to recognize their own needs—whether large or small; special purpose districts or general service governments; or found in rural, suburban, or central city environments. They range from experiments with the circuit rider concept as an attempt to provide for cost-effective professional expertise across a group of financially constrained smaller communities; to proposals for adapting the traditional technical assistance programs from their original focus on project-specific management to one emphasizing generic governmental management capacity building; to the procedural or process-oriented approaches—for example, using structured groups for better decision making. They all—it seems to me—try to raise the level of local capacity to approximate the role of full-time professional administrative officers.

All such proposals are attempts to find solutions to what Ostrowski, White, and Cole describe as

local governments [that] are finding an increasing need to develop a capacity to deal effectively with complex and difficult problems. The need is heightened by rapidly escalating costs for local services, the pressures of Reagan's ''new federalism,'' and diminishing tax bases. . . . Tightening budgets and changes in federal aid to allow for more legislative discretion are both likely to provide the incentive for councils to spend more energy on ''capacity-building''—on dealing with broader policy issues and establishing priorities.[61]

John J. Gargan has persuasively argued that ''performance results from capacity. [That is,] governing capacity is the ability of officials to do what is legally required of them and what they and relevant constituents wish to do. The level of governing capacity evident in any particular jurisdiction, therefore, will be a function of adherence to both formal-legal requirements and informal norms of a local political culture.''[62] And there appears to be substantial evidence that—for local government officials, at least—the more localized the assistance can be, the more likely that it will be recognized as relevant to the officials' own concepts of need and that it will be considered, if not always accepted.

Reactions have been decidedly mixed as to the significance of the cutbacks in the capacity-building provisions of intergovernmental grant-in-aid programs. Many local officials had—often only euphemistically—characterized existing technical-assistance programs as capacity building. Editing a recent collection of essays on building management capacity in local government, Arnold Howitt and Beth Honadle concluded that—given the retrenchment of capacity-building programs and support by the federal government, and the severely limited resources and therefore assistance offered by most state governments—

We are likely to see local governments seeking to learn from each other, through various professional associations and leagues of cities and towns, about innovative management approaches. Federal and state governments may continue to play an information-sharing role, but the burden of promoting better management is likely to fall increasingly on local governments themselves.[63]

If necessity be the mother of invention, then it is Father Time now offering a partially open window of increased opportunity for capacity building to local governments. Through a national set of trends and forces, an increasingly professional cadre of managers will likely be considering public service careers as a viable option during the next two decades. However, the demographically driven labor market forces of the Baby Boom generation, which are (at least currently) linked to and associated with the processes of CAO professionalization, along with the relatively flexible and underutilized capacity of advanced degree/preparation programs in public affairs and administration may help to make local governments a fully equal—if not the senior—partner in directly affecting the supply and nature of managers' academic preparation.

Analysts seem to agree that local government administrative capacity needs do vary, as do the capacity requirements placed on other professions by their clienteles. These needs vary by historical era, by government function, and by the scale of the individual government.[64] Still, recognition by local communities (that is, by those outside as well as inside the government) of a need for different or added management capacity building is perhaps the prerequisite condition affecting local acceptability of the professionalization of administrative personnel. Nevertheless, professionalization—however conceived of as a strategy for improving local management capacity—must often undergo many other tests and comparisons with competing concepts of capacity building (for example, the humanware versus hardware issue) that may be occurring within local political discussions.

Howitt and Honadle also noted,

The competition between instrumental effectiveness and efficiency, on one hand, and other public values, on the other, is not limited to a tension between community insiders and outsiders from other levels of government. Because there is no consensus in many communities about the appropriate balance among these values, issues of management capacity become major points of political contention. . . . Even within the administrative system of a particular community, specific plans for enhancing management capacity may be controversial and hence the focus of intense bureaucratic politics. Management improvements are rarely perceived as neutral instruments in an administrative system.[65]

I believe that there are two basic conclusions to be drawn from the analyses in this chapter. First, the search for professionalized personnel is not only a way that communities acquire and enhance their governmental management capacity, but is also how CAOs themselves become aware of and decide which occupational skills and personal capacities they may need to acquire. Moreover, this professionalization taking place within the ranks of CAOs in local governments has not been an isolated phenomenon over time, among various locations, or within the lives of the different individual managers. Rather, it is linked to a wide spectrum of demographic, social, economic, technical, and political changes and needs confronting the many different types of communities and their CAOs.

Second, there is an emerging—yet, I believe, already identifiable and coherent—set of values and skills associated with being a professional local government manager. These occupational features are becoming nationally standardized for public administration and public affairs through the accrediting guidelines recently established for university graduate degree programs and through the evolution of public service law. Nonetheless, the ultimate viability and utility of professionalized local-government management rests on "judgments about what constitutes an adequate amount of management capacity [—which] are inherently subjective and thus, in practice, are politically defined" by the local community.[66]

However, there is also a third issue that emerges from this discussion of the influence that professionalization may be having on the improvement of local management capacity. Has the occupation of full-time CAO in local government been nationally institutionalized to the point where a formal model (which legitimates its professional aspirations) can be promoted? Is there any coherence to the efforts of the network (national, state, and local governments, plus academic and associational institutions) that is attempting to develop and maintain standards of excellence; rules of conduct; recruitment and training procedures; as well as protection, promotion, and control within a recognized profession of management in local government? How can this network arrangement—which at the moment can only be described as intergovernmental, cross-institutional, and (ironically) quasi-professional—influence the development of a nationally recognizable profession, while simultaneously making its practitioners professionally adaptable and locally acceptable as part of the political decision making that—in the final analysis—determines the direction and success of management capacity building in any particular community? These important and linked issues surrounding the development of a CAO profession are the subject of Chapter 5.

## NOTES

1. Howard M. Vollmer and Donald L. Mills, *Professionalization* (Englewood Cliffs, N.J.: Prentice-Hall, 1966), pp. vii–viii.

2. Ibid., p. viii.

3. Ibid., p. xi.

4. Frederick M. Wirt, "The Dependent City? External Influences upon Local Control," *Journal of Politics* 47, no. 1 (1985), p. 104.

5. These trends were summarized by Cary Cherniss and Jeffrey S. Kane in their recent article, "Public Sector Professionals: Job Characteristics, Satisfaction, and Aspirations for Intrinsic Fulfillment through Work," *Human Relations* 40, no. 3 (1987), p. 126.

6. Historically, the notion of "job design" involves consciously specifying the tasks and work methods of a position within an organization. It is associated with a traditional school of thought called *scientific management*, and most directly with the thinking of Frederick Taylor in his classic book, *The Principles of Scientific Management* (New York: Harper and Row, 1911). More recently, human resource management and organizational behavior specialists have come to focus on redesigning, as well. For more contemporary applications, see Robert T. Golembiewski, *Public Administration as a Developing Discipline*, pt. 2: *Organizational Development as One of a Future Family of Miniparadigms* (New York: Marcel Dekker, 1977); J. Slocum and H. Sims, "A Typology of Technology and Job Redesign," *Human Relations* 33 (January 1983), pp. 193–212; and G. Oldham and J. Hackman, "Work Design in the Organizational Context," in B. Staw and L. Cummings, eds., *Research in Organizational Behavior*, 2 vols. (Greenwich, Conn.: JAI Press, 1980).

7. Edgar F. Huse and Thomas G. Cummings have defined "enriched jobs" as those which "provide people with opportunities for autonomy, responsibility, closure (doing a complete job), and feedback about performance. Such jobs are likely to be effective in situations where technical interdependence is low and uncertainty high"; they have described the process of job enrichment as that which "focuses on the attributes of the job itself." See Huse and Cummings's *Organizational Development and Change*, 3rd ed. (St. Paul, Minn.: West Publishing, 1985), p. 236. Another excellent discussion of the concept is by J. Hackman and G. Oldham, *Work Redesign* (Reading, Mass.: Addison-Wesley, 1980).

8. Described by Ralph Katz in his article, "Job Longevity as a Situational Factor in Job Satisfaction," *Administrative Science Quarterly* 23 (June 1978), p. 204.

9. Ibid.

10. Ibid., p. 205.

11. Ibid., pp. 204 and 218.

12. Based on Cherniss and Kane, "Public Sector Professionals," p. 126.

13. Ibid.

14. Ibid.

15. Ibid., p. 125.

16. For further information about these results from the 1980 ICMA/CAO questionnaire, see Amy Cohen Paul, "Local Government Managers: On the Job and Off," *Urban Data Service Report* 13, no. 9 (September 1981), p. 7.

17. The reader who wishes to review a tabular summary of the 1978 survey should see Roy E. Green and B. J. Reed, *Occupational Stress and Professional Mobility among City Managers*, Urban Data Service Report 13, no. 6 (Washington, D.C.: International City Management Association, June 1981), pp. 1–6.

18. C. Argyris and D. A. Schon, *Theory in Practice: Increasing Professional Effectiveness* (San Francisco: Jossey-Bass, 1974).

19. William R. Fannin and Don C. Moore, "Preparing for City Management Careers: What's Important?" *American Review of Public Administration* 17, no. 2/3 (Summer/Fall 1983), p. 88.

20. James F. Wolf, "Career Plateauing in the Public Service: Baby Boom and Employment Bust," *Public Administration Review* 43, no. 2 (March/April 1983), pp. 160–61.

21. Ibid., p. 161.

22. Wirt, "The Dependent City?" p. 83.

23. Ibid., pp. 102–3.

24. A number of scholars have been pointing out the rise of professions in government over the past 15 years. Four of the most prominent are Heinz Eulau, "Skill Revolution and Consultative Commonwealth," *American Political Science Review* 67 (1973), pp. 865–86; Samuel Beer, "Federalism, Nationalism, and Democracy in America," *American Political Science Review* 72 (1978), pp. 9–21; Frederick Wirt, "Professionalism and Political Conflict: A Development Model," *Journal of Public Policy* 1 (1981), pp. 61–93; and Frederick Mosher, *Democracy and the Public Service* (New York: Oxford University Press, 1982).

25. Cited by Wirt, "The Dependent City?" p. 103.

26. Frederick M. Wirt cites a paper that he coauthored with Leslie J. Christovich, entitled "Community Political Style and Professional Executive Power," presented at the annual meeting of the Midwest Political Science Association in Milwaukee, 1982.

27. James H. Svara, "Dichotomy and Duality: Reconceptualizing the Relationship between Policy and Administration in Council–Manager Cities," *Public Administration Review* 45, no. 1 (January/February 1985), pp. 221–32.

28. Katz, "Job Longevity," p. 206.

29. Based on the research and work of those who are active in the field of organizational development. Of particular interest is the research done by Rosabeth Moss Kanter, who wrote a particularly insightful analysis of the role that change agents can offer the U.S. corporation to stimulate innovation and entrepreneurship for greater productivity. Kanter's study was entitled *The Change Masters* (New York: Simon and Schuster, 1983).

30. An earlier report on some of the research and conclusions in this section appeared in an article written with B. J. Reed, under the title "Occupational Stress and Mobility among Professional Local Government Managers: A Decade of Change," in the *Municipal Year Book 1988* (Washington, D.C.: International City Management Association, 1988), pp. 35–42.

31. R. S. Lazarus, *Patterns of Adjustment*, 3rd ed. (New York: McGraw-Hill, 1976).

32. James C. Quick and Jonathan D. Quick, *Organizational Stress and Preventive Management* (New York: McGraw-Hill, 1984).

33. J. D. Adams, "Improving Stress Management," in *Social Change: Ideas and Applications* (Alexandria, Va.: N.T.L. Institute, 1978), p. 1.

34. P. D. McLean, "Depressions as a Specific Response to Stress," in T. G. Sarason and C. D. Spielberger, eds., *Stress and Anxiety* (New York: Wiley, 1976), vol. 3, p. 708.

35. D. T. DeCarlo, "Compensating Stress in the '80s," *Insurance Counsel Journal* (October 1985), p. 681.

36. Ibid., pp. 681–87.

37. J. B. Shaw and J. H. Riskind, "Predicting Job Stress Using Data from the Position Analysis Questionnaire," *Journal of Applied Psychology* 68 (1983), pp. 253–61.

38. Quick and Quick, *Organizational Stress.*

39. Green and Reed, "Stress and Professional Mobility."

40. Laurence Rutter, ed., *The Essential Community: Local Government in the Year 2000* (Washington, D.C.: International City Management Association, 1980), p. 127.

41. D. Heimovics, K. Johnson, B. Rountree and B. Rogers, "Fiscal Stringency and Stress: Experiences of City Managers," a paper presented at the National Conference of the American Society for Public Administration, Denver, 1984.

42. For a complete tabular display of manager responses categorized by age, see table 4/7 in Green and Reed, "Occupational Stress and Mobility," p. 39.

43. For complete tabular displays of manager responses categorized by career longevity, and by seniority in current position, see tables 4/8 and 4/9 in ibid., pp. 39 and 40.

44. Allie C. Kilpatrick, "Job Change in Dual-career Families: Danger or Opportunity?" *Family Relations* 31 (July 1982), p. 363.

45. Nancy C. Gilliland, "The Problem of Geographic Mobility for Dual Career Families," *Journal of Comparative Family Studies* 10, no. 3 (Autumn 1979), p. 346.

46. Ibid.

47. William T. Markham and Joseph H. Pleck, "Sex and Willingness to Move for Occupational Advancement: Some National Sample Results," *Sociological Quarterly* 27, no. 1 (1986), p. 129.

48. Ibid., p. 137.

49. For a complete tabular display of the 1986–87 responses categorized by spousal influence on the managers' general community-selection criteria, see table 4/12 in Green and Reed, "Occupational Stress and Mobility," p. 41.

50. For a complete tabular display of the 1986–87 inquiry about the importance of spouse's potential for employment in the manager's decision to relocate, see table 4/13 in ibid.

51. For a clear and concise description of discriminant function analysis, see ch. 9 in Barbara G. Tabachnick and Linda S. Fidell's *Using Multivariate Statistics* (New York: Harper and Row, 1983), pp. 292–371.

52. The first grouping of manager perceptions was based on their attitudes toward the effect of current managerial responsibilities on themselves: markedly positive effect, $N = 366$; slightly positive effect, $N = 256$; slightly negative effect, $N = 71$; and markedly negative effect, $N = 12$. The equation had a Wilk's lambda of .47 (and a chi-square of 520.97—with 99 degrees of freedom, and a significance level of zero), indicating that substantial discriminating power was present only in the first function; that is, the second function had a very large, nonsignificant lambda of .90 (and a chi-square of only 68.58—

with 64 degrees of freedom, and a significance level of .33), adding little to the explanation of variance between the groups.

Further evidence about the group differences can be derived from the group centroids. These are the mean discriminating scores for each group per function. Three distinct occupational groupings can be seen within the strong first function: markedly positive–effect group centroid = $-0.78$; slightly positive–effect group centroid = $+0.47$; slightly negative group centroid = $+1.72$; and the markedly negative group centroid = $+3.71$—the latter being statistically unreliable because of the exceedingly small number of respondents classifying themselves as members of this group.

53. The second grouping was based on manager attitudes about the effect of their official responsibilities on their families. Again, the response categories were: markedly positive, $N = 145$; slightly positive effect, $N = 353$; slightly negative effect, $N = 208$; and markedly negative effect, $N = 20$. This discriminant equation had a comparable—but slightly higher—Wilk's lambda of .53 (and a chi-square of 449.14—with 111 degrees of freedom, and a significance level of zero), indicating that substantial discriminating power is also present in the first function. But in contrast to the previous analysis, the second function in this analysis is also a useful predictor with a somewhat larger lambda of .86 (and a smaller chi-square of 108.59—with 72 degrees of freedom, and a still assuring significance level of .004).

Once again, there is additional evidence to be gained by reviewing the group centroids. Three distinct groupings can again be seen when utilizing the first function. However, the pattern is less clear after reviewing the centroids from the second function. The group mean discriminating scores for the first and the second functions—listed respectively—are: markedly positive–effect group centroid = $-1.04$ and $+0.13$; slightly positive–effect group centroid = $-0.20$ and $-0.21$; slightly negative–effect group centroid = $+0.80$ and $+0.37$; and finally, markedly negative–effect group centroid = $+2.69$ and $-1.04$. Once again, the latter (fourth) grouping is statistically unreliable because of the exceedingly small number of respondents who classified their families into this group.

54. Beth Walter Honadle, "Capacity-Building (Management Improvement) for Local Governments: An Annotated Bibliography," *Rural Development Research Report*, no. 28 (Washington, D.C.: U.S. Department of Agriculture, Economics and Statistics Service, March 1981), p. 1.

55. Leigh E. Grosenick, "Institutional Change to Improve State and Local Competencies," in Leigh E. Grosenick, ed., *The Administration of the New Federalism: Objective and Issues* (Washington, D.C.: American Society for Public Administration, 1973), p. 91.

56. Philip M. Burgess, "Capacity Building and the Elements of Public Management," *Public Administration Review* 35, Special Issue (December 1975), p. 706.

57. William A. Jones, Jr., and C. Bradley Doss, Jr., "Local Officials' Reaction to Federal 'Capacity-Building,'" *Public Administration Review*, 38, no. 1 (January/February 1978), pp. 68–69.

58. See, for example, the nationwide study conducted under the auspices of the U.S. Department of Housing and Urban Development, and reported in "Developmental Needs of Small Cities," a study required by Section 113 of the Housing and Community Development Act of 1977, HUD-PDR–374 (Washington, D.C.: U.S. Printing Office, February 1979); see also, Roy E. Green and B. J. Reed, "A Perspective on Small City Development: Local Assessments of Grant Management Capacity," *Urban Affairs Papers* 2, no. 3 (Summer 1980), pp. 23–36.

59. Jones and Doss, "Local Officials' Reaction," pp. 68 and 69.

60. Anthony Brown, "Technical Assistance to Rural Communities: Stopgap or Capacity Building?" *Public Administration Review* 40, no. 1 (January/February 1980), pp. 20–21.

61. John W. Ostrowski, Louise G. White, and John R. Cole, "Local Government Capacity Building: A Structured Group Process Approach," *Administration and Society* 16, no. 1 (May 1984), pp. 3–4.

62. John J. Gargan, "Building Local Government Capacity: University Based Capacity Builders and Strategic Planning," a paper presented at the National Conference of the American Society for Public Administration, Indianapolis, 1985, p. 1. See also his "Consideration of Local Government Capacity," *Public Administration Review* 41, no. 6 (November/December 1981), pp. 649–58; and Timothy D. Mead's "Identifying Management Capacity among Local Governments," *Urban Affairs Papers* 3 (Winter 1981), pp. 1–12.

63. Arnold M. Howitt and Beth Walter Honadle, "Conclusion," in their edited volume *Perspectives on Management Capacity Building* (Albany: State University of New York Press, 1986), p. 341.

64. Ibid., pp. 334–35.

65. Ibid., pp. 337–338.

66. Ibid., p. 336.

# 5

# PROFESSIONAL ASSOCIATES AND ASSOCIATIONS: A TOPOGRAPHY OF SERVICES, STATUS, AND STANDARDS

While running the risk of what Yogi Berra called "déjà vu all over again," I find that—to discuss the professional associates and associations of local-government CAOs—I must advisedly introduce the concept and process of *institution building*. That is, I broach the subject of institution building here only for limited heuristic purposes, because it is very difficult to avoid the many pitfalls of jargon and ambiguity common to this theoretical construct. It has more often confused than guided. But in an era of greater national optimism and confidence—the 1950s and early 1960s—institution building was associated with U.S. foreign aid as

an approach to technical assistance in developing countries that promotes developmental change by identifying a particular organization possessing technical capability, managerial skill, and an internal commitment to change and then forging linkages between this organization and the groups in its environment that provide the organization with resources, support, and outlets for its products or services.[1]

However, the social, economic, and political upheavals of the next quarter-century forced a greater national introspection and a reconsideration of internal affairs, as well as of the U.S. role in world affairs. In the 1970s and 1980s, a much greater portion of the nation's developmental enthusiasm was adapted and redirected to assessing and resolving domestic conditions and challenges. Now there is a more acute awareness than before—brought on by the many interwoven venues of foreign competition as well as intranational competition among regions, states, and localities—that the structural and functional integrity and viability of the established U.S. social, economic, and governing institutions must also be maintained and invigorated—as well as celebrated for their historical accomplishments. In this context, measures of occupational stratification and valuation have often been used by social scientists as key indicators of the changes occurring in the nation's development. National development has been dissected with a wide variety of foci on historical, social, economic, and political criteria; but most recently, predominant emphasis is along the lines of Ira Sharkansky's view of the United States as a still developing nation.[2]

Twenty-five years ago, Harold Wilensky published a now famous article that raised a still relevant question: Will this so-called age of the professionals lead to "the professionalization of everyone"?[3] In language familiar to us, Wilensky determined that professions were based on an esoteric knowledge acquired through long training, and by the existence of incumbents who were already adhering to the professional norm of a public service ideal. Established professions must—he argued—be able to offer aspiring professionals a network of professionalizing institutions that provide formal training, at universities; and national associations had to be founded; ethics codes, adopted; and licensing regulations, enacted. Comparing the historical evolution of a number of established professions (in basic characteristics, stages, and sequence of development) against the histories of a number of newer occupations at various stages of their development, Wilensky characterized the evolution of professionalization within city management in the mid–1960s as being "new," perhaps doubtful, and lacking in part because it did not have (and still does not have) any type of state-level licensing law.[4]

These were institutional processes that Wilensky considered necessary for the emergence of profession-level influence. But were they sufficient conditions to ensure the survival of the public service ideal for even the most established professions—as most of the research literature seems to assume? Or have the means of professionalization been confused with its ends? And if established, does institutionalization ensure durability of function as well as process? For example, what effect does the much discussed "postindustrial society" have on the professions and their roles and purposes? Two decades ago, Daniel Bell predicted the arrival of a professionalized, postindustrial society where university training would be the "chief determinant of the stratification system."[5]

Ten years after Harold Wilensky's paper estimated that not every occupation can become a profession (and raising considerable doubt about the future prospects for city management), Marie R. Haug took under advisement the prediction of Daniel Bell. Haug proceeded to examine the durability of Wilensky's description concerning the institutionalization of professions. She did this by considering the more contemporary trends and challenges that had not been included by Wilensky in his retrospective examination. Her empirical focus was on the prototype profession—medicine—against which all aspiring professions seem to be compared. Significantly, Haug's findings suggested that the exact opposite of Wilensky's prophecy might be occurring: "the deprofessionalization of everybody."[6]

As Haug reported,

Public education, computerization, and the sharing of expertise in new divisions of labor undermine professional claims to being the sole repositories of esoteric knowledge useful to society and the individual. [And] what of another major claim that the humanitarian ethos of the profession, the socialization to service which its incumbents undergo, and the ethical standards enforced by professional associations to justify public trust in professional judgment? To ask the question is to realize to what extent trust has been eroded in an age of consumerism and client revolt.[7]

We are reminded, then, that the established institutions of society—which here refer to the range of traditional professions as well as to the newer occupations struggling for contemporary professional legitimation—cannot be content with meeting only the historically offered types of challenges to recognition and functioning. Even established institutions must adapt in order to meet the rigors of the changing times. Wilensky showed himself to be, in fact, sensitive to these possibilities for the transformation of professions when he said,

The occupational group of the future will combine elements from both the professional and bureaucratic models; the average professional man will combine professional and non-professional orientations; the typical occupational association may be neither a trade union nor a professional association. Mixed forms of control, hybrid organizations—not a straight-line "professionalization of labor"—are the likely outcomes.[8]

And in this regard, Marie Haug was at least in partial agreement when she noted

Wilensky argued that not every occupation can become a profession because it cannot claim a monopoly of scientific knowledge. . . . Presently designated professions are rapidly losing their control over their knowledge domain as a result of inroads from computerization, new occupations in the division of labor, and increasing public and client sophistication. . . . The deprofessionalization of everyone, accordingly, would leave occupational incumbents without claims of mystery, authority, or deference. It does not, however, imply the utopian notion of the end of expertise.[9]

But Haug also acknowledged that "this is a hypothesis, not a prophecy. Like all hypotheses in social science, it can only be tested by history."[10]

Getting an institutional fix on the professionalizing of CAO standards, status, and services is essential as a contextual reference point for assessing its change. Such an approach cannot offer a determination about the inevitability of the occupation's achieving unassailable professional standing; not even the most revered of the professions is now without its doubters. However, in this regard, occupational associations and institutions have been utilized as a primary developmental marker and differentiator for properly evaluating—if not finally determining—the progression of individual vocations along the sliding scale of professionalization.

The thrust of this brief digression into the uncertain waters of institution building and professionalization has been in part to draw attention to Robert Golembiewski's caution about the organizational and occupational merits, but also the issues and costs involved, if public managers move toward full professional certification. Harold Wilensky—and many others along with him—argued that the lack of state licensing or some other formal certification process has been a major factor precluding the consideration of CAOs in local governments from the traditionally defined ranks of acknowledged professionals. As Golembiewski admonished, where existing specialities and evolving new ones seek professional status, "institution builders need always to keep the phase of development clearly in mind."[11] Marie Haug might suggest considering the external and broader societal challenges of such a step, as well.

The International City Management Association has been sensitive to these issues and inquiries. As the association's director of membership services, Laurence G. Rutter noted, "Doctors must meet rigorous standards to be certified to practice their trade. So must lawyers, planners, and architects. [And] in this respect it might appear that barbers are light years ahead of local government administrators in terms of their professionalism. . . . Today there are no nationally certified city or county managers . . . and there is not likely to be any."[12] Challenging the traditional meaning of professionalization, Rutter offered a quite different logic "for others in service in local, regional, state, and federal agencies": that the profession of local government management should move "a great distance away from the implicit and often explicit concern for professional certification that bestows external legitimacy on a calling."[13]

The rationale behind this is very enlightening from the perspective of institution building as well as from a specific interest in the professionalization of local government managers. Rutter explained,

The reason for the discrepancy is simple: different cities and counties, and different city and county elected officials need different things at different times—and both local governments and councils change with unnerving rapidity. . . . Two dimensions of competence are being required here: both different knowledge bases and different personal styles are needed to manage different communities. . . . So out of a sense of humility about the art and magic of management, local government professionals have avoided settling on a rigorous certification requirement or process.[14]

What then are to be the essential professional standards?

At a minimum, the profession considers individuals to be members if: (1) they serve in a top-management capacity in a city, county, or council of governments which the International City Management Association recognizes as having an appointed position of overall administrative responsibility . . . ; and (2) they abide by the City Management Code of Ethics and submit to its enforcement procedures. At the maximum level of standard, the profession sets as its goal continual individual development through self-evaluation and personal education as outlined by the process of application to the ICMA Academy for Professional Development.[15]

However—as examined in Chapter 2—courses offered through the academy are being increasingly challenged by the number of expanding college and university programs in public administration and, to some extent, by non-ICMA technical training institutes.

However, this is not to say that others with an official interest in the legitimacy of CAO professionalization have lost all interest in establishing a state criteria for licensure. Arthur Finkle with the Department of Civil Service, State of New Jersey, has argued,

Except for the already-licensed professions (engineer, architect, attorney, accountant, doctor), the public is not protected. The legislature has to consider the public "peace of mind" when a government hires a top policy-level general administrator or a line specialist. Indeed, how can a government assure that there are minimum education, experience, and ethical requirements which these prospective ministers of public policy possess? [Qualifications might include:] (a) graduation from an accredited or approved program; (b) acceptable performance on a qualifying examination; and/or (c) completion of given amount of work experience.[16]

After reflecting on the implications of and prospects for interjecting the state legislature into such a debate, Finkle thinks that the outcome depends "on the skill of the lobbyists and the luck of the draw. To build a state or national consensus, the public administrator will have to use the skills of bargaining and accommodation which, if his or her education and experience have been worthwhile, are the arts of the possible."[17] Such an initiative would not be without organizational risk for the association and its members, and political risks for state legislators.

Against this backdrop of debate over the broader national development issues of professionalization—deprofessionalization, this chapter focuses on description and assessment of the established (and currently active) network of nationally organized associations of local governments and officials. Institution building has been introduced here primarily because of its potential for synthesizing the issues and challenges of professionalization that have been confronting the original vision of the municipal reformers. Before proceeding toward a more complete theoretical accommodation with—and legally binding status for—the professionalization of local government management, analysts such as Golembiewski suggest that we make an assessment of the 75 years of institution-building effort and experience that have already taken place.

Notes Howard McCurdy:

The survival of [any] institution becomes the first test of success. Institutional survival ... can be achieved only if the organization develops a "support environment" that is friendly to its programs. To build an institution, organizational leaders must build "linkages" to politicians, business and labor leaders, universities, and the public. Institution builders must also increase the capacity of the institution to utilize available technology.

**Figure 5.1**
**A Network for the Professionalization of Local Government CAOs:**
**Institutionalizing a Role for the Public's Interests**

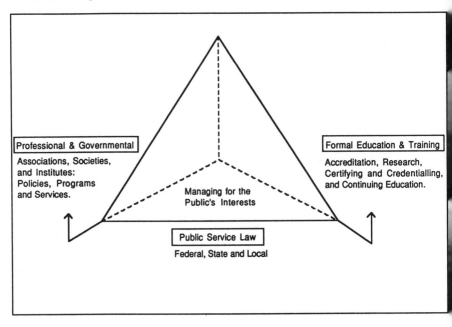

They eventually will have to strengthen internal administration. . . . Sometimes institution building is used to improve the work of agencies that provide administrative services.[18]

Our particular approach to describing and assessing the currently active network of local government CAOs is outlined in Figure 5.1. It envisions a tripartite set of institutionally related resources being invested in the development of public management as a profession. To some extent, this scheme works for all types of public managers, but it was constructed primarily from the circumstances characterizing the CAOs serving the ICMA-recognized community governments. One facet of the process emanates from the role played by a network of national associations (in particular, the ICMA) that is composed of local governments and their officials. A second facet derives from those institutions that provide nationally accredited (NASPAA) professional education programs and training in the field of public administration. The third facet pertains to the evolution and institutionalization of public service law, as now more binding on the behavior of all public sector managers (including the potential for state licensure).

The aim of focusing on this tripartite set of institutional processes is to assist us in comparing the status quo of CAO professionalization with the public service/ interest ideal espoused as the legitimating rationale for all professions. This relationship is the primary justification cited by those who promote state licensure or some other certification criteria for public managers. Particular attention must be given to the standards used historically to measure comparative development among professional associations. According to A. M. Carr-Saunders and P. A. Wilson, associations have always sought

to protect their members from undue governmental influence, encroachment of other occupational groups, and interference of the public at large. . . . A prominent aspect of these associations throughout their history has been attention to the provision of adequate training. As a corollary, almost everywhere they have been concerned ostensibly with the maintenance and improvement of adequate occupational standards [and have] attempted monopolistic arrangements to enhance their own gain.[19]

In this vein, a most interesting question can be raised with regard to the legitimating and authenticating role that the ICMA has established for itself among the public management professional associations. How successful has the ICMA been in implementing—without statutory support—the objectives and purposes described by Carr-Saunders and Wilson? And in fact, is this exactly what the ICMA has been trying to accomplish through its voluntary—but truly national—set of standards, which could be considered more uniform and therefore superior to the varying requirements that would inevitably be established, were action to be taken by 50 different state legislatures? If this national effort proved effective and in the public interest, the most appropriate role for the state legislatures would be to further strengthen the public service statutes, rather than enact a licensure process for public managers.

The notion of institution building does provide an approach to assessing the services, status, and standards of local government managers and their associations—both as institutional products of the government reform movement, and as a current network of institutional providers (and maintainers) of professionalized CAOs. But while useful for this analysis, the notion of institution building also needs to be viewed in the critical light of other research—which has not always been complimentary or supportive of the general approach, nor of the consequences of institutionalizing professionalism in government service.[20] We need only consider the title of Robert Kharasch's engaging book—which refers to the federal bureaucracy and its professional contenders as "bulky objects"— and be sobered by his opening quotation, spoken by John F. Kennedy after the Bay of Pigs fiasco: "All my life I have known better than to depend on the experts. How could I have been so stupid."[21] This is fair warning against the enveloping mystique of institution building and professionalism itself.

## FEATURES AND TRENDS

A key prerequisite for development of a professionalized occupation is its ability to maintain an important degree of influence (if not absolute control) over a tangible knowledge base. This influence involves being able to determine what the knowledge base shall encompass and who is enfranchised to learn and to exercise it (credentialled professional literacy), as well as how its informational forms are to be disseminated and under what circumstances and forms outsiders shall have access to it (the profession as "keeper of the gate"). This is a currently escalating challenge to all professions because of the expansion in more accessible public education, computerization, and telecommunications, as well as the increasing technical specialization forced partly by the explosion in research and development of all types of knowledge bases. These challenges confront the established and traditionally recognized professions, along with those occupations still seeking to emerge or further enhance their statures as professions.

The notion that information and information technology have become the newest forms of wealth in the postindustrial United States was perhaps most widely popularized by Alvin Toffler and by John Naisbitt.[22] However, there has been at least a 20-year spate of public as well as commercial and professional debate over what the legal status of information should be, both within the United States and internationally. The debate covers what U.S. information law and policy is and should be to protect the property rights and obligations of individuals and institutions (and in this context, professional interests), while at the same time protecting legitimate public interests with regard to access, costs, equity, and control.[23]

Public policy is perpetually trying to catch up to the information revolution— or what the private sector's Information Industry Association has called the *infostructure*.[24] At issue are the essential characteristics that can make knowledge, information bases, and their users a form of wealth and privilege as well as a source of legal obligation and public responsibility. How information managers respond to these boom conditions also serves to differentiate between the business entrepreneur and the professional. The key questions separating the "infopreneur" from the professional necessarily involve: Who shall be allowed to participate in information creation as well as in the management of its uses? What is the information's life cycle, in terms of its development, management and dissemination? How are knowledge bases to be institutionally organized in terms of goods and services provided? And finally, how are these information/knowledge/expertise-based institutions to be legally defined within the U.S. political economy? This economy now ranges from the public agency, to the not-for-profit organization, to professionals and their respective associations, and to the commercial enterprise.

However—we note in passing—being classified as a "fee-for-service" professional, such as a lawyer or a physician, does not obviate one's mandate to provide a bona fide public (interest) service. Nor should being a professional in public administration diminish one's occupational responsibility and commitment to the development, management, and competent use of expertise. The age of information presents new dimensions of risk assessment and added questions of liability, ethics, and choice. The information society raises issues of expanding and binding relevancy to those occupations who would become professionalized in this age of professionals!

Most research and thinking on the challenges posed by the information age to the knowledge base of professional associations (formation, structure, and functioning) has focused on the attributes and relative influence of these groups on centralized governmental authority—typically, at federal, state, and metropolitan levels. And these levels as listed probably represent the descending order of frequency of activities among the various professional interest groups. This is not too surprising insofar as there has been an obvious and substantial growth in all forms of government since World War II, and that this growth has been most pronounced and systematic at the federal, state, and metropolitan levels— in that order. If there be any truth to the notion that influence follows money, then the coterminous increase in research interest with the growth of national associations is understandable. The fact remains that, even after the efforts of Presidents Carter and Reagan, the federal government remains an important source of public policy formation and implementation, with a major and direct influence on local affairs.

And there have been important research results culminating from these efforts. For example, Theodore Lowi's influential book, *The End of Liberalism*, has raised much interest and promoted a great deal of additional inquiry into the policy consequences of this concentration of professional-interest groups operating at the federal level.[25] While associational influence on expanding federal and state intervention into local and individual affairs represents both cause and consequence, research into their rise in influence and numbers has been largely limited to case studies. Very little systemic information is available about the ways the interest groups came to be created, how they have worked to survive as national institutions, or how they have attempted to exercise influence on their memberships as well as on public policy. This is in no small part due to the difficulty in trying to identify the universe of national associations, and the difficulty in locating any reliable information about them.

Within this arena, then, Jack Walker's pioneering research efforts have served to advance our understanding of which factors are most key to meeting the primary test of an association's institutionalization. Walker's assessments were based on a survey conducted in 1980–81 of all voluntary associations listed in the *Congressional Quarterly*'s *Washington Information Directory*. His survey sample included those organizations that were open to membership and concerned with some aspect of public policy at the national level. From the *CQ Directory* and his national survey, Walker constructed a fourfold classification for the responding groups (private, mixed, nonprofit, and citizen). Excluded from the study were organizations such as trade unions and business corporations. Analyzing his "typology of occupational roles"—that is, based on the occupation features of the membership (public- or private-sector requiring credentials, or else open to all citizens), Walker confirmed that the first occupational groups were founded in the middle of the nineteenth century, and that it took almost another century to create the first half of these groups. The remainder of the occupational groups in [his] sample were founded since World War II. In contrast, the first half of the citizen groups did not come into existence until 1960; then, during the next 20 years, there was a period of explosive growth during which citizen groups multiplied at twice the rate of all types of occupationally based groups.[26]

In general agreement with interest-group theorist David Truman, Walker said that "the propensity to form groups increases during periods of general social upheaval, as in the 1930s and 1960s." But he reported, "Many other groups in fields like education, mass transportation, and environmental protection also sprang up after the passage of dramatic new legislation that established the major outlines of public policy in their areas."[27] In addition—although his research and survey were conducted before much of the Reagan administration's cutbacks could have been felt—Walker found that

in the not-for-profit sector, groups often come about at the urging of federal officials who need to have regular contact with administrators of state or local agencies receiving aid from some new federal program. There is a need to share information, develop standard administrative practices, create model bills for adoption by cities or states, and of course, work to expand support for their programs in the Congress.[28]

Walker's categorical separation and summary of the nonprofit occupational associations informs the following analysis. There appears to be an active associational network of local government officials, within which the International City Management Association has been working to establish and maintain itself as the major institutional source of professionalization for local public managers. Like all institutions, the ICMA has developed and adjusted with the changing times and conditions. At this point, the reader may wish to review Figures 1.1 and 2.1 in order to compare and contrast the sources of change, and the overlapping or simultaneous timing of the changes, that have been confronting individual practitioners as well as their national network of management associations.

After researching various national association directories, encyclopedias, and source books and a number of special libraries and information centers, the author also made a content survey of the governmental and public administration listings in the 1988 edition of the *Encyclopedia of Associations*.[29] The *Encyclopedia* enabled me to identify and examine the basic institutional features of a broad collection of nonprofit membership associations and professional societies with a primary interest in local government. And specifically, I was able to select a cross section of local government associations that had a nationwide scope of organized activities and memberships. Organizations did not need to have a presence in Washington, D.C., to be included in the analysis, although an overwhelming proportion did. See Appendix B for a list of all the organizations characterized in Figure 5.2. In the appendix, these groups are listed by formal

**Figure 5.2**
**Development Histogram for the Currently Active Network of Local Officials' Associational Affiliations**

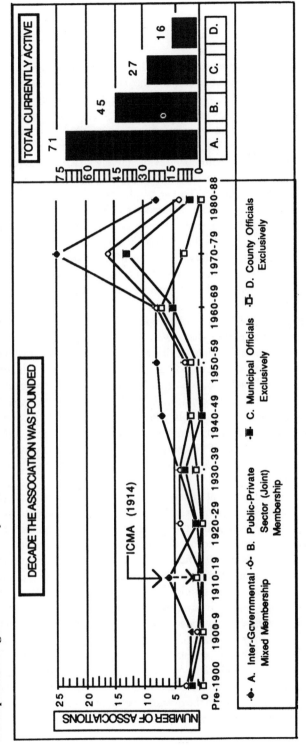

*Note:* A complete listing of the organizations included in Figure 5.2 is provided in Appendix B.

*Source:* Compiled by the author from a content survey of organization entries in "Section 3: Legal, Governmental, Public Administration, and Military Organizations," in Karin E. Koek, Susan B. Martin, and Annette Novallo, eds., *Encyclopedia of Associations, 1988* (Detroit: Gale Research, 1988), pp. 437–508.

name, primary field of interest, founding date, and according to a four-category membership typology.

As observed in earlier chapters, the occupational characteristics of in-service professional local government managers, and the realities within which they have been operating, have changed in a number of significant ways since the council–manager form of government was first introduced in 1912. Some of these changes have been a product of how and when managers entered the field; many others have been a product of where managers initiated their careers, and what occupation they had been pursuing beforehand. Collectively, "what" the profession is and "who" the individual professional is at any one point in time are in many ways the product of these factors. The bar graph portion of Figure 5.2 reveals that the individual today considering a career as a full-time local government manager has access to an information network of more than 150 national organizations whose memberships include local officials, and that have some direct interest in the responsibilities of local government. And this does not include the agencies of the federal and state governments, nor any private sector organization, nor any of the independently organized regional, state, and local associations.

The bar graph portion of Figure 5.2 classifies the national associations into four categories of membership. There were 10 percent of the organizations composed of various types of officials serving exclusively in county governments, while another 17 percent were composed of officials serving exclusively in municipal governments. Thus, about one-fourth of this local government network has exclusive single-source memberships. However, the other three-fourths are national organizations with fields of policy interest directly tied to local government—but whose memberships are composed of a mixture of local, state, and federal officials (approximately 45 percent), or that are organizations where local officials have joined with members from private and other public sector sources (the remaining 28 percent).

While the fields of interest that characterize these organizations are—by selection—relevant to officials serving in local government, this tabulation suggests that, in terms of professionalization, only slightly more than a quarter of these national organizations is composed of, and therefore serves exclusively, a particular type of local government official or level of local government. It is noteworthy that these organizations are not the area of greatest group density.

At least one additional point should be made regarding the bar graph in Figure 5.2. Increasingly, local government CAOs are likely to have had some subordinate-level government experience before being promoted to their first position as manager. They are therefore also likely to have some experience with one or more of the national organizations that serve these more specialized responsibilities, as well as with other general-purpose organizations. It would seem that the cumulative weight of these national service associations must inevitably be having some effect on the overall level of professionalization among CAOs serving in local governments.

Another facet of institution building that pertains to the question of increased CAOs is the historical presence, survival, exclusivity, and interassociational positioning of the primary occupational association. The histogram portion of Figure 5.2 depicts the ICMA at the time of its founding in 1914 as being an exclusively municipal-level membership organization (see Chapter 2), but accounts for it topographically in terms of its contemporary membership composition. Organizational history (some would say prestige or lineage) is often considered to be an important factor in assessing an association's role, and in accounting for its influence as a source of professional legitimation. And the institutional pedigree of an association is relevant to the debate over who should have authority to recognize practicing professionals within an occupation, and what position an association may choose to take on the necessity for public licensure. This may be one aspect of Laurence Rutter's opposition to state licensure of public managers in local government.

Among the 159 national organizations represented by the histogram in Figure 5.2, only ten were founded before the decade in which the ICMA was officially established. By the end of the 1910–19 decade, ICMA was one of only 17 such national organizations for local officials (and only one of three organizations then in the exclusively municipal category). Today, the ICMA is one of 71 mixed local government membership groups represented here. Changing an organization's criteria for membership to make it more inclusive and influential as an institution for professionalization can also raise broader policy questions about the association's mission and the sources of its legitimacy.

Similar to the basic findings of Jack Walker's study—although based on a different source and cross section of organizations—there is evidence in Figure 5.2 that expansions in the number of these associations has been linked to the societal upheavals of the 1930s and the 1960s. The dates of their foundings seem to reflect national issue trends at the local level, and a conjunction of federal efforts with state and local governments to address the problems.

Of the national organizations founded since 1960 and still active in 1988, 20 have an exclusively municipal membership (of the 27 municipal total); 10 have an exclusively county membership (of the 16); 49 have a mixed level of government membership (of the 71); and 22 have a public–private sector membership (of the 45). If the growth rate of citizen groups in the 20-year period between 1960 and 1980 was at twice the rate of occupational groups—as Walker reported —then it is relevant that nearly two-thirds of the organizations in this national sample were also founded after 1960. The magnitude of the change seems significant because (as noted above) there has been a substantial increase in both the nationalization and competition among occupational/professional groups as well as among consumer/citizen groups. They all operate within the infostructure. Therefore, there has been a truly fundamental change in the structure of public affairs.

Since 1980, however, the creation of new national nonprofit occupational organizations has slowed down to only about 25 percent of the number that were being established during the 1970s. One major limitation of this data, however, is that the *Encyclopedia of Associations* and the *CQ Directory* do not maintain entries for organizations that have become defunct. It is more difficult to study the factors leading to the demise of an organization, therefore.

Furthermore, the 159 local government associations in the *Encyclopedia* are categorized under 42 special-interest rubrics. But here again, the density is revealing. We find nine fields of institutionalized interest with five or more of the associations present. Ranking eight of the groups in descending order by frequency (but excluding, for current purposes, the forensic sciences as an independent field), they are: law enforcement (30 without the 7 forensic-science organizations), municipal government (14), county government (11), planning and fire fighting (each with 9), public administration (8), and building codes and civil service (each with 5). Not surprisingly, the general jurisdictional authorities and the traditional local government service functions are the fields of interest where there is the greatest density of organizational activity.

Maybe there is an analogy to be drawn here between Aaron Wildavsky's concern about the high density of federal agencies in policy spaces and the consequences flowing from the increased density of associations that now actively view local government as a primary interest.[30] Looking back 70 years and then to the current institutional space occupied by the ICMA, one must ask whether the presence of so many new associations has encroached on its exclusivity as the primary (if not sole) provider of services, status, and standards for CAOs. Or has the ICMA been able to retain its institutional imperative—as it implicitly claims through its recognition system?

Figure 5.3 allows us to consider these questions more closely through a number of key institutional dimensions for a cross-sectional core of nationally organized local government management associations. An organization was selected for this closer study if it was: (1) included in the *Encyclopedia of Associations* as still active in 1988; (2) focused specifically on some type or level of official local government management; and (3) included one or more of the major municipal, county, or COG service function areas in its specific focus.

Groups were first classified by type of officials, level of governmental affiliation, and local government function. Then the groups were assigned to four broad categories. The first category includes umbrella associations (single level of government, but across executive positions—elected and appointed); the second category is specifically for local government function associations (local official function and responsibility); the third category covers groups with major local function responsibilities but that are organized within extralocal government associations (composed of mixed levels of government officials with similar functional responsibilities); and the fourth category includes pertinent public-administration resource associations (composed of cross-positional and/or mixed government-level groups of public officials, and/or private sector memberships whose field of interest is the furtherance of public administration).

In a number of instances, there were two or more associations that qualified under these guidelines and had the same specific focus. (For example, in the area of fire fighting, the choice ultimately came down to the International Association of Fire Chiefs and the Fire Marshall's Association of North America.) The group that seemed to represent the broadest range of local managers or managerial interests was then selected for this study. Of all 159 possible groups, only the ICMA defined its membership as representing exclusively

professional positions [that] are defined by a set of criteria describing the characteristics of overall professional management. The present criteria include a statement for recognition of a position in the council–manager form of government and of a position of general management which applies to a wide variety of governmental forms, councils of governments, and state municipal leagues.[31]

While this research strategy was systematic, it also ultimately had to be judgmental—and dependent on the information provided by the associations in their entry descriptions in the *Encyclopedia*.

An overview of the 29 organizations selected for inclusion in this matrix of executive-oriented groups—represented in Figure 5.3—reveals that there are 4 umbrella associations, 5 specifically local-government function associations, 13 groups with major local-functional responsibilities but organized within extra-local government associations, and 7 public-administration resource associations with an established interest in the quality of local government and its management. In this instance, slightly less than half (13) were founded or had been merged into their current forms before 1960. Thus—even among this core selection of major local-government management associations—more than half have emerged since 1960. Today's local government CAO must deal with an increasingly sophisticated environment of expanded local and intergovernmental responsibilities, a labyrinth of established consumer/citizen action groups, as well as a broad spectrum of local-government management associations.

Comparing the institutional attributes of the ICMA with the rest of the matrix, we see that—in terms of national staff size (as a surrogate measure for capacity and financial base), professional recognition (annual awards for excellence), promotional activities (including annual national conventions), and membership services, resources, and programs—the ICMA is clearly among the most well established of these organizations. Certainly, its dues-paying membership (to which is added its nonmember affiliates) is among the largest; and it offers one of the most well developed book and periodical series and computer information networks. Further, the ICMA Training Institute (founded in 1934) is among the most well defined and tested in the field; and its research resources (including statistical data bases and library) are extensive by comparison with the descriptions offered for the other selected organizations. An examination of the ICMA's affiliations within the association network, and through its various exchange programs and local-government consortia, suggests that it does retain effectiveness and a relatively exclusive role as the primary conduit to and for its membership.

Figure 5.3

## A Core Matrix of Major Local-Government Management Associations and Key Dimensions of Their National Institutionalization

| TYPE AND LEVEL OF LOCAL GOV'T ASSOCIATION | BASELINE FEATURES | | | | INFRASTRUCTURE | | | |
|---|---|---|---|---|---|---|---|---|
| | Organiz. Founded | Number of Members | HQ Staff | Nat'l Budget (000's) ($) | # of Reg. State Local Groups | # of Sects., Divs. | # of Prog., Comm-ittees, Panels | Affiliated Organiz-ations |
| **Umbrella Associations:** | | | | | | | | |
| National Association of Counties | 1935 | 2100 Counties | 50 | NL | 50 State | NL | 12 | NL |
| Nat'l Association of Towns/Townships | 1963 | 13000 State/ Local Organiz. | NL | NL | M'mbr-ship | 1 | NL | NL |
| National League of Cities | 1924 | 1400 State/ Leagues & Cities | 65 | NL | M'mbr-ship | 1 | 5 | NL |
| Nat'l Association of Regional Councils | 1967 | 400 COG's, Libraries & Regional Organiz. | 13 | NL | NL | 3 | NL | NL |
| **Specifically Local Government Function Associations:** | | | | | | | | |
| Public Housing Directors Association | 1979 | 800 Directors | 2 | 190 | NL | NL | 3 | NL |
| International City Management Association | 1914 | 7000 City, County/ COG's/Mgrs./Direct. | 65 | NL | NL | 1 | NL | NL |
| Nat'l Inst. of Munic'pl Law Officers | 1935 | 2000 Municipalities | 5 | NL | NL | 6 | 28 | NL |
| U.S. Conference of Mayors | 1932 | 600 from cities over 30000 | 50 | 3800 | NL | 4 | 8 | NL |
| Munic'pl Treasurers Ass'n,U.S./Canada | 1965 | 1500 City Deputy Trs./Fin.Drs/Cmptrs. | 3 | 250 | NL | NL | 1 | NL |
| **Major Local Functional Responsibilities Found Within Extra-Local Government Associations:** | | | | | | | | |
| Bld. Officials & Code Admin. Internat'l | 1915 | 8000 Mgrs. and Agencies | 44 | 4500 | NL | NL | 11 | NL |
| National Association of Gov't Communicators | 1976 (54-61-71) | 1000 Employees & Students | 1 | 100 | 2 Local | 3 | NL | NL |
| Internat'l Association of Fire Chiefs | 1873 | 8000 Chiefs: City, State, Mil., Industry | 15 | NL | 8 Region. | NL | 13 | NL |
| Amer. Economic Devel. Council (U.S./Canada) | 1926 | 1250 Indust./Econ. Mgrs/Dirs/Agencies | 6 | 550 | NL | NL | 5 | NL |
| Public Risk & Insur. Mgt. Associations | 1978 | 1000 Mgrs: Cities, Counties, Sp.Districts | 4 | NL | 17 State | 1 | NL | NL |
| Internat'l Association of Chiefs of Police | 1893 | 14000 Police Executives | 60 | 4500 | NL | 5 | NL | NL |
| American Park & Recreation Society Assn. | 1966 (1898-1938) | 5000 Directors | 1 | NL | NL | NL | 22 | Nat. Rec. Prk Asn. |
| Amer. Society for Personnel Admin. | 1948 | 40,000 Personnel/ Indust. Rel. Execs. | 68 | 9100 | 52 St. 600 Lcl | NL | 12 | Personnel Acr. Inst. |
| Nat'l Ass'n of County Planning Directors | 1965 | 860 Chief Advisors | 1 | NL | NL | NL | 2 | Nat. Assoc. of C'nties |
| American Public Works Association | 1894 | 24000 Dirs/Admins/ Heads/Individuals | 52 | NL | 62 State | NL | 15 | NL |
| National Institute of Government Purchasing | 1944 | 1500 Federal, State, Local Agencies | 10 | 750 | NL | NL | 4 | NL |
| Nat'l Coord. Council on Emergency Mgt. | 1952 | 2000 City, County Governments | NL | 90 | 10 Reg. 50 St. | NL | 2 | NL |
| Fed. of Gov't Info. Processing Councils | 1978 | 12000 Federal, State Local Managers | NL | 25 | 3 Reg. 4 St. | NL | 4 | US Gen'l Svc. Adm. |
| **Pertinent Public Administration Resource Associations:** | | | | | | | | |
| Law & Society | 1964 | 2400 Academics & Gov't Administrators | 3 | NL | NL | NL | NL | NL |
| National Civic League | 1894 | 3000 Civic Leagues; Public Officials | 15 | 700 | NL | NL | 2 | NL |
| Amer. Society for Public Admin. | 1939 | 16600 Public Admin/ Off./Educ./Res. | 18 | NL | 10 Reg. 122 Lcl. | 17 | 4 | Nat. Assoc. of Schls. |
| Ass'n of Mgt. Analysts in State/Local Gov't | 1972 | 265 Analysts: Bus/ Educ/St/Local Gov't | NL | NL | NL | NL | 3 | NL |
| National Academy of Public Admin. | 1967 | 369 Recognized Scholars/Admins. | 13 | NL | NL | NL | 4 | NL |
| Nat'l Assoc. of Schools of Public Affairs/Admin. | 1970 1958 | 240 Univ/Gov't Agencies | 10 | 380 | NL | 5 | 2 | Pi Alpha Alpha |
| American Political Science Associations | 1903 | 12000 Educ/Lawyers Pub.Off/Researchers | 20 | NL | NL | NL | NL | NL |

*Note*: NL indicates that this type of data was not listed by the organization in providing information for the *Encyclopedia*.

*Source*: Compiled by the author from a content survey of organization entries in "Section 3: Legal, Governmental, Public Administration, and Military Organizations," in Karin E. Koek, Susan B. Martin, and Annette Novallo, eds., *Encyclopedia of Associations, 1988* (Detroit: Gale Research, 1988), pp. 437–508.

| PROFESSIONAL RECOGNITION | | MEMBERSHIP SERVICES | | | | | | | |
|---|---|---|---|---|---|---|---|---|---|
| Awards for Excellence | Speaker's Bureau Services | # of Serial Publs. | # of Periodical Publs. | Establ. Training Prog. | Research Svcs. | Select Computerized Svcs. | Select Telecomm. Svcs. | # of Annual Conventions/Meetings | Placement Svcs. |
| Yes | NL | NL | 2 | NL | Yes | NL | NL | 1 Annual | NL |
| Yes | NL | 1 | 1 | Yes | Yes | NL | NL | 1 Annual | NL |
| NL | NL | 3 | 2 | Yes | Yes | NL | NL | 1 Annual | NL |
| Yes | NL | 2 | 2 | Yes | Yes | NL | NL | 1 Annual | NL |
| NL | NL | 1 | 1 | Yes | Yes | NL | NL | 5 Annual | NL |
| Yes | NL | 4 | 4 | Yes | Yes | Yes | NL | 1 Annual | Yes |
| NL | NL | 3 | 3 | Yes | Yes | NL | NL | 2 Annual | NL |
| Yes | NL | 2 | 2 | Yes | Yes | NL | NL | 2 Annual | NL |
| Yes | Yes | 2 | 1 | Yes | Yes | Yes | NL | 1 Annual | NL |
| Yes | NL | 11 | 3 | Yes | Yes | NL | NL | 1 Annual | Yes |
| Yes | NL | 1 | 1 | NL | NL | NL | NL | 1 Annual | Yes |
| Yes | NL | NL | 2 | Yes | Yes | NL | NL | 1 Annual | NL |
| Yes | NL | 1 | 3 | Yes | Yes | NL | NL | 1 Annual | NL |
| NL | NL | 1 | 1 | NL | Yes | NL | NL | 1 Annual | NL |
| Yes | Yes | 3 | 2 | Yes | Yes | NL | NL | 1 Annual | NL |
| Yes | Yes | NL | 1 | Yes | Yes | NL | Yes | 1 Annual | NL |
| Yes | Yes | 2 | 2 | Yes | Yes | Yes | Yes | 1 Annual | NL |
| NL | NL | 1 | NL | NL | Yes | NL | NL | 2 Annual | NL |
| Yes | NL | 2 | 1 | Yes | Yes | Yes | NL | 2 Annual | NL |
| Yes | Yes | NL | 2 | Yes | Yes | NL | Yes | 1 Annual | NL |
| Yes | Yes | 1 | 2 | Yes | Yes | NL | NL | 2 Annual | NL |
| Yes | Yes | 1 | 1 | Yes | Yes | NL | NL | 1 Annual | NL |
| Yes | NL | NL | 2 | Yes | Yes | NL | NL | 1 Annual | NL |
| Yes | NL | 1 | 1 | NL | Yes | Yes | NL | 1 Annual | NL |
| NL | NL | NL | 2 | NL | Yes | NL | NL | 1 Annual | NL |
| NL | NL | 3 | 2 | Yes | Yes | NL | NL | 2 Annual | NL |
| Yes | Yes | 1 | 1 | Yes | Yes | NL | NL | 2 Annual | Yes |
| NL | NL | 1 | 2 | Yes | Yes | NL | NL | 1 Annual | NL |
| Yes | NL | 1 | 3 | Yes | Yes | NL | NL | 1 Annual | Yes |

So far, the ICMA has met the tests of historical presence and survivability. By dint of its 1914 founding, it has clearly been able to maintain itself. Furthermore, during the 1970s and 1980s the association extended its sphere of community governments and state leagues, where its recognition system has been applied. Through this process of institution building, it has achieved for itself and its membership a considerable measure of stature with other public sector occupational associations (partially demonstrated through a number of jointly administered programs, such as the PTI-NET electronic messaging services), as well as more generally.

But has it been able to meet the historical tests offered by Carr-Saunders and Wilson: "to protect [its] members from undue governmental influence . . . and interference of the public at large"?[32] Important experiential aspects of this issue have been described through the survey responses of in-service managers—as reported in Chapters 2, 3, and 4. Next we consider the evolution in public service law and its constraining influence on the CAOs in local governments, as well as on the associational network within which they have various options to participate.

## PUBLIC CONSTRAINTS

The two decades of the 1960s and the 1970s saw a marked increase in political activity within the arena of consumer affairs. This activity was represented by and encouraged through a proliferation of citizen action groups at the national, state, and local government levels. While it appears that the rate of expansion may now have levelled off—as it seems to have in the development of other categories of groups—the tests of institutional survival and influence continue to focus public attention on the extensiveness and the legitimacy of their governmental access. For example, in his study of interest groups operating at the federal level in 1980, Jack Walker found "that there are many more interest groups operating in Washington today than in the years before World War II, and that citizen groups make up a much larger proportion of the total than ever before."[33]

Several major changes that are directly pertinent to the public service role of professionals and their professional associations seem to have evolved in concert with this nationalization—and, in fact, institutionalization—of citizen action groups. These changes represent the third facet of the tripartite institutional arrangement outlined in Figure 5.1—focusing attention on the influence of public service law on the professions, and on the particular profession of CAO in local government. For clarity's sake, we can separate out public service law across the continuum of relevant interests—that is, the range of public constraints linking the legal notion of public service (and interest) to the functional roles of professionals and to the roles of their professional associations.

Therefore, we will first consider the individual CAO's relationship to public service law, and then how professional associations are being scrutinized by the judiciary under antitrust statutes. Once again, the institutional approach and roles of the ICMA in promoting professionalized public management in local government will represent the empirical case study. Notice that crosscutting the continuum of public service law are the dual (both individual and association) legal issues associated with property rights within the infostructure as well as the concerns of the particular local government over the contemporary status of Dillon's Rule (the jurisdictional authority of local government).

David H. Rosenbloom—a leading scholar in the field—argued that studying the origins, values, structures, and views toward the individual citizen that are reflected in public service law is one of three major approaches to public administration. The other two are the managerial and the political approaches—examined in this book as a politics–administration dichotomy. But the legal approach—noted Rosenbloom—"has historically been eclipsed by the other approaches, especially the managerial. Nevertheless, it has a venerable tradition and has recently emerged as a full-fledged vehicle for defining public administration."[34]

Rosenbloom described public service law as being derived primarily from three interrelated sources—all of which pertain to individuals serving in public administration generally, but which are particularly significant for those in positions of managerial authority. These three sources are: (1) administrative law (authorities granted to agencies and specific public functionaries); (2) the internal "judicialization" of public administration (procedures for safeguarding individual rights during the processes of administrative decision making); and constitutional law ("procedural, equal protection and substantive rights and liberties of the citizenry vis-à-vis public administrators").[35] Rosenbloom based his characterization of public service law somewhat on the views of Kenneth Davis, who had promoted the notion that "an administrative agency is a governmental authority, other than a court and other than a legislative body, which affects the rights of private parties through either adjudication, rule-making, investigating, prosecuting, negotiating, settling, or informally acting."[36]

More recently, Rosenbloom made an observation of particular relevancy to the relationship of public service law and administrative professionalism:

The term "public service law" would not have encompassed a great deal three decades ago. [But] today, this body of law defines the substantive and procedural rights of public employees, their right to equal protection, remedies for breaches of their rights, and their liabilities and immunities in civil suits for damages. It also provides guidance on more general moral obligations of public employees.[37]

One final point from Rosenbloom's examination of federal and state publicservice statutes and judicial precedents must be cited:

Each of the three constitutional branches of government has adjusted its structure and/or role to deal with the emergence of bureaucratic power. [But] public service law has also undergone remarkable change in recent years as the discrepancy between administrative processes and values on the one hand and those of democratic constitutionalism, on the other, became more evident and increasingly troublesome. . . . At present, legal developments in the areas of liability/immunity, the right to disobey, and whistleblowing strongly reinforce the potential for such a professionalism to emerge.[38]

Depending on which statutory or constitutional question is at hand, the evolution, purview, and particular applicability of public service law emanating from either the federal or state level often has direct consequences for local government officials. In no other area of law or judicial precedence is this point more poignantly demonstrated than in the continuing debate over the jurisdictional authority of local governments. While certainly not held singularly responsible, the CAO is considered the chief law enforcement officer of a local government—which has increased the position's knowledge-base requirements substantially since the turn of the century. These demands become particularly clear when we consider the growth in the number and types of locally administered service functions.[39]

As Doyle Buckwalter explains,

A recent study of state control of local government structure and operations clearly revealed the breadth of state influence on forms of government, annexation, consolidation, elections, administrative procedures, financial practices, and personnel management. [However,] an analysis of 904 major state legislative actions between 1970 and 1979 revealed that 681 (74 percent) expanded local control over property taxation, land use, fiscal procedures, bonding, employee salaries, training, unionization, home rule, utilities, intergovernmental relations, transportation, community development, governmental structures, etc.[40]

Buckwalter raises a further point about the impact of the Reagan administration's version of the New Federalism: "Local governments, preoccupied with federal-local relations during the last two decades, have begun demanding a reexamination of state-local relations, including functional delineation, fiscal equity, political accountability and partnership with and participation in state policy processes."[41]

Having acknowledged the context of perpetually evolving conditions and challenges faced by CAOs in ICMA-recognized community governments (as well as by others in the field of public administration generally), we must now also appraise the role of the professional association in this same light. Earlier I made reference to a rather unique philosophical position established by the ICMA— a position that differentiates it from the other established professional associations in the field. This distinction was clear, particularly with regard to using certification or licensure to authenticate professionalization status and to empower individual professionals. In Chapter 1, there was mention made of the research of William Trombetta, a deputy attorney general with the antitrust section/division of criminal justice for the State of New Jersey. We now employ his framework more extensively to review the antitrust statutes and judicial precedents as constraints on the prerogatives of the traditional professions. These precedents may become ever more important as public managers consider the costs and benefits of pursuing state licensure (as well as other attributes of the traditional model for professionalization). In this regard, however, our analysis is only hypothetical in that Trombetta's assessment was limited to evaluating the "impact of antitrust law on anticompetitive conduct in the traditionally established professions"—and, as such, precluded occupations that currently do not have formal licensing requirements.[42]

Nonetheless, it is instructive to consider recent antitrust statutes and judicial decisions concerning licensing requirements, barriers to entry and exclusionary practices, price-fixing, stifling of innovative delivery systems, and restrictions on the scope of public service as they have been applied to the traditional professions' associations and to other licensed occupations. Our review may also offer some insight into the future of professional associations, as they attempt to comply with their historical goal of protecting members from undue government regulation, the encroachment of other occupational groups, and too much intervention by the general public. However, it has certainly not only been the licensed private sector occupations that have demonstrated a concern over the potential for future conflicts between the courts and themselves; this has been a matter of some concern to public administrators, as well.[43]

One stream of antitrust cases relates directly to professionals and the policies of their associations (in regard to group boycotts, price-fixing, minimum fee schedules, competitive bidding, relative-value guides, codes of ethics, access/delivery/group practice, and the scope of professional practice). Trombetta reports that, "in the past, courts have been frustrated by three obstacles in attempting to apply the antitrust laws to the professions."[44] The first two obstacles pertain to the nature and status of professionalism: The first involves jurisdictional complications ("is professional practice a trade and, if so, does it satisfy the interstate commerce requirement?"); while the second obstacle is the "learned profession exemption," which "leaves an 'out' for a kind of anticompetitive professional conduct that may actually benefit the public and does not solely involve a commercial motive."[45]

A second stream of cases relates to the implementation of state occupational regulations (licensing, residency, reciprocal licensing, and citizenship), and corresponds to the third obstacle that has inhibited the judicial application of antitrust statutes to the professions. That obstacle is where "a state action exemption can provide a barrier to antitrust challenge if (1) competition is deemed not to be in the public interest, (2) the anticompetitive conduct is actively supervised by state officials, and (3) the authority of a state agency is received by legislative command."[46] However—Trombetta concludes—"in those situations where anticompetitive conduct is allowed at the initiation of a professional group and then merely 'rubber stamped' by a state agency which gives such groups the authority to set entry requirements and fees and allocate markets among its members, such conduct should not qualify for a state action exemption."[47] In this context as well as in others, if a professional association (like the ICMA) could set and enforce employment contracts, it probably would be controlled by the courts in a manner similar to the handling of fees-for-service issues.

In the instance of all three recognized obstacles hindering the courts' application of the antitrust statutes to the traditional professions—Trombetta convincingly documents—

Virtually all immunities and loopholes that have previously stood in the way of applying antitrust law to the professions have been eroded. [However, while] the professions' interest in maintaining high standards is certainly a legitimate one, as is the public's right to allow qualified practitioners to offer services . . . when exclusionary practices exceed what is reasonably necessary to accomplish a legitimate purpose, their members subject themselves to antitrust liability.[48]

To resubmit William Goode's provocative question: What are "the theoretical limits of professionalization" if the ground rules that govern the two basic characteristics of the established professions—knowledge base (expertise), and the ideal of service (public interest)—have themselves been altered by changes in the law?[49] Are we to conclude that, in a culmination of two or three decades of legislative and judicial activity, the utility and meaning of the professions will go the way of Marie Haug's prognostication regarding "the deprofessionalization of everyone"? Or will the infostructure and the evolving definition of public service yet provide some new and unanticipated developments? Part of the answer seems to lie in Carr-Saunders and Wilson's question about how well professional associations are protecting their members. This issue can now be considered in view of the evolution of public service law and the expanding scrutiny of antitrust statutes and citizen/consumer action groups.

One indication about where and how professional associations can play a different and unanticipated role will be keyed to how they respond to the privatization issue (initiated in different ways by both the Carter and Reagan administrations). In recent years, the founding of the Information Industry Association (established only in 1969) suggests just how significant policy questions regarding the value of information have become. As pictured by the Information Industry Association, the players in this information society include the information industry itself, associations, societies, citizen groups, academic institutions, local, state, and federal government agencies, congressional committees, and others both in the United States and abroad. The stakes are seen as the specific policy challenges that confront the nation as a whole, or specific sectors of the economy or society. And the information marketplace itself represents the arena where the game's changes are taking place.[50]

One role that may be increasingly played by professional associations is in the realm of information managers. As Barry Bozeman—a well-known information management specialist—noted, "it is getting more and more difficult to know what's going on. Potentially helpful means of alleviating this problem include computerized information systems, humanware, and policy analysis."[51] Under pressure, it is most important to be able to find out what types of experiences, experiments, and research is in progress elsewhere so that immediate— if circumscribed—information can be accumulated for use in making decisions. Often, what is going on outside the individual agency or government is of critical concern to the public manager. And frequently enough, the information of concern cannot be acquired through the traditional depositories of information in a timely fashion.

Professional competency requires more than just access to information. It also demands the ability to use information and innovation in increasingly complex social, economic, technological, and political community environments—just as professional literacy means more than just sharing information, but also acquiring the ability to understand the more technical information associated with current and changing occupational responsibilities. The individual public manager and the professional associations are now—and will need to be even more—concerned with the legal status of information and its uses—including provisions of the Freedom of Information Act and the Privacy Act; First Amendment freedoms; fair information practices; mode and media codes, telecommunications, computerization, and so forth; and—occasionally—copyright, secrecy, censorship, and unfair practices issues. These additional responsibilities come with new risks and liabilities, as well as with questions of ethics and choice.

In this regard, the ICMA's membership, policies, and role seem to be evolving within—and, in fact, largely in support of—the newer professional constraints of public service law, the scrutiny of antitrust statutes, and the emerging legal regulation regarding the infostructure. The association continues to define its primary purposes as being "to enhance the quality of local government and to nurture and assist professional local government administrators in the U.S. and other countries." It has revised its code of ethics to meet contemporary conditions: Since its original adoption in 1924, the code is currently in its sixth amended version. ICMA has now grown to include "over 7,500 appointed chief management executives [who] serve cities, towns, counties, villages, boroughs, townships, and councils of governments at the direction of elected councils and governing bodies" in the United States and several other countries.[52]

According to a recent *Fact Sheet on ICMA*, the council–manager plan "is growing faster than any other form of local government," and has been "adopted (on the average) more than once every week by a city or county since 1945 (65 adoptions annually)." However, the fact sheet did not report rechartering trends in the opposite direction. But by the end of 1987, this meant that the association had recognized 2,587 council–manager cities and 93 council–manager counties along with 898 other cities, another 182 counties, 146 councils-of-governments, and 15 state/provincial associations of local governments with "overall professional management responsibilities in the United States."[53]

To compare these developments with the record of antitrust cases and decisions reviewed by William Trombetta, the author initiated a search for relevant cases involving the ICMA (all the way back to its founding in 1914)—utilizing the computerized "Lexis" legal data-base system. Also included in my search were possible cases involving the ICMA in questions over the legal status of the information (its collection, use, and dissemination; or in conjunction with the contract research that it occasionally undertakes for some other governmental entity or organization) or other services provided by the association for—or on behalf of—its members.[54]

The broadest possible Lexis case-search strategy was introduced: A request was made for all federal and state cases released by the courts anywhere in the United States with any of the names or acronyms used by the International City Management Association, and for any type of case. The association was mentioned in nine federal cases and eight state cases—but never as a principle party.

Specifically, the Lexis search uncovered no instance where the ICMA was a principle party to any case concerning antitrust, property rights, copyrights, freedom of information, privacy, codes of ethics, the First Amendment, fair/ unfair information practices, computerization or telecommunications, liability and immunity, the right to disobey, whistleblowing, due process, equal protection, or contracts-of-employment issues. Despite the fact that, for example, the ICMA does conduct "six to eight mail surveys each year on local government operations and governance issues [including studies such as] alternative service delivery, organizational structure and decision making, salaries and fringe benefits, and city–military installation relationships" and does publish and otherwise disseminate the survey results through electronic services, it has never been a principle party to any case involving membership boycotts, price-fixing, minimum-fee schedules, competitive bidding, relative-value guides, its code of ethics, or access/delivery/group practice—or for restricting the scope of professional practice in assisting its membership with employment agreements or otherwise.[55]

And because of the fact that individuals who now hold CAO positions in communities recognized by the ICMA are not required to be licensed or otherwise officially certified by the state or by affiliation with the association, there have been no cases involving the issues of state and reciprocal licensing. Membership in the ICMA is not required even on the part of CAOs serving in recognized communities (although it is certainly encouraged by the association), nor is it required by the state statutes.

Peer review is another area of increasing interest to the professions. Robert Golembiewski contends that "major progress toward a public service profession will be more clearly signalled by a broadly-accepted and reasonably systematized periodic peer review of both academic programs and individuals."[56] Looking at this trend from the perspective of the overall professionalization of the management team serving in local government, Golembiewski reports,

Many observers foresee a closer approach to the just society via the growing professionalization of law enforcement officers. . . . In addition, moves toward professionalization via certification or accreditation have been made in diverse areas relevant to managerial efficiency and effectiveness: in personnel administration, in organization development and consultancy, and so on. [However,] despite such awesome momentum, the specific case for professionalization as leading to more or better performance is far from clear or consistent.[57]

At contract renewal intervals, CAOs are periodically—if not otherwise constantly—assessed by the councils or commissions that employ them, and by the general community that elects the council—and, thus, indirectly also by the other public servants who work for and with them. Few analysts would try to argue that the current conditions of professionalization among CAOs in ICMA-recognized communities are overbalanced on the side of protectionism (at least in terms of the antitrust statutes). As we have seen, the evolution of both protections and obligations under public service law, the growing jurisdictional responsibilities of local governments, the expanded and institutionalized information/association network that provides support programs and services, and the increasing (though still seemingly noncompulsory) career requirements are all encouraging greater professionalization. However, this is not to suggest that the costs would—by definition—outweigh any or all benefits that might accrue from mandating state licensing or certification procedures in an effort to standardize the entrance and maintenance of professional competence in selected public management positions.

However, the traditional professions—too—have demonstrated a desire to enhance occupational compensation through collective (and sometimes questionable) action, and also to raise their occupational standards by ''peer'' (professional) monitoring of precareer training programs. Both goals have involved a number of the established professions in litigation. There is also a concern among the traditional professions over personal standards of behavior (codes of ethics), which can be understood as increasing both the status and standard of performance. These are matters that pertain to the education facet of the tripartite set of institutional processes depicted in Figure 5.1.

## PURPOSES AND GOALS

In the midst of the 1960s–1970s academic debate over the professionalization/deprofessionalization of everyone, another important development was being watched and measured. Martin Oppenheimer observed that, ''among professional workers, [a number of] lawyers, professors, school administrators, engineers and scientists, physicians, and many others have broken away from traditional professional societies to join trade unions, or else professional societies themselves have affiliated with unions.''[58] This—he argued—has resulted in professional autonomy being taken away by administrators through the standardization of all workers in bureaucracies, in terms of work conditions, financial compensation, methods of evaluation, and the threat of unemployment. As evidence,

Oppenheimer reported that between 1960 and 1970 there was a proportionate increase of white-collar workers among all American unionists (up from 12 to 16 percent, in a decade in which there was an actual decline in the proportion of the U.S. labor force that was unionized—down from 23.6 percent to 22.6 percent).[59]

This convergence of factors and forces has required that public sector managers—a subset of whom are the primary focus of this book—perform for their communities an important collective-bargaining role with the salaried professionals within their own organizations. While it is outside the purview of this study to assess the further implications of this trend on the public sector as a whole (or the local government CAO), it does offer a significant test of the historical role played by all professionals (including professionalized local government managers) and their professional associations. For the latter, that test is how best to respond to this challenge and yet still promote the values of expertise, autonomy, commitment, and responsibility for their memberships. As Archie Kleingartner has noted:

When we consider the array of methods that salaried professionals have used to achieve their goals, collective bargaining has been, in a historical sense, one of the least used. . . . Others, such as informal consultations with management, lobbying, mutual aid, publication of professional journals, and promulgations of codes of ethics, continue to serve a useful purpose. [But] most salaried professionals recognize that professionalism must in its concrete aspects be obtained primarily from the employer.[60]

There are two types of indicators that can help to pinpoint where CAOs serving in ICMA-recognized communities stand on these issues. One axis is a dual measure of how the occupational goal of achieving predictable (competitive) rewards for being employed (satisfactory income, fringe benefits, suitable working conditions, fair treatment, and a measure of job security) can be or is balanced by the unique—and perhaps more long-term—career goal of being a member of a recognized profession. And a crosscutting second axis measures how the profession is attempting to internalize and maintain values of expertise, autonomy, commitment, and responsibility among its practitioners during the course of their careers.

Research has never uncovered any serious evidence of an organized effort to unionize the ICMA membership. However, Archie Kleingartner reported in a study for the U.S. Department of Labor that most public service professional groups were pursuing goals in their bargaining and contracts with employers that included—but went beyond—the usual labor issues. Included in the additional contract provisions are several well known professional goals: "(1) autonomy, (2) occupational integrity and identification, (3) individual satisfaction and career development, and (4) economic security and enhancement."[61]

Predicted Kleingartner:

Salaried professionals have made it clear that they want real authority to make decisions affecting not only their own status and career aspirations but the basic character, quality, and amount of services provided to the recipients of their professional services. . . . Consultation, negotiation, and bargaining which result in a genuine redistribution of authority are becoming part of everyday management in the public sector. The groups on the cutting edge of this revolution are the salaried professions. The implications of this revolution are a tall challenge to public management and employee organizations alike.[62]

Significantly, CAOs in ICMA-recognized communities are often required to negotiate with the representatives of different occupational groups within the civil service. However, these managers must negotiate directly with their councils when it comes to their own substantive labor and professional goal provisions. What role, then, has and does the ICMA play for its membership—given the statutory and judicial changes that have occurred?

ICMA's assistance to its members who are seeking positions and negotiating employment agreements—and thereby its promotion of professionally beneficial arrangements—has been stimulative in nature: That is, it promotes fair competition among locally screened, well-qualified candidates. The association produces a set of guidelines for interested local governments (or their appointed or hired representatives) who are searching for an appointive CAO. It has also developed guidelines for managers who are getting ready to negotiate an employment agreement. In addition, members have access to annually generated summary information on manager and department-head salaries and fringe benefits throughout the country. Further, the ICMA lists available positions in its publications as well as through the informational services offered at its annual conference and state league meetings. Finally, the association offers a referral service for what it considers "qualified job candidates from its minorities/women's talent bank to local governments, public interest groups, and executive search firms seeking to fill management positions."[63]

Notice that the ICMA does not negotiate on behalf of individual members, nor attempt to establish and enforce collective standards for levels of compensation—practices that have been the subject of antitrust cases involving other professional associations. It does, however, keep its membership informed and current about traditional and innovative trends, through its annual surveys. And it does offer optional retirement benefit plans, through the affiliated ICMA Retirement Corporation.

What roles are being played by professional associations and institutions of higher education in promoting the ethical pursuit of efficiency and effectiveness in the performance of a public manager's duties? In particular, how are the institutions of higher education—whose goal it is to provide nationally accredited and recognized professional degree programs and training in the field of public administration—meeting these challenges, in light of the public service ideal?

As already seen, many values and skills of professionalism in local government management are associated by practitioners with their formal years of education and training, along with other collegial processes and continuing education.

However, the traditional values of professionalism continue to be challenged by changing social, economic, political, technological, and organizational developments. While the ICMA does operate its own training institute—and while it does not officially endorse any particular university or college-based program— it has worked with the National Association of Schools of Public Affairs and Administration (NASPAA) to bridge the gap between practitioners and educators in the field of urban management.

In particular, in the mid–1970s the U.S. Department of Housing and Urban Development (HUD) contracted with the ICMA and NASPAA to construct a strategy for a better understanding of the "the mutual problems of the scholar and the practitioner of urban management, the reasons for their inability to effect closer cooperation in meeting the problems, and to explore strategies that might stimulate interaction and facilitate a drawing together."[64] This project was concurrent with a number of others—like the Urban Observatory Program, the Urban Information Systems Inter-agency Committee, and the Urban Technology System—being funded or otherwise supported by various governmental agencies and private foundations. The HUD project has been viewed as a response to the upheavals of the 1960s; it was part of a national mobilization by the federal government and other levels of government to find mechanisms for developing more capable and effective local government managers.[65]

To that end, the ICMA/NASPAA/HUD venture established a national committee of scholars and local managers to study the problems and develop approaches for bridging the academic–practitioner gap. This led to the formation of 20 university-local community pilot projects with a goal of strengthening urban-management education programs; the projects were monitored by staffs of the two professional associations. In the final analysis, the joint venture's major insights are probably best summed up in the following two excerpts. One comment is from a team of participating academics, who observed, "The question, how do you balance a program of a strong theoretical basis with the need for specific skills, was asked. The answer was that a strong commitment from the consumers of MPAs was needed." And the second observation comes from a participating practitioner: "I am not and most of my peers are not really competent to tell the academic people what they should teach in order to produce what we want, but the academicians visiting our cities and seeing our needs should be able to go back and do a better job in preparing the students for their future."[66]

But—while there do seem to have been clear benefits to the project's participants—a lack of university and association financial resources, the cutbacks in federal funding, faculty and manager turnover, and the differing organizational demands and systems of reward for local managers and for academics all continue to hamper most efforts at initiating similar national projects for others to experience. There have been occasional efforts to duplicate these linkages through in-service local government training programs, university-based governmental training-development programs (typically offered as continuing-education or certification programs), state agency training and development programs (typically located in departments of community affairs or development), and some statewide associations (for example, state leagues of cities).

However, these in-service training and development programs are often only loosely associated with—and are sometimes in actual competition with—the training programs and services offered through the national network of public-management associations described earlier. Harold Holtz—chief administrator of the well-regarded governmental training division at the Institute of Government, University of Georgia—noted, "An overview of most training programs for local government officials reveals a variety of activities—all of which function in a more-or-less haphazard manner, with little systematic coordination of efforts among programs and institutions."[67] In contrast, on the up side of efforts to institutionalize professional training in the fields of public administration has been the decision by the Council on Postsecondary Accreditation to recognize NASPAA as a specialized agency for accrediting M.P.A. programs in colleges and universities.

One final aspect of this focus on the purposes and goals of professional associates and associations is tied to their codes of ethics. At issue is the role that the code of ethics is thought to play in establishing and maintaining professional, internalized standards of behavior for individual practitioners. As noted earlier, in the case of a number of traditional professions, permutations of their codes of ethics have brought them to the attention of the courts—via antitrust litigation. However, while there have been occasional instances where members have brought code-of-ethics allegations before the ICMA, my Lexis search uncovered no evidence that the association has ever been charged with violating public service law protections afforded to its members or to the communities served.

If—as is generally held—a code of ethics is one of the most desirable standards by which to measure professionals and to hold them accountable (in tandem with performance expectations for their expertise), then—logic dictates—learning about ethical behavior and its meanings within a professional context cannot be separated from the broader discussion of professionalization as a continuing process of knowledge development and enhancement. How can a code of ethics be enforced without systematically teaching what ethical behavior is about? But ultimately, does the code of ethics mean more than what is in the federal and state constitutions, or codified in public service law?

No issue in the field of public administration has generated more debate than that focused on the meaning and exercise of occupation-specific codes of ethics. Once again, the issue is multidimensional in nature. One dimension of the debate pertains to just how a code of ethics can actually guide individuals in their public service, and what types of structures and processes should be used to encourage and enforce subscription to the code's precepts. The generic purpose of codes of ethics is intuitively clear: They encourage practitioners of a profession to administer to their responsibilities in pursuit of the public interest, rather than primarily for individual gain. It is in the specifics of code application and enforcement that the principles, structures, and processes get more complex and controversial.[68]

However, ICMA moved to adopt its first code of ethics only ten years after its founding. This adoption was partly a result of the association's heritage in the municipal reform movement, and of the reformers' commitment within the early association to establishing standards of professionalization for its membership (and meeting, in the process—if not in historical sequence—one of the primary criteria of the traditional professions).[69] Since its original adoption of a code of ethics, the ICMA has occasionally censured, suspended, and even expelled members for violating one or more of the basic principles found in the code (currently organized into 12 articles). In 1981, William Besuden reported that "the enforcement of the code as it affects individual members has been a relatively recent development. For many years the profession was small and closely knit . . . , and formal enforcement procedures were not necessary. Even today, in fact, the number of ethical cases is small, never exceeding 20 a year and probably averaging about 10.''[70]

The ICMA has established a two-tiered structure to implement its code of ethics. On the support side, a Committee on Professional Conduct developed an initial set of guidelines in 1972 for interpreting the code—guidelines that have since been updated. The committee also offers advisory opinions to members with regard to the code's application in particular instances. On the enforcement side, the association's constitution provides that the ICMA Executive Board— after following established rules of due process in its investigation of a complaint—has the responsibility for determining whether disciplinary actions will be required against any member. It is important to note, however, that an ICMA censure, suspension, or expulsion from membership does not directly or necessarily result in the loss of a CAO appointment. A manager's loss of position remains exclusively in the hands of the local council or board, and perhaps a court.

There is another important institution-building aspect of the ICMA code-of-ethics apparatus—having nothing to do with its internal enforcement role. This is the association's capacity to provide investigative services through its Committee on Professional Conduct and the Executive Board—services that may offer some protection to members who are under unfair local criticism in regard to the performance of their duties. Notes Besuden:

The code has been used in several cases since 1975 to reaffirm the ethical conduct of a member who was under attack locally. These cases involved court action that could easily have left a question about a member's integrity if the committee had not, at the member's request, investigated the steps leading to court action and found the member had acted honorably, according to professional ethics as stated in the code.[71]

This observation is substantiated by my search of federal and state cases: A substantial proportion of them were amici curiae (friend of the court) briefs. In these proceedings, the ICMA—while not itself a party in the litigation—filed a legal brief to advise the court on some matter of law that was at issue in the case. The courts' willingness to invite and to accept amici curiae briefs from the ICMA is another form of governmental (judicial) recognition of its standing as a professional association—and, implicitly, a recognition of the standards of its membership.

A second dimension of the ethics debate pertains to the occupational consciousness raising and reinforcement that takes place in the process of code development and revision. At the same time, there arises the countervailing risk of group divisiveness (and its potential for deleterious effects on the other purposes of the professional association). In this regard, the ICMA has undergone five successful amendment proceedings since it originally adopted a code of ethics in 1924 (having amended its code in 1938, 1952, 1969, 1972, and 1976). Measures of the impact of the code revision discussions on the CAOs serving in ICMA-recognized communities were not included in any of the surveys supporting this study. However, it seems reasonable to assume that code revision matters discussed in the ICMA publications and at its annual meetings would—at a minimum—focus members' attention on the whole issue of ethics and the implications of their being codified.

The third dimension of the debate approaches ethics from a cross-institutional perspective—focusing on the issues of ethics education in professional degree programs and within in-service training, rather than just on codification. Here we encounter the difficulties in discerning effective methods by which the ethical behavior of particular professions may be taught and—correspondingly—learned. The themes of two relatively recent articles perhaps best grab the horns of this dilemma. In one of them—"Ethics in the Public Service: Codification Misses the Real Target"—Gerald Caiden argues,

In short, no codifiers of ethics have ever claimed that codification alone would solve anything. It was merely a beginning of a wider venture to impress on civil servants the need to be aware of public service traditions and the dangers inherent in deviant behavior. It was not a substitute for good government or good people in government. It was merely an additional instrument for implementing the traditional policy of deterrence in American public administration.[72]

On the other hand, in their essay "Ethics and Public Administration: Teaching What 'Can't Be Taught,' " John Worthley and Barbara Grumet report,

The National Association of Schools of Public Affairs and Administration (NASPAA) guidelines for public administration programs contain an ethics requirement, and both the American Society for Public Administration (ASPA) and the International Association of Schools and Institutes of Administration (IASIA) have stressed the importance of ethics education and sensitivity. [Nevertheless], a Ford Foundation Study found great uncertainty in public administration schools over how to teach ethics, recent ASPA conference panels reported considerable frustration in teaching ethics, and [our] own current survey of NASPAA schools found widespread difficulties with the subject.[73]

In particular, the Worthley and Grumet survey of NASPAA schools suggested that there have emerged four basic approaches in public administration programs for teaching ethics: "1. analysis of 'horror' stories . . . with a fairly clear 'right–wrong' element, 2. study of codes of conduct . . . , 3. emphasis on law: ethics is avoiding anything illegal, or anything for which you can be sued, or anything for which you can be fired, [and] 4. study of the great philosophers."[74]

Clearly, to study a professional association's codes of ethics and not examine the structures, processes, and alternative roles that the code may play within the association and for its membership—and in the professional degree programs offered at universities—would necessarily result in an underassessment of its potential value as a codeterrence educational vehicle along with evolving public service law. The latter observation comes under the maxim that "ignorance of the law is no excuse." While there may not yet be (or ever be) a general consensus on the best way to teach ethics (or—for that matter—on how to learn ethical behavior in advance of the events that require it), addressing ethical issues and problems in some fashion as part of a professional public-administration degree program is a step in the right direction. The continuing focus of academics and professional associations on these issues, should not be allowed to cause too much frustration, but should prove helpful and can be considered as a mark of professionalization in itself.

Insofar as the system of higher education has established a national accreditation system for professional degree programs in public administration, and since communities (through the marketplace) have been increasingly recruiting these accredited public managers—who often also possess or will secure (or will be encouraged by the community to apply for) membership in a professional association with a code of ethics—it is clearly evident that a highly professionalized CAO corp is now available for service in local government. They have increasingly become the norm, although localities have not had state licensure requirements constraining their choices. Professionalized public management remains, however, only one of a number of local capacity-building options and strategies. Cost and competition continue to be important factors in a local government's considerations.

## CAO CAREER PATH AND ASSOCIATIONAL AFFILIATION

There has been a significant movement by local governments toward hiring CAOs with advanced degrees. And there appears to be an increasing acceptance of the M.P.A. degree as the professional credential of choice. Confirming our earlier analysis in Chapter 2, another review of graduation and placement reports indicates the following:

The number of graduate public administration degrees annually awarded grew rapidly from 1973 ($N$ = 2,403) to 1981 ($N$ = 6,736). Since 1981, the number has averaged around 6,250 per year. [However, only] approximately 55 percent of those graduates accepted positions at some level of government (NASPAA, 1986). According to a recent study by Lewis (1987), only a law degree is more valuable than the MPA in terms of civil service grade and pay. Lewis also finds that the number of MPA degree holders in the federal bureaucracy is growing at a much higher rate than other fields.[75]

Some of the information within these studies refocuses attention on the perennial issue of curriculum relevancy (in the skill areas as well as within the study of professional ethics). It also raises a number of issues about the importance of student and postgraduation affiliations and about the placement services of host colleges and universities, as well as those of the professional associations. It is perhaps in the recruitment/placement of M.P.A. graduates and experienced managers where the processes of institutionalization are least developed, and yet have much in common with the traditional professions. One consequence of this underdevelopment—in the context of a growing emphasis on public–private sector cooperation—is that it can lead to divergence in M.P.A. program curricula. This may come from the increased possibilities or pressures for intercareer mobility among public managers with advanced training, and may portend a type of professional identity crisis for both M.P.A. programs and graduate students that could not have been anticipated prior to the arrival of the Baby Boom generation.

Earlier we engaged in this discussion from the perspective of the public manager's historical career pathways and a concern over career plateauing. We acknowledged the evolving need for continuing education that is in evidence for all the professions. The topic is revisited here from the public interest perspective: the need for competitive access to a well-qualified and adequately supplied pool of public managers.

The interdependent notions of educational utility/career and recruitment/placement would seem to describe an area of keen interest to the professional associations in public administration. Neil Brady reminds us of what—on the one hand—an institutionally diluted professional curriculum that responds only to demand and competition can bring.

[Public administrators] may possess a profound understanding of the theory and concepts underlying [their] profession without consistently being able to exhibit good judgment in the use of that knowledge. . . . This lack of systematic understanding leaves only the hope that the unsupported implication between conceptual skill and administrative success is reversible and that success implies the possession of skill. Consequently, public administration programs often rely on placement of graduates to justify their claims to curriculum adequacy.[76]

On the other hand, there is a countervailing supply problem. Public management career counselors and educators—like James Wolf—report from experience that, while cutback management in the 1980s has been "meant to describe a creative process of finding new and cheaper ways to do old business, the reality is too often a meat-ax approach to budgets and personnel."[77] As a consequence, Wolf and other educators and consultants now counsel preprofessional students as well as in-service public managers that they should control their career options by identifying themselves with attached or adjoining occupations ("role sub-identities that match the . . . career clusters that are relevant to him/her").[78]

The impact of student enrollments and job placements on future M.P.A. program concentrations and curriculum developments may well prove to be an important public interest test for the movement to seek state licensure for public managers. The continued emphasis given to the "public" in M.P.A. programs, as well as the availability of program resources (faculty and classes) and concentrations in areas such as local government management will be interesting to monitor. Depending on how these developments proceed, there are other possible routes to institutionalized professionalization, outside of M.P.A. credentialling—alternatives that already exist in an embryonic stage. One can envision—for example—a reinvigorated, expanded, and perhaps even nationally organized network (maybe in conjunction with state licensing procedures) that would be based on various government nondegree certification programs offered through universities, colleges, private institutes, and professional associations such as the ICMA.[79]

Because the M.P.A. seems to have become more marketable as a professional degree for nongovernmental occupations (nonprofit and private sectors) as well as for government service, there may be increasing competition away from public service—particularly in smaller communities—for the most recently trained individuals in the field of public affairs/administration. As previously noted, there have been indications that the educational preparation and initial appointments and experiences of city managers exercise substantial influence over the subsequent course of their public management careers.[80] An increased focus on M.P.A. preparation and recruitment patterns would seem to be very much in the public's interest. However, it has only been in recent years that colleges and universities offering professional degree programs in public administration have begun to examine how their graduates actually found an initial position and went about developing a public service career, or else took a nongovernmental position or reprogrammed and replaced an early public service career. Neither has there been much systematic research on the placement services offered by professional associations in the field of public administration.[81]

Two teams of researchers have done pioneering work in this basically uncharted area. The first—Samuel Yeager, Jack Rabin, and Thomas Vocino—focused on the responses of M.P.A. degree holders that were included in the 1980 National Longitudinal Study of graduates of political science, public administration, and public affairs programs. Yeager, Rabin, and Vocino report,

Analyses of our data indicate that there are no meaningful differences in how MPAs in the following categories found their jobs: males vs. female, white vs. black, MPAs vs.

equivalent degrees, NASPAA member institution vs. non-NASPAA member institution, recent graduate vs. past graduates (5–10, 10–15, and 15 or more years since graduation), supervisory status vs. nonsupervisory status, and young vs. middle vs. older age groups.[82]

However, what they did find was that the "use of information sources varies so much at different points in the MPA's careers that we find it necessary to examine MPAs in their first and subsequent positions separately."[83]

Yeager, Rabin, and Vocino discovered from these M.P.A. respondents that friends and faculty were the sources of information that had most often led to their first job. With regard to professional associations,

relatively few master's level students belong to appropriate professional organizations, much less attend their national meetings where most association-assisted recruiting is done. . . . Regional associational meetings are even less helpful since virtually no recruiting occurs there. . . . Professional association placement activities are more helpful to those further along in their careers than new MPAs looking for their first job.[84]

More M.P.A. holders seem to get their second and subsequent positions through promotion, by asking for a job on answering an ad, and through recruitment by an employer than by assistance from friends or faculty advisors. This clearly demonstrates the importance of having an acceptable service record.

The myriad of positions open in local government—let alone, the specific management positions—can present a formidable obstruction to potential job candidates. While there are both public and private sector placement services and listings for federal and state civil service and appointive positions, there are only a limited number of national services that supply information about local governments. These sources are primarily found in the national network of local officials' associations; and at present, they have not undertaken responsibility for providing comprehensive coverage about position availability. In the instance of city and county managers, periodic listings are provided by the ICMA and the American Society for Public Administration, on a submission (versus survey-of-source) basis.

The market, however, is national; and the recruiting budget of governments is often very limited—particularly as population size of the community falls into the smaller categories. The scope of advertising in newspapers , most magazines, and the publications of the regional public administration societies, state municipal leagues, and management associations (as well as their meetings, where positions may also be listed) is limited by the services that they offer and by the nature of the regional or state audiences that they attract. University and college placement services are even more unpredictable as sources of information about local government management positions.

A second team of research pioneers—David Ammons and James Glass— reported an apparent increase in the use of executive search firms for management-level positions in local government; but the limited increase is mostly

restricted to the larger communities with populations over 50,000, and to jurisdictions that employ the council–manager form of government. After surveying
local government jurisdictions that had advertised positions in ICMA's biweekly
newsletter, Ammons and Glass forecasted that "if search firm activity in local
government increases, that expansion will likely occur in two areas: more jurisdictions recruiting their chief executive with search firm assistance and increased use of search firms in the recruitment of department heads and assistant
city or county managers."[85] However, this expansion is likely to be constrained
by the costs typically associated with such services—estimated to run "when
provided by a major firm . . . in the neighborhood of $12,000 plus expenses for
a single search."[86] Since the search for positions and personnel is one reason
that draws potential members to the ICMA itself, these trends offer both an
opportunity for further associational development and a challenge to that development.

While due-process and equal-opportunity clauses established within public
service law mandate open and fair competition based on merit, competency, and
experience, there remain major marketplace obstacles to a more efficient, effective, and mutually beneficial national system for recruitment/placement. This
is particularly true for the professional capacity needs of the smaller governmental
jurisdictions. In another of their series of studies, Yeager, Rabin, and Vocino
reported that—once in service—government employees

use a wide range of sources of information to find jobs. When these information sources
are grouped into formal, direct application and informal sources, government professionals
rely more heavily on formal than on the other sources of job information. This result
differs significantly from earlier studies of non-governmental employees, which indicate
that professionals rely most heavily on informal sources of information. This may reflect
the fact that formal information sources are more extensive and readily available in
government than in much of the private sector. It may also reflect legal mandates that
these formal processes be used. The formal processes insure equal protection of the laws
and make equal employment opportunity possible.[87]

## THE NET EFFECT

Analysis of the information structured around the notion of a tripartite network
for professionalization of local government managers—as depicted in Figure 5.1,
summarized in Figure 5.2, and illuminated by the key institutions presented in
Figure 5.3—suggests an increasing institutional sophistication as well as complexity in the dynamics of network development. The composition and nature
of the network is likely to continue evolving, particularly with regard to the
associations formed during the past two decades. The density of associational
foundings and rediversy of their activities across time—as illustrated with the
case of the ICMA (particularly in the structures, processes, and uses of its code
of ethics apparatus)—shows that the nationally (vertically) organized, local
government management network of professional associations (operating in tan-

dem with the increased numbers of national consumer/citizen action groups) continues to change in response to the evolving perceptions of the public and their memberships.

The different perspectives of Frederick Wirt (about local decision making) and Theodore Lowi (federal decision making) and the warnings of Robert Golembiewski (on professional protectionism) all imply that there are likely to be both positive and negative consequences of this increase in type, configuration, and density of national interest and occupational groups. Each of the national associations must meet the tests of survival to remain a force for the professionalization of public service in government in its own right. Conflicts and contractions within the network, as well as its institutionalization or expansion, merit close monitoring.

The availability of a nationally recognized set of professional credentials, a more fully institutionalized network of professionalizing associations, and the development and precedence being established through evolving public service law are all indicators that there have been significant new developments over the past two decades. These changes can be associated with an increase in the standards, status, services, and responsibilities of local public managers and their associations. But they are not guarantees of performance. There is always room for improvement; and there will be challenges ahead in adjusting to the unanticipated consequences of current arrangements and external dynamics.

Opportunities for more contemporary, balanced, and useful measures of professionalization in public service will continue to emerge from the tripartite set of institutional forces in public service law, higher education, and professional associations. And it is safe to say that developments will be anything but equal, constant, unambiguous, and implemented with unanimous consent. Nonetheless, as it stands today (even without anticipating future challenges), the process has led to increased numbers of CAOs entering the field of local public management with professional (M.P.A.) degrees from accredited programs in institutions of higher education. Once in service, these graduates frequently become members of an association that was established three quarters of a century ago to promote professional local government management: ICMA. And when accepted for membership in that association, professionals are governed and served by a code-of-ethics system as well as emerging body of public service law.

## NOTES

1. Howard E. McCurdy, *Public Administration: A Synthesis* (Menlo Park, Calif.: Cummings Publishing, 1977), p. 404.

2. Ira Sharkansky, *The United States: A Study of a Developing Country* (New York: David McKay, 1975).

3. Harold L. Wilensky, "The Professionalization of Everyone?" *American Journal of Sociology* 60, no. 2 (September 1964), pp. 137–58.

4. Wilensky identified city management initially as a unique, full-time occupation

within the council–manager plan for government. That was in 1912—only two years before the International City Management Association was formed. The first training school for city managers was established in 1921, and the first university school was established in 1948. See table 1 in Wilensky, "Professionalization of Everyone?" p. 143.

5. Daniel Bell, "The Measurement of Knowledge and Technology," in Eleanor B. Sheldon and Wilbert E. Moore, eds., *Indicators of Social Change* (New York: Russell Sage Foundation and Ford Foundation, 1968), pp. 145–246.

6. Marie R. Haug, "The Deprofessionalization of Everyone?" *Sociological Focus* 8, no. 3 (August 1975), pp. 197–213.

7. Ibid., p. 206.

8. Wilensky, "Professionalization of Everyone?" p. 157.

9. Haug, "Deprofessionalization?" p. 211.

10. Ibid., p. 212.

11. Robert T. Golembiewski, "Toward Professional Certification?" *Bureaucrat* 12, no. 2 (Summer 1983), p. 54.

12. Laurence G. Rutter, "Art and Magic: Local Government Management's Standards of Professionalism," *Bureaucrat* 6, no. 2 (Summer 1977), p. 52.

13. Ibid., p. 53.

14. Ibid., p. 54.

15. Ibid., p. 53.

16. Arthur L. Finkle, "A Discipline in Search of Legitimacy," *Bureaucrat* 13, no. 2 (Summer 1984), p. 60.

17. Ibid.

18. McCurdy, *Public Administration*, pp. 310–11.

19. A. M. Carr-Saunders and P. A. Wilson, "The Historical Development of Professional Associations," in Howard M. Vollmer and Donald L. Mills, *Professionalization* (Englewood Cliffs, N.J.: Prentice-Hall, 1966), p. 153.

20. See, for example, D. Woods Thomas et al., *Institution Building* (Cambridge, Mass.: Schenkman Publishing, 1973), or Warren F. Illchman and Norman T. Uphoff, *The Political Economy of Change* (Berkeley: University of California Press, 1969); and for an integrated overview, see Milton J. Esman and John D. Montgomery, "Systems Approaches to Technical Cooperation: The Role of Development Administration," *Public Administration Review* 29, no. 5 (September/October 1969), pp. 507–39.

21. Cited by Robert N. Kharasch, *The Institutional Imperative: How to Understand the United States Government and Other Bulky Objects* (New York: Charterhouse Books, 1973), p. xi.

22. See Alvin Toffler, *Future Shock* (New York: Random House, 1970), and John Naisbitt's *Megatrends: Ten New Directions Transforming Our Lives* (New York: Warner Books, 1984).

23. Forest Woody Horton, Jr., ed., *Understanding U.S. Information Policy: The Infostructure Handbook* (Washington, D.C.: Information Industry Association, 1982).

24. Commercial practitioners have now come to characterize themselves as *infopreneurs*—defined as a person "who gathers, organizes, and disseminates information as a business venture or as a value-added service." See H. Skip Weitzen, *Turning Data into Dollars* (New York: John Wiley and Sons, 1988), p. 2.

25. Theodore J. Lowi, *The End of Liberalism: The Second Republic of the United States*, 2nd ed. (New York: W. W. Norton, 1979).

26. Jack L. Walker, "The Origins and Maintenance of Interest Groups in America," *American Political Science Review* 77, no. 2 (June 1983), p. 394.

27. Ibid., p. 403.

28. Ibid., p. 398.

29. Karin E. Koek, Susan B. Martin, and Annette Novallo, eds., "Section 3: Legal, Governmental, Public Administration, and Military Organizations," *Encyclopedia of Associations: 1988* (Detroit: Gale Research, 1988), pp. 437–508.

30. Of particular interest is Aaron Wildavsky's description of the "law of large solutions in public policy"; see his *Speaking Truth to Power: The Art and Craft of Policy Analysis* (Boston: Little, Brown, 1979), pp. 63–67.

31. "Inside the Year Book," in the *Municipal Year Book 1988* (Washington, D.C.: International City Management Association, 1988), p. xii.

32. Carr-Saunders and Wilson, "Development of Professional Associations," p. 153.

33. Walker, "Interest Groups in America," p. 395.

34. David H. Rosenbloom, "Public Administrative Theory and the Separation of Powers," *Public Administration Review* 43, no. 3 (May/June 1983), p. 222.

35. Ibid., pp. 222–23.

36. See Kenneth Davis, *Administrative Law and Government* (St. Paul, Minn.: West Publishing, 1975), p. 6.

37. David H. Rosenbloom, "Public Administrative Professionalism and Public Service Law," *State and Local Government Review* 16, no. 2 (Spring 1984), p. 55.

38. Ibid., pp. 55–56.

39. Doyle W. Buckwalter, "Dillon's Rule in the 1980s: Who's in Charge of Local Affairs," *National Civic Review* 71, no. 8 (September 1982), p. 400.

40. Ibid., pp. 405–6.

41. Ibid., p. 406.

42. William L. Trombetta, "The Professions under Scrutiny: An Antitrust Perspective," *Journal of Consumer Affairs* 16, no. 1 (Summer 1982), p. 105.

43. For a review of the court-related concerns, see Phillip J. Cooper, "Conflict or Constructive Tension: The Changing Relationship of Judges and Administrators," *Public Administration Review*, Special Issue (November 1985), pp. 643–52; Gregory D. Foster, "Law, Morality, and the Public Servant," *Public Administration Review* 41, no. 1 (January/February 1981), pp. 29–34; Melvin Hill, Jr., "The 'Littler Hatch Acts': State Laws Regulating Political Activities of Local Government Employees," *State Government* 52, no. 4 (Autumn 1979), pp. 161–68; and J. Jackson Walter, "The Ethics in Government Act, Conflict of Interest Laws and Presidential Recruiting," *Public Administration Review* 41 (November/December 1981), pp. 659–65.

44. Trombetta, "Professions under Scrutiny," p. 89.

45. Ibid., pp. 89 and 91.

46. Ibid., p. 91.

47. Ibid., pp. 91–92.

48. Ibid., pp. 107 and 109.

49. William J. Goode, "The Theoretical Limits of Professionalization," in Amitai Etzioni, ed., *The Semi-professions and Their Organizations: Teachers, Nurses, Social Workers* (New York: Free Press, 1969), pp. 299–313.

50. For an excellent overview of the economy in terms of the information marketplace, see Horton, *Understanding U.S. Information Policy*, pp. xv–xix.

51. Barry Bozeman, *Public Management and Policy Analysis* (New York: St. Martin's Press, 1979), p. 361.

52. *Fact Sheet on ICMA*, revised November 1987 (Washington, D.C.: International City Management Association, 1987), p. 1.

53. "Facts on the Council–manager Plan," in the *Fact Sheet on ICMA*, p. 5.

54. The search was initiated on January 14, 1989, through the School of Law at the University of Oregon. For further information on the Lexis data base and its uses, see *Learning Lexis: A Handbook for Modern Legal Research* (Dayton: Mead Data Central, 1986).

55. "Facts on Council–manager Plan," p. 5.

56. Robert T. Golembiewski, "Professionalization, Performance, and Protectionism: A Contingency View," *Public Productivity Review* 7, no. 3 (September 1983), p. 256.

57. Ibid., p. 251.

58. Martin Oppenheimer, "The Unionization of the Professional," *Social Policy* 5, no. 5 (January/February 1975), p. 34.

59. Ibid., pp. 40 and 35.

60. Archie Kleingartner, "Collective Bargaining between Salaried Professionals and Public Sector Management," *Public Administration Review* 33, no. 2 (March/April 1973), p. 169.

61. Ibid., p. 167.

62. Ibid., pp. 171–72. One can begin to see how a new synthesis may be emerging in terms of the value and rewards of being a member of a profession, even within an organizational framework. See again the findings reported in Chapter 3 from the research of Mary E. Guy, *Professionals in Organizations: Debunking a Myth* (New York: Praeger Publishers, 1985).

63. "Professional Activities," in *Fact Sheet on ICMA*, revised November 1987 (Washington, D.C.: International City Management Association, 1987), p. 3.

64. See the introduction by Lynn S. Miller and Laurence Rutter to "A Special Symposium: Strengthening the Quality of Urban Management Education," *Public Administration Review* 37, no. 5 (September/October 1977), p. 569.

65. See ch. 2, "Attempts to Advise," in Peter Szanton, *Not Well Advised* (New York: Russell Sage Foundation and Ford Foundation, 1981), pp. 17–56.

66. Cited by Miller and Rutter in their introduction to "Special Symposium," p. 630.

67. See the introductory comments by Harold Holtz in "A Symposium: Local Governmental Training: Practices and Perspectives," *State and Local Government Review* 13 no. 2 (May 1981), p. 43.

68. While the organization of and conclusions drawn in this section are my own, I am indebted to the thoughtful essays written by Elizabeth M. Gunn, "Ethics and the Public Service: An Annotated Bibliography and Overview Essay," *Public Personnel Management Journal* 10 (1981), pp. 172–78, and by James S. Bowman, "The Management of Ethics: Codes of Conduct in Organizations," *Public Personnel Management Journal* 10 (1981), pp. 59–66—as well as to the research head start provided by Bowman's "Ethics and the Public Service: A Selected and Annotated Bibliography," *Public Personnel Management Journal* 10 (1981), pp. 179–99.

69. While a bit dated, a report written by Joseph F. Zimmerman, "Ethics in Local Government," *Management Information Service Report* 8, no. 8 (Washington, D.C.: International City Management Association, August 1976), proved quite useful for laying

out the issues linking the association's code-of-ethics policies, structures, and processes with those of emerging state and local government codes of ethics.

70. William E. Besuden, "The Profession's Heritage: The ICMA Code of Ethics," *Public Management* 63, no. 3 (March 1981), p. 5.

71. Ibid., p. 4.

72. Gerald E. Caiden, "Ethics in the Public Service: Codification Misses the Real Target," *Public Personnel Management Journal* 10 (1981), p. 149.

73. John A. Worthley and Barbara R. Grumet, "Ethics and Public Administration: Teaching What 'Can't Be Taught,' " *American Review of Public Administration* 17, no. 1 (Spring 1983), p. 54. See also Worthley's earlier "Ethics and Public Management: Education and Training," *Public Personnel Management Journal* 10 (1981), pp. 41–47.

74. Worthley and Grumet, "Ethics and Administration: Teaching," p. 57.

75. Reported by Richard C. Kearney and Chandan Sinha as fn. 5 in "Professionalism and Bureaucratic Responsiveness: Conflict or Compatibility?" *Public Administration Review* 48, no. 1 (January/February 1988), p. 577.

76. Neil Brady, "Conceptual Skills and the Public Administrator: Good Judgment and the Logic of Principles," *American Review of Public Administration* 16, no. 1 (Spring 1982), pp. 3 and 4.

77. James F. Wolf, "Public Management Careers—Understanding and Options," *American Review of Public Administration* 17, no. 2/3 (Summer/Fall 1983), p. 91.

78. Wolf, "Public Management Careers," p. 100.

79. See—specifically—the Georgia experience with tax assessors and appraisers in John F. Azzaretto, Howard Smith and Judith Mohr, "The Role of Higher Education in Training and Development for Local Governments," pp. 62–67, and—more generally—the rest of the symposium on "Local Governmental Training: Practices and Perspectives," *State and Local Government Review* 13, no. 2 (May 1981), pp. 42–71.

80. See William R. Fannin and Don C. Moore, "Preparing for City Management Careers: What's Important?" *American Review of Public Administration* 17, no. 2/3 (Summer/Fall 1983), pp. 79–90; Carin S. Weiss, "The Development of Professional Role Commitment among Graduate Students," *Human Relations* 34, no. 1 (1981), pp. 13–31; and Chris Argyris and D. A. Schon, *Theory and Practice: Increasing Professional Effectiveness* (San Francisco: Jossey-Bass, 1974).

81. In this regard, pioneering research has been done by the team of Samuel J. Yeager, Jack Rabin, and Thomas Vocino in a multireport series that utilized the 1980 National Longitudinal Study of graduates from political science, public administration, and public affairs programs as the basis for analysis. See their "Professional Values of Public Servants in the United States," *American Review of Public Administration* 16, no. 4 (Winter 1982), pp. 402–12; "Sources of Information Used by Professionals in Government to Find Jobs: Effectiveness and Impact," *Review of Public Personnel Administration* 4, no. 1 (Fall 1983), pp. 100–13; "How Do MPAs Find Jobs?" *Bureaucrat* 13, no. 2 (Summer 1984), pp. 48–52; and "Employee Perceptions of State and Local Government Evaluation and Reward Systems," *State and Local Government Review* 16, no. 2 (Spring 1984), pp. 58–62.

82. See Yeager, Rabin, and Vocino, "How Do MPAs Find Jobs?" p. 52, fn. 4.

83. Ibid., p. 49.

84. Ibid., p. 50.

85. David N. Ammons and James J. Glass, "Headhunters in Local Government: Use

of Executive Search Firms in Managerial Selection,'' *Public Administration Review* 48, no. 3 (May/June 1988), p. 692.

   86. Ibid., p. 687.
   87. Yeager, Rabin, and Vocino, ''Sources of Information,'' p. 112.

# 6

# PROFESSIONAL MARKS ON A NATION OF COMMUNITIES: HOW WELL ADVISED?

The "rediscovery" of various municipal and other local officials, and of the government jurisdictions in which they serve, is a periodically recurring theme among academics, the national mass media, and—at times—even state and federal government officials. It does not seem that citizens and the local media in each jurisdiction need any such reintroduction to their local government—at least if you talk to any of the locally elected or appointed officials who have management-level responsibilities and who look at their mail and the newspaper![1] However, if we consider the historical moment of each of these rediscoveries— in terms of the greatest volume of media air time and page space—we also uncover some basic reasons why the local arena became newsworthy at that time. The social upheavals of the 1930s and 1960s led to major expansions in national and state involvement in local affairs; and the late 1980s has been an era in which—for philosophical and financial reasons—the federal government has been attempting to reduce its level of local involvement.

But to the serious student of local government, the absence of widespread social trauma or of a sudden shift in intergovernmental relations is not the only reason for the intermittent lapses in attention. The dearth of systematically collected information on local issues, organizations, and actors has also limited the ability to monitor national trends. To compensate for the lack of continuous tracking information, elapsed-time data (typically, toward the end of each decade) have been substituted so that, by cross-sectional analysis, at least the most pronounced changes will be identified—unless there has been an interim systemic change that is affecting a significant number or type of local jurisdictions simultaneously.

When public administration is judged as a generic discipline or field, the inescapable fact that there is an overbalance of opinion and theory in a void of systematic and integrated empirical information has often resulted in debate without evidence or direction. Theory and principle as well as empirical research and experience are both invaluable in the research context, and this seems particularly true in discussions over the level(s) of professionalism within public administration.[2] Specifically, the study of local government management has also been frustrated by a lack of field data, and—to some extent—thwarted by similar types of questions.

Merging the CAO surveys of the ICMA with the 1986–87 Green-Reed survey has allowed us to make some progress beyond the rhetorical—and often paradoxical—discussion of professionalism at the field level of public administration. This study has focused on the management team of local government—in particular, on the position of chief administrative officer. I hope that it has presented a meaningful perspective on the impact of current changes, and on what some of the costs and benefits of the increasing professionalization of CAOs are likely to be. It does not claim to make inviolate, irrevocable, or irreversible conclusions about the inevitability of current trends. Further, this study has attempted to assess the utility of comparing CAOs serving in community governments recognized by the ICMA—as a specific reference group—against the professional model as it has been evolving within the field of public administration generally. The model's basic dimensions are derived from the values of professionalism represented within the traditionally recognized professions—values of expertise, autonomy, commitment, and responsibility.

However, the traditional measures of professional development were adapted to the circumstances of local government management. These circumstances were the role and function responsibilities identified by most state and city codes, by the ICMA, and by the National Institute of Municipal Law Officers. Thus, the basic set of position elements and job functions of CAOs included: oversight and management of personnel matters, preparation of the budget and other financial reports, acting as the primary law enforcement officer, providing for policy analysis, and otherwise assisting the local council with its deliberations and meetings.[3]

In the ICMA/CAO surveys conducted in 1973–74 and again in 1984, the managers confirmed that budgeting and finance, administration, personnel, and public relations were the most useful areas of educational preparation for becoming a modern manager. And—when managers were asked in the 1980 ICMA/ CAO survey how they evaluated the importance of various skill categories today and for the year 2000—budgeting and finance, management and control of programs, and personnel and labor relations were ranked first, second, and third, respectively. Public relations was again ranked among the top seven in both estimations. It seems clear, therefore, that these are in fact the core skill areas of the CAO occupation. The suggestion that there is no widely shared consensus on what should be considered as a basic set of skills necessary to becoming a professional local government manager is contradicted by analysis of the ICMA/ CAO and Green–Reed survey data.

Particular attention was also paid here to impacts of the environmental changes that have had some influence on public interests in and toward local government, and toward the nature and discharge of the CAOs' duties and responsibilities. Time waits for no man or woman—nor for governments or public officials! Time has brought a considerable amount of change to communities in terms of demographic, economic, technological, social, and political events, shifts, and trends. Other impacts include the changes occurring in advanced and continuing education programs based on evolving management theory, experiences, and expectations. Also scrutinized were possible shifts in the educational, occupational, and personal affiliations and associations of practitioners. Of particular interest were the developments in teaching, learning, enforcement, and professional protection offered and demanded by the occupational codes of ethics and the expanding public service law.

Essentially, we have argued that professional local government managers— like professionals in other occupations—must and have adapted their repertoire of expertise in order to meet the changing times. These adaptations have been attempted—and, it seems, increasingly accomplished—to increase the CAO's professional utility. We conclude that, while changes have indeed been occurring within the auxiliary functions of professional local government managers, this has not happened to any marked extent through a substitution of the traditional core of expertise associated with the field—but, rather, through skill expansion. The diversification of CAO skill seems to be coupled with a necessary delegation of some authorities and responsibilities to better trained and experienced administrative staff. It does not seem to mean—as some had feared—that a basic change in the social, economic, or political context of modern community life has altered the basic core of skills, expertise, or roles associated with and sought from professional local government managers.

However, the move toward greater professionalism among the CAOs in ICMA-recognized communities does not mean—by definition—that, if all communities do not desire or have the same need or ability to pay for professional management, then a profession does not exist because it is not universally mandated by law. In this context, state licensing is not necessarily synonymous with the professional ideal, nor with the existence of a practicing professional cadre of local government managers. State licensing represents but one approach to identifying—and protecting the public's interest and trust in—those who would claim to be professionals. In the field of public administration, licensing may now be genuinely extraneous as a professional criteria, where its essential purpose is already being met in a different manner. Some argue that such a system is present in the evolution of public service law, as well as through the vehicles of governmental and associational codes of ethics—and in the contemporary marketplace, which can now utilize the NASPAA criteria for evaluating professional-level credentials.

While some of the findings in this study reveal stability and consistency, there are also areas of substantial variation among the managers in ICMA-recognized communities. Professional local government managers show a great stability and coherency in the range of managerial styles that they have practiced over the 14-year period of the surveys. But all professionals are not alike—even those who are members of the most traditionally acknowledged occupations of medicine, law, and education. Community and career variables (values) are important considerations in explaining why particular individuals within a particular profession differ or deviate from the dominate professional style (characterized in terms of values, roles, and activities).

A scale of professional mobility was developed to capture and group the CAOs' role orientations through a classification of differences in their career and community attachments. There were, indeed, important differences in role orientations among the managers in the field; but it seems reasonable to consider these differences as measures of professional style and career stage, as well as representing differences in the individual community and the general market—rather than as a disproof of professionalism. When shifts occur in the manager's career or community role orientation, these appear to be associated with transition points in career choice: that is, changes in professional style occur when different stages of professional expectation are either obtained or frustrated.

Perhaps one of the most significant findings to come out of this study is that the types of functions performed by managers do not seem to be predicated on any particular pattern of orientations toward career or community. Regardless of their own career motivations and their levels of personal commitment to individual communities, managers demonstrate a substantial professional commitment to accommodating the particular management deficiencies of their governments. When multiple roles were reported by the CAOs, they were primarily from among the four traditional core skill areas.

Nevertheless, professionalization of the field of local government management is a double-edged sword for practitioners and their communities. In fact, it is in this process—linking the personal world of a local government manager together with the changes occurring in the occupational world—where the real utility of using the professional model becomes most apparent. In this capacity, the model also doubles its utility by establishing a framework for making systematic comparisons possible across occupations. Seeking professionalized personnel is not only a process by which communities acquire and enhance their governmental management capacity; it is also the constant process by which CAOs become aware of and decide on occupational skills and personal capacities that they may need, to supplement their core skills. However, the professionalization taking place within the ranks of our study's CAOs indicates that the process is not static—nor without cost and risk. Rather, it is linked to a wide spectrum of changes and needs confronting both the many different types of communities being served and the various styles of individual managers.

Managers do sense changes and challenges in the workplace differently depending on their ages and the levels of their professional experience. They are also affected by their own career motivations and expectations for career mobility.

The timing and variation in the career development of managers, and their abilities to match professional expectations with job appointments, may result in personal and familial side effects that lead to unequal professional, personal, and family benefits. Occupational mobility seems to be a significant requirement for having a long-term career as a local government CAO. And the mobility factor also reveals a number of important dimensions to the scope and direction of CAO professionalization. That is, local government managers serving in ICMA-recognized communities are facing greater competition among more highly educated and experienced colleagues for proportionately fewer available positions. The frequency and other conditions associated with occupational mobility, then—as well as the expectations and responsibilities of actually being a professional local government manager—represent a number of different and potentially very stressful factors that have a complex influence on the manager's professional capacities, career choices, and longevity.

According to our analysis of the 1986–87 Green–Reed survey, managers perceive the degree of occupationally induced stress under which they labor to be so intense that—even with increasing maturity and after increasing amounts of professional-level experience—they continue to leave the occupation before completing a full work-life career. The timing of career choices and selected aspects of professional preparation seem to be important factors affecting the comparative stress levels felt by local government managers. And variations in perceived levels of occupationally induced stress are ultimately linked with differences in personality types; professional expectations, requirements, and conditions; familial circumstances; and the nature of individual work environments. These are important risk considerations for those charged with evaluating candidates for the CAO position in various community types at different points in time. These factors seem just as important to the individual manager considering career options and strategies.

Analysis of the ICMA/CAO and Green–Reed surveys indicates that there has been a steadily emerging, identifiable, and coherent set of skills and values associated with being a professional local government manager. These occupational features are becoming nationally standardized for public administration and public affairs through the graduate degree accrediting guidelines supervised by NASPAA, via the evolution of public service law, and by competition and the placement of managers in the marketplace. However, the ultimate test of the viability and utility of professionalized local government managers rests with the judgments of the hiring jurisdictions.

A final source of change and evolution in the professionalization of local government management—as examined in this study—is the associational network for qualifying fellow practitioners. Getting an institutional fix on this professionalizing network seems essential to gaining perspective. The notion of institution building was introduced here primarily because of its potential for synthesizing the issues and challenges of professionalization that have been confronting the original vision of the municipal reformers. The worth of the professional association lies not so much in its founding, then, as in the manner in which it performs its functions. But the occupational association is facing a new day in its task to establish, promote, and provide professionalizing standards, status, and services for those whom it identifies as members.

A tripartite set of institutionally based developments and resources was introduced in Chapter 5; this scheme was based primarily on the homogenizing (in the sense of standard- and status-raising) circumstances characterizing the CAOs serving in ICMA-recognized community governments. In this context, we considered the roles of a national network of local government officials' associations, NASPAA-accredited professional degree programs, and other occupational certification processes, as well as the evolution of public service law in relation to the implementation of occupational ethics. Our aim in focusing on this tripartite set of institutional processes was to compare the status quo of professionalization among CAOs currently in the field, with the public service (interest) ideal espoused as the primary rationale for the existence of all professions. One outstanding issue to watch in the future is how the debate over state licensure for selected classifications of public managers will be resolved. Or—that is—whether the current voluntary set of national standards will be maintained through the same informal network of occupational associations. Perhaps a new course will be set; but at this juncture, resolution of the issue is still very much up in the air.

Today's managers must deal with an increasingly sophisticated environment of expanded local and intergovernmental responsibilities, a labyrinth of national networks of established consumer/citizen action groups, as well as a cross section of local government associations. When the institutional attributes of the ICMA are compared with those of other local government management associations, it appears that its membership base and uniqueness; financial stability and staff capacities; service activities, resources, and program offerings; and its interassociational activities, all mark the ICMA as one of the most well established in the public sector—and comparable to many in the private sector. Each of the national organizations in this local government network must meet the tests of survival to remain a force for the professionalization of public service in government. Conflicts and contractions within and between elements of the network, as well as its further institutionalization or expansion, are developments that merit close monitoring.

In fact, further analysis of the tripartite outline describing professionalization suggests that the composition and nature of the network will indeed continue to change. This part of the study adds another interpretation to the issue of associational buildup beyond that presented by Lowi, Wildavsky, and the Walkers. There are likely to be both positive and negative consequences to its evolution. The implications of associational influence on expanding or contracting federal and state intervention into local and individual affairs seems to represent both cause and consequence—and case in point.

However, the availability of a nationally recognized set of postgraduate professional credentials, a more fully institutionalized network of professionalizing associations, and the development and precedence being established through the evolving public service law are all indicators that there have been significant new developments during the past two decades. In this regard, the ICMA's membership, policies, and role seem to be evolving within—and largely in support of—the newer professional constraints of public service law. This conclusion is based on a comprehensive computer search of published federal and state court cases—conducted by the author in 1989. I was unable to locate a single case where the ICMA was a principle party to any litigation concerning antitrust statutes, property rights, copyrights, freedom of information, privacy, codes of ethics, the First Amendment, fair/unfair information practices, computerization or telecommunications, liability and immunity, the right to disobey, whistleblowing, due process, equal protection, or contract-of-employment issues.

The trends noted in this study do not offer any determination about the inevitability of the occupation's achieving unassailable professional standing. While all these changes have been linked to increases in the standards, status, services, and responsibilities of public managers in local government—and the associational network—they are not in any ultimate sense guarantees of professional performance. They do, however, seem to increase its prospects and probabilities. Insofar as the system of higher education has established a national accreditation system for professional degree programs in public administration, and since communities (through the marketplace) have increasingly been able to recruit this level of manager—who often possesses or will secure membership in one or more professional associations—there is evidence that an increasingly professionalized CAO corp is available for service in local government.

As noted, there is always room for improvement, and there will be challenges in adjusting to the unanticipated consequences of current arrangements and to external dynamics. The room for improvement is perhaps best illustrated in the recruitment/placement of M.P.A. graduates, and also in the position exchanges of in-service managers—an area that has been only partially institutionalized. One of the possible consequences of this underdevelopment is that it may lead to further divergence in M.P.A. curricular focus. Such a risk is partially associated with the competitive nature of the job market itself. In the end, this research does not conclude with the sense of futility that some others seem to feel about the usefulness of making a comparison between public sector managers and the professional model. Nor is there disappointment over the level of professional competency available to local communities. Quite the contrary. There seems to have been substantial progress made.

We have attempted to pay particular attention here to factors of stability and to the changes occuring over the past 20 years. And so in conclusion, I hope that this study presents a new perspective on these changes without attempting to provide any final conclusion for what is actually an ongoing story. This type of analysis need not be particularly unique, because there are other complementary resources within the information network of various research, occupational, and governmental associations. Interaction between public administrationists and public administrators is the key to access—and a requirement. In summary, I concur with the remarks of another analyst in the field, when he said that "the involvement and contributions of all [local government] officials will expand in the future. The demands on the manager for a fuller range of competences and heightened sense of responsibility will make the position even more challenging."[4]

## NOTES

1. James H. Svara, "The Rediscovery of Municipal Officials," *Public Administration Review* 48, no. 6 (November/December 1988), pp. 1005–11.

2. Darrel L. Pugh, "Professionalism in Public Administration: Problems, Perspectives, and the Role of ASPA," *Public Administration Review* 49, no. 1 (January/February 1989), pp. 1–8.

3. Doyle W. Buckwalter and J. Ivan Legler, "City Managers and City Attorneys: Associates or Adversaries?" *Public Administration Review* 47, no. 5 (September/October 1987), p. 395.

4. James H. Svara, "Is There a Future for City Managers? The Evolving Roles of Officials in Council–manager Government," *International Journal of Public Administration* 12, no. 2 (1989), p. 207.

# Appendix A

# MANAGERS ON LOCAL GOVERNMENT MANAGEMENT: A BASE OF SURVEY RESEARCH

Research for writing this analysis was completed in two stages. In the winter of 1986–87, this investigator undertook with Professor B. J. Reed—a research colleague at the University of Nebraska—Omaha—a 50 percent random-sample survey of the ICMA listing of recognized communities with professional city, county, and council-of-government managers. The instrument was developed to collect information on five key occupational dimensions thought to be reflective of managerial experience within varying community environments: (1) individual demographic information, (2) career path history, (3) spousal occupational status and family characteristics, (4) professional choice/mobility factors, and (5) occupational stress and conflict factors. The response rate was 67 percent of the mailing sample, or 34 percent of the total number of these professional managers serving in communities recognized by the association.

In the summer of 1986, the International City Management Association provided this writer with their chief administrative officer (CAO) data files from 1973–74, 1980, and 1984 surveys. Each of the three surveys (with response rates never below 50 percent of the association's total listing of managers or directors serving in recognized communities) provided information on individual profiles, career patterns, education and training, employment provisions and benefits, leisure time, work patterns, and responsibilities, as well as the managers' attitudes about the profession's current and future trends.

During the summers of 1986 and 1987, the three ICMA/CAO survey files were merged ("matched") with each other and with the Green–Reed survey conducted in 1986–87. By using the ICMA survey community-identifier system—which allowed for the matching of surveys from the same communities—this writer could make comparisons on the characteristics, perceptions, roles, and activities of different managers serving in the same community over time, and (to a limited extent) could study the evolution of professional local government managers during the course of their careers. The longitudinal component of the study was limited to those managers who stayed in service within a single community for two or more of the survey intervals. The major limitation of data organized in this fashion is that it does not allow the investigator to track individual managers when they change positions, except through the vehicle of their memories. Nonetheless, the information collected from the surveys and integrated in this fashion did allow for an intriguing look into the development of local government management over the past decade and a half.

# Appendix B

# CURRENTLY ACTIVE NETWORK OF LOCAL OFFICIALS' ASSOCIATIONAL AFFILIATIONS: BY PRIMARY MEMBERSHIP, ORGANIZATIONAL NAME, FIELD OF INTEREST, AND FOUNDING DATE/MERGERS

## MUNICIPAL OFFICIALS

1. Association of Major City Building Officials (building codes), 1974
2. Emergency Planning Committee (civil defense), 1950
3. Afro-American Police League (law enforcement), 1968
4. American Federation of Police (law enforcement), 1961
5. American Policy Academy (law enforcement), 1977
6. Committee on Uniform Crime Records (law enforcement), 1930
7. International Association of Chiefs of Police (law enforcement), 1893
8. National Association of Police Organizations (law enforcement), 1979
9. National Black Police Association (law enforcement), 1972
10. National Disabled Law Officers Association (law enforcement), 1971
11. Police Executive Research Forum (law enforcement), 1975
12. Police Foundation (law enforcement), 1970
13. Police Management Association (law enforcement), 1980
14. Police Marksman Association (law enforcement), 1976
15. American Association of Small Cities (municipal government), 1975
16. Hispanic Elected Local Officials (municipal government), 1976
17. National Association of Towns and Townships (municipal government), 1963
18. National Center for Municipal Development (municipal government), 1974
19. National Conference of Black Mayors (municipal government), 1974
20. National Institute of Municipal Law Officers (municipal government), 1935
21. National League of Cities (municipal government), 1924

22. United States Conference of Mayors (municipal government), 1932

23. Women in Municipal Government (municipal government), 1974

24. Association of Metropolitan Water Agencies (natural resources), 1981

25. Municipal Treasurers Association of the U.S. and Canada (public finance), 1965

26. United States Conference of Local Health Officers (public health), 1960

27. International Municipal Signal Association (safety), 1896

## COUNTY OFFICIALS

1. National Association of County Office Employees (agriculture), 1959

2. National Association of County Agricultural Agents (agriculture), 1915

3. Council of Intergovernmental Coordinators (county government), 1966

4. National Association of Black County Officials (county government), 1975

5. National Association of Counties (county government), 1935

6. National Association of County Administrators (county government), 1959

7. National Association of County Civil Attorneys (county government), 1963

8. National Association of County Information Officers (county government), 1965

9. National Association of County Recorders and Clerks (county government), 1948*

10. National Council of County Association Executives (county government), 1967

11. National Council of Elected County Executives (county government), 1970

12. National Organization of Black County Officials (county government), 1975

13. National Association of County Park and Recreation Officials (parks and recreation), 1964

14. National Association of County Planning Directors (planning), 1965

15. National Association of County Treasurers and Finance Officers (public finance), mid–1940s*

16. National Association of County Health Officials (public health), 1965

## INTERGOVERNMENTAL (MIXED) MEMBERSHIP

1. Association of Government Accountants (accounting), 1950

2. Governmental Accounting Standards Board (accounting), 1984

3. Building Officials and Code Administrators International (building codes), 1915

4. Council of American Building Officials (building codes), 1972

5. International Conference of Building Officials (building codes), 1922

6. National Academy of Code Administration (building codes), 1970

7. National Coordinating Council on Emergency Management (civil defense), 1952

8. Blacks in Government (civil service), 1975

9. Council of Jewish Organizations in Civil Service (civil service), 1946

10. National Association of Civil Service Employees (civil service), 1973

11. National Conference on Public Employee Retirement Systems (civil service), 1942

12. Public Employees Roundtable (civil service), 1982

13. National Association of Government Communicators (communications), 1976: 1954/ 1961

14. National Association of Consumer Agency Administrators (consumers), 1976

15. International Association of Clerks, Recorders, Election Officials and Treasurers (county government), 1971

16. Society of Government Economists (economics), 1970

17. International Association of Personnel in Employment Security (employment), 1913

18. Fire Marshals Association of North America (fire fighting), 1906

19. International Association of Arson Investigators (fire fighting), 1951

20. International Fire Service Training Association (fire fighting), 1933

21. Association of Food and Drug Officials (food and drugs), 1897

22. International Narcotic Enforcement Officers Association (food and drugs), 1960

23. American Association of Policy Polygraphists (forensic sciences), 1977

24. International Association for Identification (forensic sciences), 1915

25. Council of Large Public Housing Authorities (public housing), 1981

26. Public Housing Authorities Directors Association (public housing), 1979

27. International Association of Official Human Rights Agencies, (human rights), 1949

28. Federation of Government Information Processing Councils (information management), 1978

29. Government Management Information Sciences (information management), 1971

30. National Association of Government Inspectors and Quality Assurance Personnel (inspectors), 1955

31. National Board of Boiler and Pressure Vessel Inspectors (inspectors), 1919

32. Public Risk and Insurance Management Association (insurance), 1978

33. Society of Professional Investigators (investigation), 1955

34. National Public Employer Labor Relations Association (labor), 1971

35. Law and Society Association (law), 1964

36. Airborne Law Enforcement Association (law enforcement), 1968

37. Commission on Accreditation for Law Enforcement Agencies (law enforcement), 1979

38. International Association of Law Enforcement Firearms Instructors (law enforcement), 1981

39. International Association of Women Police (law enforcement), 1915

40. Justice System Training Association (law enforcement), 1974

41. National Association of Police Community Relations Officers (law enforcement), 1969

42. National Law Enforcement Council (law enforcement), 1978

43. National Organization of Black Law Enforcement Executives (law enforcement), 1976

44. National Police Bloodhound Association (law enforcement), 1962

45. National Police Officers Association of America (law enforcement), 1955

46. National Sheriffs' Association (law enforcement), 1940

47. National United Law Enforcement Officers Association (law enforcement), 1970

48. North American Police Work Dog Association (law enforcement), 1977

49. United States Police Canine Association (law enforcement), 1971

50. International City Management Association (municipal government), 1914

51. International Institute of Municipal Clerks (municipal government), 1947

52. National Black Caucus of Local Elected Officials (municipal government), 1970

53. National Association of Urban Flood Management Agencies (natural resources), 1977

54. American Park Rangers Association (parks and recreation), 1981

55. League of Federal Recreation Associations (parks and recreation), 1958

56. National Association of Development Organizations (planning), 1967

57. American Society for Public Administration (public administration), 1939

58. National Academy of Public Administration (public administration), 1967

59. National Young Professionals Forum (public administration), 1981

60. Public Technology (public administration), 1970

61. Section for Women in Public Administration (public administration), 1971

62. Government Finance Officers Association of United States and Canada (public finance), 1906

63. Association for Vital Records and Health Statistics (public health), 1933

64. American Public Works Association (public works), 1894

65. Association of Metropolitan Sewerage Agencies (public works), 1970

66. National Institute of Governmental Purchasing (purchasing), 1944

67. International Association of Assessing Officers (taxation), 1934

68. National Association of Telecommunications Officers and Advisors (telecommunications), 1980

69. American Public Power Association (utilities), 1940

70. National Resource Recovery Association (waste), 1982

71. National Association of Regional Councils (regional government), 1967

## PUBLIC–PRIVATE SECTOR (JOINT) MEMBERSHIP

1. American Association for Budget and Program Analysis (budgeting), 1976

2. American Civil Defense Association (civil defense), 1962

3. National Emergency Management Association (civil defense), 1950

4. National Association of Blacks within Government (civil service), 1982

5. Fellowship of Christian Firefighters, International (fire fighting), 1978

6. Fire Department Instructors Conference (fire fighting), 1928

7. International Association of Black Professional Fire Fighters (fire fighting), 1970

8. International Association of Fire Chiefs (fire fighting), 1873

9. International Society of Fire Service Instructors (fire fighting), 1960

10. Joint Council of Fire Service Organizations (fire fighting), 1970

11. American Academy of Forensic Sciences (forensic sciences), 1948

12. American Polygraph Association (forensic sciences), 1966

13. American Society of Questioned Document Examiners (forensic sciences), 1942

14. Forensic Sciences Foundation (forensic sciences), 1969

15. International Society of Stress Analysts (forensic sciences), 1973

16. National Health Lawyers Association (health law), 1971

17. Association of Local Housing Finance Agencies (housing), 1982

18. National Association of Housing and Redevelopment Officials, (housing), 1933

19. Public Agency Risk Managers Association (insurance), 1974

20. International Association of Credit Card Investigators (investigation), 1968

21. International Association of Law Enforcement Intelligence Analysts (investigation), 1981

22. International Association Auto Theft Investigators (law enforcement), 1951

23. International Footprint Association (law enforcement), 1929

24. International Law Enforcement Stress Association (law enforcement), 1978

25. Local Government Center (municipal government), 1976

26. National Civic League (municipal government), 1894

27. American Park and Recreation Society (parks and recreation), 1966: 1898/1938

28. American Economic Development Council (planning), 1926

29. American Institute of Certified Planners (planning), 1978

30. American Planning Association (planning), 1978

31. Center for Design Planning (planning), 1973

32. Metropolitan Association of Urban Designers and Environmental Planners (planning), 1968

33. Planning and the Black Community (planning), 1980

34. Urban Land Institute (planning), 1936

35. Association of Management Analysts in State and Local Government (public administration), 1972

36. National Association of Public and Private Employer Negotiators and Administrators (public administration), 1970

37. National Association of Schools of Public Affairs and Administration (public administration), 1970: 1958

38. Council on Municipal Performance (public finance), 1973

39. Associated Public-Safety Communications Officers (safety), 1935

40. React International (safety), 1962

41. National Tax Association–Tax Institute of America (taxation), 1973: 1907/1932

42. National Committee on Uniform Traffic Laws and Ordinances (traffic), 1926

43. International Bridge, Tunnel, and Turnpike Association (transportation), 1932

44. American Clean Water Association (utilities), 1978

45. Governmental Refuse Collection and Disposal Association (waste), 1961

*Note*: The two organizational founding dates with asterisks beside them were provided by the National Association of Counties because they had not been listed with the *Encyclopedia*.

*Source*: Compiled by the author for inclusion in Figure 5.2 from a content analysis of "Section 3: Legal, Governmental, Public Administration, and Military Organizations," in Karin E. Koek and Susan Boyles Martin, eds., *Encyclopedia of Associations 1988*, 22nd ed. (Detroit: Gale Research, 1988), vol. 1, pt. 1, pp. 437–508.

# BIBLIOGRAPHY

## BOOKS

Anderson, Wayne F., Chester A. Newland, and Richard J. Stillman II. *The Effective Local Government Manager*. Municipal Management Series. Washington, D.C.: International City Management Association, 1983.

Argyris, Chris, and D. A. Schon. *Theory in Practice: Increasing Professional Effectiveness*. San Francisco: Jossey-Bass Publishers, 1974.

Banfield, Edward C., and James Q. Wilson. *City Politics*. New York: Vintage Books, 1963.

Barfield, Claude E. *Rethinking Federalism: Block Grants and Federal, State, and Local Responsibilities*. Washington, D.C.: American Enterprise Institute for Public Policy Research, 1981.

Barnard, Chester. *The Functions of the Executive*. Cambridge, Mass.: Harvard University Press, 1938.

Bell, Daniel. "The Measurement of Knowledge and Technology." In *Indicators of Change*, edited by B. Sheldon and Wilbert E. Moore, 145–246. New York: Russell Sage Foundation, 1968.

Bledstein, Burton J. *The Culture of Professionalism: The Middle Class and the Development of Higher Education in America*. New York: W. W. Norton, 1976.

Bloom, Allan. *The Closing of the American Mind*. New York: Simon and Schuster, 1987.

Bok, Sissela. *Lying: Moral Choice in Public and Private Life*. New York: Vintage Books, 1978.

Booth, David A. *Council–Manager Government in Small Cities*. ICMA Research Reports. Washington, D.C.: International City Management Association, 1968.

Bozeman, Barry. *Public Management and Policy Analysis*. New York: St. Martin's Press, 1979.

Bradbury, Katharine L., Anthony Downs, and Kenneth A. Small. *Urban Decline and the Future of American Cities*. Washington, D.C.: Brookings Institution, 1982.

Brown, Lawrence D., James W. Fossett, and Kenneth T. Palmer. *The Changing Politics of Federal Grants*. Washington, D.C.: Brookings Institution, 1984.

Burke, John P. *Bureaucratic Responsibility*. Baltimore: Johns Hopkins University Press, 1986.

Burke, W. Warner. *Organizational Development: Principles and Practices*. Boston: Little, Brown, 1982.

Burns, Ruth Ann. "Women in Municipal Management: Opportunities and Barriers." In *Municipal Year Book 1981*, 167–73. Washington, D.C.: International City Management Association, 1981.

Caiden, Gerald E. *The Dynamics of Public Administration: Guidelines to Current Transformations in Theory and Practice*. Hinsdale, Ill.: Dryden Press, 1971.

Carr-Saunders, A. M., and P. A. Wilson. "The Historical Development of Professional Associations." In *Professionalization*, edited by Howard M. Vollmer and Donald L. Mills, 153–58. Englewood Cliffs, N.J.: Prentice-Hall, 1966.

Davis, Kenneth. *Administrative Law and Government*. St. Paul, Minn.: West Publishing, 1975.

Eads, George C., and Michael Fix, eds. *The Reagan Regulatory Strategy: An Assessment*. Washington, D.C.: Urban Institute Press, 1984.

Edelman, Murray. *The Symbolic Uses of Politics*. Chicago: University of Illinois Press, 1964.

Fainstein, Susan S., et al. *Restructuring the City: The Political Economy of Urban Redevelopment*. New York: Longman, 1983.

Fink, Stephen S., Stephen Jenks, and Robin D. Willits. *Designing and Managing Organizations*. Homewood, Ill.: Richard D. Irwin, 1983.

Floyd, Michael. *Policy-making and Planning in Local Government: A Cybernetic Perspective*. Brookfield, Vt.: Gower Publishing, 1984.

Fosler, R. Scott, and Renee A. Berger, eds. *Public–Private Partnership in American Cities: Seven Case Studies*. Lexington, Mass.: Lexington Books, 1982.

French, Wendell L., and Cecil H. Bell, Jr. *Organizational Development: Behavioral Science Interventions for Organizational Improvement*, 3rd ed. Englewood Cliffs, N.J.: Prentice-Hall, 1984.

Frendreis, J. P. "Patterns of Reputation and Personal Interaction among City Managers." In *Municipal Year Book 1981*, 159–62. Washington, D.C.: International City Management Association, 1981.

Golembiewski, Robert T. *Public Administration as a Developing Discipline*, Part 2: *Organizational Development as One of a Future Family of Miniparadigms*. New York: Marcel Dekker, 1977.

Goode, William J. "The Theoretical Limits of Professionalization." In *The Semi-professions and Their Organizations: Teachers, Nurses, Social Workers*, edited by Amitai Etzioni, 299–313. New York: Free Press, 1969.

Gordon, George J. *Public Administration in America*, 3rd ed. New York: St. Martin's Press, 1986.

Green, Roy E., and B. J. Reed. "Occupational Stress and Mobility among Professional Local Government Managers: A Decade of Change." In *Municipal Year Book 1988*, 35–42. Washington, D.C.: International City Management Association, 1988.

Grosenick, Leigh E. "Institutional Change to Improve State and Local Competencies." In *The Administration of the New Federalism: Objectives and Issues*, edited by

Leigh E. Grosenick, p. 91. Washington, D.C.: American Society for Public Administration, 1973.

Gross, Edward. *Work and Society*. New York: Thomas Y. Crowell, 1958.

Guy, Mary E. *Professionals in Organizations: Debunking a Myth*. New York: Praeger Publishers, 1985.

Hackman, J., and G. Oldham. *Work Redesign*. Reading, Mass.: Addison-Wesley, 1980.

Hall, Richard H. *Occupations and the Social Structure*. Englewood Cliffs, N.J.: Prentice-Hall, 1969.

Harlow, LeRoy F. *Servants of All: Professional Management of City Government*. Provo, Utah: Brigham Young University Press, 1981.

Harrigan, John J. *Political Change in the Metropolis*, 3rd ed. Boston: Little, Brown, 1985.

Haskell, Thomas L., ed. *The Authority of Experts: Studies in History and Theory*. Bloomington: Indiana University Press, 1984.

Hauptman, Arthur M. *Students in Graduate and Professional Education: What We Know and Need to Know*. Washington, D.C.: Association of American Universities, 1986.

Hawley, Amos H., and Sara Mills Mazie, eds. *Nonmetropolitan America in Transition*. Chapel Hill: University of North Carolina Press, 1981.

Henry, Nicholas. *Public Administration and Public Affairs*. Englewood Cliffs, N.J.: Prentice-Hall, 1975.

Hirsch, E. D., Jr. *Cultural Literacy: What Every American Needs to Know*. Boston: Houghton Mifflin, 1987.

Horton, Forest Woody, Jr., ed. *Understanding U.S. Information Policy: The Information Policy Primer*. Washington, D.C.: Information Industry Association, 1982.

Houle, Cyril O. *Continuing Learning in the Professions*. Jossey-Bass Series in Higher Education. San Francisco: Jossey-Bass Publishers, 1980.

Howitt, Arnold M., and Beth Walter Honadle. "Conclusion." In *Perspectives on Management Capacity Building*, edited by Arnold M. Howitt and Beth Walter Honadle, 334–41. Albany: State University of New York Press, 1986.

Huntley, Robert J., and Robert J. Macdonald. "Urban Managers: Organizational Preferences, Managerial Styles, and Social Roles." In *Municipal Year Book 1975*, 151–59. Washington, D.C.: International City Management Association, 1975.

Huse, Edgar F., and Thomas G. Cummings. *Organizational Development and Change*, 3rd ed. St. Paul, Minn.: West Publishing, 1985.

Illchman, Warren F., and Norman T. Uphoff. *The Political Economy of Change*. Berkeley: University of California Press, 1969.

International City Management Association. *FYI: Resources on Local Government 1983–85*. Washington, D.C.: International City Management Association, 1986.

———. "Inside the Yearbook." In the introduction of the *Municipal Year Book 1985*, xvii and xviii. Washington, D.C.: International City Management Association, 1985.

———. "Inside the Yearbook." In the introduction of the *Municipal Year Book 1988*, xii. Washington, D.C.: International City Management Association, 1988.

Jackson, J. A., ed. *Professions and Professionalization*. Sociological Studies, no. 3. New York: Cambridge University Press, 1970.

Jennings, Edward T., Jr., Dale Krane, Alex N. Pattakos, and B. J. Reed, eds. *From*

*Nation to States: The Small Cities Community Development Block Grant Program.* Albany: State University of New York Press, 1986.

Judd, Dennis R. *The Politics of American Cities: Private Power and Public Policy*, 2nd ed. Boston: Little, Brown, 1984.

Kanter, Rosabeth Moss. *The Change Masters.* New York: Simon and Schuster, 1983.

Kaufman, H. G. *Professionals in Search of Work: Coping with the Stress of Job Loss and Underemployment.* New York: John Wiley and Sons, 1982.

Kaufman, Herbert. *The Forest Ranger: A Study in Administrative Behavior.* Baltimore: Johns Hopkins University Press, 1960.

Kelly, John E. *Scientific Management, Job Redesign, and Work Performance.* London: Academic Press, 1982.

Kharasch, Robert N. *The Institutional Imperative: How to Understand the United States Government and Other Bulky Objects.* New York: Charterhouse Books, 1973.

Kirkpatrick, Jeane. *Private Virtues Public Vices.* Ethics and Public Policy Essay 41. Washington, D.C.: Ethics and Public Policy Center, 1982.

Koek, Karin E., Susan B. Martin, and Annette Novallo, eds. "Section 3: Legal, Governmental, Public Administration, and Military Organizations." *Encyclopedia of Associations: 1988*, 437–808. Detroit: Gale Research, 1988.

Larson, Magali Sarfatti. *The Rise of Professionalism.* Berkeley: University of California Press, 1977.

Lazarus, R. S. *Patterns of Adjustment*, 3rd ed. New York: McGraw-Hill, 1976.

Le Breton, Preston P., ed. *The Assessment and Development of Professionals: Theory and Practice.* Seattle: University of Washington, 1976.

Levy, John M. *Economic Development Program for Cities, Counties, and Towns.* New York: Praeger Publishers, 1981.

Liebert, Roland J. *Disintegration and Political Action: The Changing Functions of City Governments in America.* New York: Academic Press, 1976.

Little, Thomas C., ed. *Making Sponsored Experiential Learning Standard Practice.* New Directions for Experiential Learning Series, no. 20. San Francisco: Jossey-Bass Publishers, 1983.

Loveridge, Ronald O. *City Managers in Legislative Politics.* New York: Bobbs-Merrill, 1971.

Lowi, Theodore J. *The End of Liberalism: The Second Republic of the United States*, 2nd ed. New York: W. W. Norton, 1979.

Lustig, R. Jeffrey. *Corporate Liberalism: The Origins of American Political Theory 1890–1920.* Berkeley: University of California Press, 1982.

McCurdy, Howard E. *Public Administration: A Synthesis.* Menlo Park, Calif.: Cummings Publishing, 1977.

McLean, P. D. "Depressions as a Specific Response to Stress." In *Stress and Anxiety*, Volume 3, edited by T. G. Sarason and C. D. Spielberger, 708. New York: John Wiley and Sons, 1976.

Marando, Vincent L., and Robert D. Thomas. *The Forgotten Governments: County Commissioners as Policy Makers.* Gainesville: University Presses of Florida, 1977.

Martin, David L. *Running City Hall: Municipal Administration in America.* Tuscaloosa: University of Alabama Press, 1982.

Mayhew, Lewis B. *Changing Practices in Education for the Professions.* Southern Regional Education Board Research Monograph, no. 17. Atlanta: Southern Regional Education Board, 1971.

Meier, Kenneth J. *Regulation: Politics, Bureaucracy, and Economics*. New York: St. Martin's Press, 1985.

Moore, Barbara H., ed. *The Entrepreneur in Local Government*. Practical Management Series. Washington, D.C.: International City Management Association, 1983.

Morgan, David R. *Managing Urban America: The Politics and Administration of American Cities*. North Scituate, Mass.: Duxbury Press, 1979.

Mosher, Frederick. *Democracy and the Public Service*. New York: Oxford University Press, 1982.

Naisbitt, John. *Megatrends: Ten New Directions Transforming Our Lives*. New York: Warner Books, 1984.

Nyre, Glenn F., and Kathryn C. Reilly. *Professional Education in the Eighties: Challenges and Responses*. AAHE-ERIE/Higher Education Research Report, no. 8. Washington D.C.: American Association for Higher Education, 1979.

Oldham, G., and J. Hackman. "Work Design in the Organizational Context." In *Research in Organizational Behavior*, edited by B. Staw and L. Cummings, 2 vols. Greenwich, Conn.: JAI Press, 1980.

Palmer, John L., and Isabel V. Sawhill, eds. *The Reagan Experiment: An Examination of Economic and Social Politics under the Reagan Administration*. Washington, D.C.: Urban Institute Press, 1982.

———. *The Reagan Record: An Assessment of America's Changing Domestic Priorities*. Cambridge, Mass.: Ballinger Publishing, 1984.

Pavalko, Ronald M. *Sociology of Occupations and Professions*. Itasca, Ill.: F. E. Peacock Publishers, 1971.

Porter, Paul R., and David C. Sweet, eds. *Rebuilding American Cities: Roads to Recovery*. New Brunswick, N.J.: Center for Urban Policy Research, 1984.

Quick, James C., and Jonathan D. Quick. *Organizational Stress and Preventive Management*. New York: McGraw-Hill, 1984.

Rapp, Brian W., and Frank M. Patitucci. *Managing Local Government for Improved Performance: A Practical Approach*. Boulder, Colo.: Westview Press, 1977.

Ridley, Clarence E., and Orin F. Nolting. *The City Manager Profession*. Chicago: University of Chicago Press, 1934.

Ritterbush, Philip C., ed. *Talent Waste: How Institutions of Learning Misdirect Human Resources*. Washington, D.C.: Acropolis Books, 1972.

Ritzer, George. *Man and His Work: Conflict and Change*. New York: Meredith Corporation, 1972.

Rosenbloom, David H. *Public Administration and the Law*. New York: Marcel Dekker, 1983.

Ross, Michael J. *State and Local Politics and Policy: Change and Reform*. Englewood Cliffs, N.J.: Prentice-Hall, 1987.

Rueschemeyer, Marilyn. *Professional Work and Marriage: An East–West Comparison*. New York, St. Martin's Press, 1981.

Rutter, Laurence. *The Essential Community: Local Government in the Year 2000*. Municipal Management Series. Washington, D.C.: International City Management Association, 1980.

Schein, Edgar H. *Professional Education: Some New Directions*. Series of Profiles Sponsored by the Carnegie Commission on Higher Education, no. 10. New York: McGraw-Hill, 1972.

Schellinger, Mary A. "Local Government Managers: Profile of the Professionals in a

Maturing Profession." In *Municipal Year Book 1985*, 181–93. Washington, D.C.: International City Management Association, 1985.

Schultze, William A. *Urban Politics: A Political Economy Approach.* Englewood Cliffs, N.J.: Prentice-Hall, 1985.

Sharkansky, Ira. *The United States: A Study of a Developing Country.* New York: David McKay, 1975.

Slayton, Philip, and Michael J. Trebilcock, eds. *The Professions and Public Policy.* Toronto: University of Toronto Press, 1978.

Solomon, Arthur P., ed. *The Prospective City: Economic, Population, Energy, and Environmental Developments.* Cambridge, Mass.: MIT Press, 1980.

tern, Milton R., ed. *Power and Conflict in Continuing Professional Education.* Belmont, Calif.: Wadsworth Publishing/Continuing Education, 1983.

Stever, James. *The End of Public Administration: Problems of the Profession in the Post-Progressive Era.* Dobbs Ferry, N.Y.: Transnational Publishers, 1988.

Stillman, Richard J., II. *The Rise of the City Manager: A Public Professional in Local Government.* Albuquerque: University of New Mexico Press, 1974.

———. "Local Public Management in Transition: A Report on the Current State of the Profession." In *Municipal Year Book 1982*, 162–73. Washington, D.C.: International City Management Association, 1982.

Stone, Clarence N., Robert K. Whelan, and William J. Murin. *Urban Policy and Politics in a Bureaucratic Age*, 2nd ed. Englewood Cliffs, N.J.: Prentice-Hall, 1986.

Szanton, Peter. *Not Well Advised.* New York: Russell Sage Foundation and Ford Foundation, 1981.

Tabachnik, Barbara G., and Linda S. Fidell. *Using Multivariate Statistics.* New York: Harper and Row, 1983.

Taylor, Frederick. *The Principles of Scientific Management.* New York: Harper and Row, 1911.

Thomas, D. Woods, et al. *Institution Building.* Cambridge, Mass.: Schenkman Publishing, 1973.

Toffler, Alvin. *Future Shock.* New York: Random House, 1970.

Verba, Sidney, and Norman H. Nie. *Participation in America: Political Democracy and Social Equality.* New York: Harper and Row, 1972.

Vollmer, Howard M., and Donald L. Mills, eds. *Professionalization.* Englewood Cliffs, N.J.: Prentice-Hall, 1966.

Walker, David B. *Toward a Functioning Federalism.* Boston: Little, Brown, 1981.

Weitzen, H. Skip. *Turning Data into Dollars.* New York: John Wiley and Sons, 1988.

Wildavsky, Aaron. *Speaking Truth to Power: The Art and Craft of Policy Analysis.* Boston: Little, Brown, 1979.

Wilson, James Q. *The Amateur Democrat: Club Politics in Three Cities.* Chicago: University of Chicago Press, 1968.

Wolfinger, Raymond E. *The Politics of Progress.* Englewood Cliffs, N.J.: Prentice-Hall, 1974.

Zeigler, Harmon, Ellen Kehoe, and Jane Reisman. *City Managers and School Superintendents: Response to Community Conflict.* New York: Praeger Publishers, 1985.

## ARTICLES AND PERIODICALS

Abney, Glenn. "Local Chief Executives: Roles in the Intergovernmental Administrative Process." *Administration and Society* 11, no. 4 (February 1980):393–410.

Abney, Glenn, and Thomas P. Lauth. "Councilmanic Intervention in Municipal Administration." *Administration and Society* 13, no. 4 (February 1982):435–49.

———. "Influence of the Chief Executive on City Line Agencies." *Public Administration Review* 42, no. 2 (March/April 1982):135–43.

Adams, J. D. "Improving Stress Management." *Social Change: Ideas and Applications* 8, no. 4 (1978):1–4, 9–12.

Adrian, Charles R., and James F. Sullivan. "The Urban Appointed Chief Executive, Past and Emergent." *Urban Interest* 1, no. 1 (Spring 1979):3–9.

Aleshire, Fran. "Moving Again." *Public Management* 59, no. 10 (October 1977):5–7.

Allan, Peter, and Stephen Rosenberg. "Getting a Managerial Performance Appraisal System Under Way: New York City's Experience." *Public Administration Review* 40, no. 4 (July/August 1980):371–79.

Almy, Timothy A. "Local–Cosmopolitanism and U.S. City Managers." *Urban Affairs Quarterly* 10, no. 3 (March 1975):243–72.

Ammons, David N., and James J. Glass. "Headhunters in Local Government: Use of Executive Search Firms in Managerial Selection." *Public Administration Review* 48, no. 3 (May/June 1988):687–93.

Ammons, David N., and Joseph C. King. "Professionalism and Local Government Administration." *American Review of Public Administration* 16, no. 4 (Winter 1982):386–401.

Anna, Henry J. "The Agency Perspective and the Future of Local Government Administration." *International Journal of Public Administration* 12, no. 2 (1989):251–63.

"ASPA [American Society for Public Administration] Code of Ethics Guidelines." *Bureaucrat* 14, no. 4 (Winter 1985):27–29.

Axelrod, Regina. "Decentralized Service Delivery: Role of the District Manager." *National Civic Review* 69, no. 6 (June 1980):321–22.

Azzaretto, John F., Howard Smith, and Judith Mohr. "The Role of Higher Education in Training and Development for Local Governments." *State and Local Government Review* 13, no. 2 (May 1981):62–68.

Banfield, Edward C. "Corruption as a Feature of Governmental Organization." *Journal of Law and Economics* 18, no. 3 (December 1975):587–605.

Barnett, Camille Cates. "The Ox and Me: A View from Atop an Organization." *Public Administration Review* 44, no. 6 (November/December 1984):525–30.

Beer, Samuel. "Federalism, Nationalism, and Democracy in America." *America Political Science Review* 72 (1978):9–21.

Bennett, James T., and Manuel H. Johnson. "Tax Reduction without Sacrifice: Private Sector Produce of Public Services." *Public Finance Quarterly* 8, no. 4 (October 1980):363–96.

Bennett, L. "City Politics in the 1970's: The Struggle for Control of Shrinking Public Services." *Urbanism Past and Present* 6 (Summer/Fall 1981):40–49.

Bergmann, Thomas J., Joyce L. Grahn, and Robert Wyatt. "Relationship of Employment Status to Employee Job Satisfaction." *Akron Business and Economic Review* 17, no. 2 (Summer 1986):45–51.

Berman, David R., and Bruce D. Merrill. "Citizen Attitudes toward Municipal Reform Institutions: A Testing of Some Assumptions." *Western Political Quarterly* 29, no. 2 (June 1976):274–83.

Besuden, William E. "The Profession's Heritage: The ICMA Code of Ethics." *Public Management* 63, no. 3 (March 1981):2–5.

Biller, Dr. Robert P. "Turning Conflicts into Challenges." *Public Management* 64, no. 1 (January 1982):2–4.

Black, Richard L. "Full Partnership for Counties." *Public Management* 63, no. 12 (December 1981):2–4.

Blumenauer, Earl, Donn Shelton, and Charles Watt, Jr. "Regional Solutions for Local Government." *National Civic Review* 68, no. 6 (June 1979):292–95.

Bobowski, Rita Cipalla. "Molding the New Breed Public Officials." *American Education* 13, no. 10 (December 1977):22–27.

Borgsdorf, Del D. "The Small City Scene." *Public Management* 59, no. 9 (September 1977):11–13.

Bowles, Samuel. "Relations of State to Municipal Government and the Reform of the Latter." *Journal of Social Science* 9 (January 1878):140–46.

Bowman, James S. "Ethics and the Public Service: A Selected and Annotated Bibliography." *Public Personnel Management Journal* 10 (1981):179–199.

———. "The Management of Ethics: Codes of Conduct in Organization." *Public Personnel Management Journal* 10 (1981):59–66.

Boyle, John, and David Jacobs. "The Intracity Distribution of Services: A Multivariate Analysis." *American Political Science Review* 76, no. 2 (June 1982):371–79.

Boyton, Robert Paul, and Deil S. Wright. "Mayor–Manager Relationships in the Large Council–Manager Cities: A Reinterpretation." *Public Administration Review* 31, no. 1 (January/February 1971):28–36.

Brady, Neil. "Conceptual Skills and the Public Administrator: Good Judgement and the Logic of Principles." *American Review of Public Administration* 16, no. 1 (Spring 1982):3–14.

Brint, Steven. " 'New-Class' and Cumulative Trend Explanations of the Liberal Political Attitudes of Professionals." *American Journal of Sociology* 90, no. 1 (1984):30–71.

Brown, Anthony. "Technical Assistance to Rural Communities: Stopgap or Capacity Building?" *Public Administration Review* 40, no. 1 (January/February 1980):18–23.

Brown, Brack. "Purpose and Pedagogy for Courses about Change and Innovation." *Teaching Political Science* 11, no. 2 (Winter 1983–84):70–77.

Brown, Robert W. "The Black Tax: Stresses Confronting Black Federal Executives." *Journal of Afro-American Issues* 3, no. 2 (Spring 1975):207–18.

Brudney, Jeffrey L., and Robert E. England. "Analyzing Citizen Evaluations of Municipal Services: A Dimensional Approach." *Urban Affairs Quarterly* 17, no. 3 (March 1982):359–69.

Buckwalter, Doyle W. "Dillon's Rule in the 1980's: Who's in Charge of Local Affairs?" *National Civic Review* 71, no. 8 (September 1982):399–406.

Buckwalter, Doyle W., and J. Ivan Legler. "City Managers and City Attorneys: Associates or Adversaries?" *Public Administration Review* 47, no. 5 (September/October 1987):393–95.

Bunker, Barbara Benedict, and Edith Whitfield Seashore. "Breaking the Sex Role Stereotypes." *Public Management* 57, no. 7 (July 1975):5–11.

Burgess, Philip M. "Capacity Building and the Elements of Public Management." *Public Administration Review* 35, Special Issue (December 1975):705–16.

Caiden, Gerald E. "Ethics in the Public Service: Codification Misses the Real Target." *Public Personnel Management Journal* 10 (1981):146–52.

Cartwright, John. "Experience of a Small City in Managing the Consultant Process." *Public Administration Review* 39, no. 3 (May/June 1979):214–18.

Chandler, Ralph Clark. "The Problem of Moral Illiteracy in Professional Discourse: The Case of the Statement of Principles of the American Society for Public Administration." *American Review of Public Administration* 16, no. 4 (Winter 1982):369–86.

Cherniss, Cary, and Jeffrey S. Kane. "Public Sector Professionals: Job Characteristics, Satisfaction, and Aspirations for Intrinsic Fulfillment through Work." *Human Relations* 40, no. 3 (1987):125–36.

Cleveland, Harlan. "Control the Twilight of Hierarchy." *New Management* 3 (Fall 1985):14–21.

Conklin, Hal. "A View from the Top." *Public Management* 69, no. 2 (February 1987):9–10.

Cooper, Harlan T. "Service-learning through Internships and Research for State Government," *New Directions for Higher Education* 5, no. 18 (Summer 1977):37–52.

Cooper Phillip J. "Government Contracts in Public Administration: The Role and Environment of the Contracting Officer." *Public Administration Review* 40, no. 5 (September/October 1980):459–68.

———. "Conflict or Constructive Tension: The Changing Relationship of Judges and Administrators." *Public Administration Review* 45, Special Issue (November 1985):643–52.

Coulter, Philip B. "Measuring the Inequity of Urban Public Service: A Methodological Discussion with Applications." *Policy Studies Journal* 8, no. 5 (Spring 1980):683–97.

Cranston, Ross F. "Regulating Conflict of Interest of Public Officials: A Comparative Analysis." *Vanderbilt Journal of Transitional Law* 12 (Spring 1979):212–16.

Davis, Michael. "The Use of Professions." *Business Economics* 22, no. 4 (October 1987):5–10.

DeCarlo, D. T. "Compensating Stress in the '80s." *Insurance Counsel Journal* (October 1985):681–87.

Deeb, Michael S. "Municipal Council Members: Changing Roles and Functions." *National Civic Review* 68, no. 8 (September 1979):411–16.

DeMarie, Gene A. "Manager Mobility: What the ICMA Newsletter Can Tell You." *Public Management* 59, no. 10 (October 1977):8–11.

Denhardt, Robert B. " Public Administration: Sub-Field? Profession? Discipline?" *American Review of Public Administration* 16, no. 1 (Spring 1982):15–21.

Dersin, A. "What Kind of Schools for Public Management? The State of Affairs in the USA, 1980." *International Review Administrative Sciences* 47, no. 2 (November 2, 1981):151–69.

De Young, Tim, and Bruce J. Perlman. "Teaching Research Methodology in Public Administration." *Teaching Political Science* 11, no. 2 (Winter 1983–84):63–69.

Donaldson, William V. "Continuing Education for City Managers." *Public Administration Review* 33, no. 6 (November/December 1973):504–8.

Dugan, Terry. "The Statewide Association's Role in Training and Development for Local Government." *State and Local Government* 13, no. 2 (May 1981):51–56.

Dunn, Delmer D., Frank K. Gibson, and Joseph W. Whorton, Jr. "University Commitment to Public Service for Local Governments." *Public Administration Review* 45, no. 4 (July/August 1985):503–9.

Durant, Robert F., and William A. Taggart. "Mid-career Students in MPA Programs: Implications for Pre-service Student Education." *Public Administration Review* 45, no. 2 (March/April 1985):301–8.

Dwivedi, O. P. "Ethics and Values of Public Responsibility and Accountability." *International Review of Administrative Sciences* 51, no. 1 (1985):61–66.

Eadie, Douglas C. "Putting a Powerful Tool to Practical Use: The Application of Strategic Planning in the Public Sector." *Public Administration Review* 43, no. 5 (September/October 1983):447–52.

Eastland, Michael R. "Stretching Services to Fit Available Revenue." *Public Management* 63, no. 6 (June 1981):8–9.

Edwards, J. Terry, and Thomas D. Galloway. "Freedom and Equality: Dimensions of Political Ideology among City Planners and City Managers." *Urban Affairs Quarterly* 17, no. 2 (December 1981):173–93.

Edwards, J. Terry, John Nalbandian, and Kenneth R. Wedel. "Individual Values and Professional Education: Implication for Practice and Education." *Administration and Society* 13, no. 2 (August 1981):123–43.

Epstein, Paul D., and Alan Leidner. "Technology Transfer in the Trenches." *National Civic Review* 76, no. 1 (January/February 1978):130–36.

Esman, Milton J., and John D. Montgomery. "Systems Approaches to Technical Cooperation: The Role of Development Administration." *Public Administration Review* 29, no. 5 (September/October):507–39.

Eulau, Heinz. "Skill Revolution and Consultative Commonwealth." *American Political Science Review* 67 (1973):169–91.

Evans, Richard, and Robert Weinstein. "Ranking Occupations as Risky Income Prospects." *Industrial and Labor Relations Review* 35, no. 2 (January 1982):252–59.

Fannin, William R., and Don C. Moore. "Preparing for City Management Careers: What's Important?" *American Review of Public Administration* 17, no. 2/3 (Summer/Fall 1983):79–90.

Finkle, Arthur L. "A Discipline in Search of Legitimacy." *Bureaucrat* 13, no. 2 (Summer 1984):58–60.

Fisher, Fred. "The New Entrepreneurs: Public, Persistent, and Prevailing in the Decade Ahead." *Public Management* 63, no. 6 (June 1981):2–7.

Fletcher, Thomas W. "Is Consolidation the Answer?" *Public Management* 62, no. 4 (May 1980):15–17.

Fosler, R. Scott. "Providing Community Services: What Role for Whom?" *National Civic Review* 71, no. 6 (June 1982):288–97.

Foster, Gregory D. "Law, Morality, and the Public Servant." *Public Administration Review* 41, no. 1 (January/February):29–34.

Frazier, Mark. "Privatizing the City." *Policy Review* 12 (Spring 1980):91–108.

Fredrickson, H. George. "The Lineage of New Public Administration." *Administration and Society* 8, no. 2 (August 1976):149–74.

Gadbaw, Holly. "The C–M Plan Works: A Case in Point." *Public Management* 69, no. 2 (February 1987): 7–8.

Galloway, T. D., and J. T. Edwards. "Critically Examining the Assumptions of Espoused

Theory: The Case of City Planning and Management." *American Plan Association Journal* 48 (Spring 1982):184–89.

Gargan, John J. "Consideration of Local Government Capacity." *Public Administration Review* 41, no. 6 (November/December 1981):649–58.

Gilliland, Nancy C. "The Problem of Geographic Mobility for Dual Career Families." *Journal of Comparative Family Studies* 10, no. 3 (Autumn 1979):345–58.

Gold, Kenneth A. "Managing for Success: Comparison of the Private and Public Sectors." *Public Administration Review* 42, no. 6 (November/December 1982):568–75.

Golembiewski, Robert T. "Toward Professional Certification?" *Bureaucrat* 12, no. 2 (Summer 1983):50–55.

———. "Professionalization, Performance, and Protectionism: A Contingency View." *Public Productivity Review* 7, no. 3 (September 1983):251–68.

———. "The Pace and Character of Public Sector Professionalization: Six Selected Questions." *State and Local Government Review* 16, no. 2 (Spring 1984):63–68.

Goode, S. "The Changing Nature of Local Government Liability under Section 1983." *Urban Law Annual* 22 (1981):71–104.

Goode, William J. "Community within a Community: The Professions." *American Sociological Review* 22, no. 2 (April 1957):194–200.

Gray, Richard N. "Ethical Problems at the State Level." *Public Management* 63, no. 3 (March 1981):17–18.

Green, Roy E., and B. J. Reed. "A Perspective on Small City Development: Local Assessments of Grant Management Capacity." *Urban Affairs Papers* 2, no. 3 (Summer 1980):23–36.

Greene, Kenneth R. "Municipal Administrators' Receptivity to Citizens and Elected Officials' Contracts." *Public Administration Review* 42, no. 4 (July/August 1982):346–53.

Greenhill, Muriel, Charles Metz, and Philip Stander. "Performance Based Public Administration: A Viable Approach to Adult Learning." *Teaching Political Science* 9, no. 4 (Summer 1982):197–204.

———. "The Case for Competence-based Public Administration Curriculum for Urban Managers." *Alternative Higher Education: The Journal of Non-traditional Studies* 7, no. 1 (Fall/Winter 1982):27–43.

Greenwood, Ernest. "Attributes of a Profession." *Social Work* 2, no. 3 (July 1957):45–55.

Grizzle, Gloria A. "Essential Skills for Financial Management: Are MPA Students Acquiring the Necessary Competencies?" *Public Administration Review* 45, no. 6 (November/December 1985): 840–44.

Guess, George M. "Toward a Theory of Public Administration Instruction." *Teaching Political Science* 11, no. 2 (Winter 1983–84):54–62.

Gundry, K. G., and T. A. Heberlein. "Do Public Meetings Repress the Public?" *Journal of American Planning Association* 50 (Spring 1984):175–82.

Gunn, Elizabeth M. "Ethics and the Public Service: An Annotated Bibliography and Overview Essay." *Public Personnel Management Journal* 10, (1981):172–78.

Gunnell, John G. "Reflections on Public Policy and Academic Discourse." *Teaching Political Science* 11, no. 2 (Winter 1983–84):84–87.

Halachmi, Arie. "Evaluating Training Policy in Local Governments." *State and Local Government Review* 13, no. 1 (January 1981):33–37.

Halperin, Michael J. "The Relevance of Public Administration Education in the 1980's." *American Review of Public Administration* 16, no. 2/3 (Summer/Fall 1983):261–64.

Harper, Robert. "Black Administrators and Administrative Law." *Journal of Afro-American Issues* 3, no. 2 (Spring 1975):173–79.

Harris, Charles. "COG's: A Region Response to Metro-Urban Problems." *Growth and Change* 6, no. 3 (July 1975):9–15.

Hatry, Harry P. "Would We Know a Well-Governed City If We Saw One?" *National Civic Review* 75, no. 3 (May/June 1986):142–46.

Haug, Marie R. "The Deprofessionalization of Everyone?" *Sociological Focus* 8, no. 3 (August 1975):197–213.

Hein, C. J. "Contracting Municipal Services: Does It Really Cost Less?" *National Civic Review* 72, no. 6 (June 1983):321–26.

Henderson, Dee W. "Enlightened Mentoring: A Characteristic of Public Management Professionalism." *Public Administration Review* 45, no. 6 (November/December 1985):857–63.

Henning, Kenneth K. "Certification as a Recognition of Professional Development." *State and Local Review* 13, no. 2 (May 1981):69–72.

Heper, Metin. "Notes on Public Administration 'Training' for the Potential Bureaucratic Elites of the Transitional Societies." *Social Science Journal* 27, no. 1 (1975):163–73.

Herbert, Adam W. "The Evolving Challenges of Black Urban Administration." *Journal of Afro-American Issues* 3, no. 2 (Spring 1975):173–79.

Herrick, Neal Q. "QWL: An Alternative to Traditional Public-sector Management Systems." *National Productivity Review* 3, no. 1 (Winter 1983–84):54–67.

Hetland, James L., Jr. "Restructuring Service Delivery: The Basic Issues for Government." *National Civic Review* 71, no. 2 (February 1982):67–74, 90.

Hill, Melvin, Jr. "The 'Littler Hatch Acts': State Laws Regulating Political Activities of Local Government Employees." *State Government* 52, no. 4 (Autumn 1979):161–68.

Hillenbrand, Bernard F. "The Most Rapidly Changing Form of Government." *Public Management* 63, no. 12 (December 1981):8–9.

Hinton, Robert. "Getting Along with the Media." *Public Management* 64, no. 1 (January 1982):16–17.

Holtz, Harold. Introductory comments in "A Symposium: Local Governmental Training: Practices and Perspectives." *State and Local Government Review* 66, no. 5 (May 1981):42–43.

Howard, Lawrence C. "Black Praxis of Governance: Toward an Alternative Paradigm of Public Administration." *Journal of Afro-American Issues* 3, no. 2 (Spring 1975):143–59.

Howell, James M. "Banking on Local Economic Development." *Public Management* 64, no. 1 (January 1982):10–12.

Hy, Ronald John, William L. Waugh, Jr., and Peter B. Nelson. "Statistical Backgrounds and Computing Needs of Graduate Students in Political Science and Public Administration Programs." *Teaching Political Science* 8, no. 2 (January 1981):201–12.

ICMA Executive Board, 1972. "ICMA Code of Ethics with Guidelines." *Public Management* 63, no. 3 (March 1981):6–8.

ICMA Executive Board, 1977. "ICMA Code of Ethics: Rules of Procedure." *Public Management* 63, no. 3 (March 1981):9–11.

Johnson, K. F., and C. J. Hein. "Assessment of the Council–Manager Form of Government Today: Managers Meet the Challenge through Balance." *Public Management* 67, no. 7 (July 1985): 4–6.

Johnson, Verne, and Ted Kolderie. "Public/Private Partnerships: Useful but Sterile." *Foundation News* 25, no. 2 (March/April 1984):29–33.

Jones, Garth N. "Rise and Fall of a Professional Ideal: Particulars Concerning Public Administration." *American Review of Public Administration* 16, no. 4 (Winter 1982): 305–19.

Jones, William A., Jr., and C. Bradley Doss, Jr. "Local Officials' Reaction to Federal 'Capacity-building.' " *Public Administration Review* 38, no. 1 (January/February 1978):64–72.

Kane, Thomas J., Jr. "City Managers View Intergovernmental Relations." *Publius* 14, no. 3 (Summer 1984):121–33.

Katz, Ralph. "Job Longevity as a Situational Factor in Job Satisfaction." *Administrative Science Quarterly* 23 (June 1978):204–23.

Keane, Mark E. "The Quality of Life." *Public Management* 64, no. 1 (January 1982):5–6.

Kearney, Richard C., and Chandon Sinha. "Professionalism and Bureaucratic Responsiveness: Conflict or Compatibility?" *Public Administration Review* 48, no. 1 (January/February 1988):571–79.

Keeley, Michael. "A Social-justice Approach to Organizational Evaluation." *Administrative Science Quarterly* 23, no. 2 (June 1978):272–92.

Kellar, Elizabeth K. "What Every Manager Should Know about Being Fired." *Public Management* 61, no. 2 (February 1979):2–5.

Keller, Lawrence F. "City Management, Public Administration, and the American Enlightenment." *International Journal of Public Administration* 12, no. 2 (1989):213–49.

Kilpatrick, Allie C. "Job Change in Dual-Career Families: Danger or Opportunity?" *Family Relations* 31, no. 3 (July 1982):363–68.

Kipp, Robert A. "Mayors and Councils—The New Breed." *Public Management* 59, no. 9 (September 1977):2–4.

Klaus, George H., Jr. "Role of the State Department of Community Affairs in Training and Development for Local Governments: Pennsylvania's Experience." *State and Local Review* 13, no. 2 (May 1981): 56–61.

Kleingartner, Archie. "Collective Bargaining between Salaried Professionals and Public Sector Management." *Public Administration Review* 33, no. 2 (March/April 1973):165–72.

Klerman, Gerald L., M.D. "Fighting the Management Blues." *Public Management* 64, no. 1 (January 1982):13–15.

Klitgaard, Robert. "Managing the Fight Against Corruption: A Case Study." *Public Administration and Development* 4 (January/March):77–98.

Knapp, Elaine S., ed. "A Woman's Place Is in the Capitol." *State Government News* 27, no. 7 (September 1984):4–9.

Koehler, Cortus T. "Policy Development and Legislative Oversight in Council–Manager

Cities: An Information and Communication Analysis." *Public Administration Review* 33, no. 5 (September/October 1973):433–41.

Landry, Lawrence D. "City Councils as Policy Makers: Myths That Destroy Effectiveness." *National Civic Review* 66, no. 11 (December 1977):553–57.

Lau, Alan W., Arthur R. Newman, and Laurie A. Broedling. "The Nature of Managerial Work in the Public Sector." *Public Administration Review* 40, no. 5 (September/October 1980):513–20.

Leffler, Mary. "ICMA's Role with County Managers." *Public Management* 63, no. 12, (December 1981):10–11.

Legge, Jerome S., Jr., and James Devore. "Measuring Productivity in U.S. Public Administration and Public Affairs Programs 1981–1985." *Administration and Society* 19, no. 2 (August 1987):147–56.

Levine, Charles S., Irene S. Rubin, and George G. Wolohojian. "Resource Scarcity and the Reform Model: The Management of Retrenchment in Cincinnati and Oakland." *Public Administration Review* 41, no. 6 (November/December 1981):619–28.

Levine, Marvin J. "Regulating the Off-duty Employees: Constitutional Issues." *Journal of Collective Negotiations* 14, no. 4 (1985):359–75.

Lewis, Carol W., and Anthony T. Logalbo. "Cutback Principles and Practices: A Checklist for Managers." *Public Administration Review* 40, no. 2 (March/April 1980):184–88.

Lineberry, Robert L., and Edmund P. Fowler. "Reformism and Public Policies in American Cities." *American Political Science Review* 61, no. 3 (September 1967):701–16.

Logan, John R., ed. "Urban Theory and National Urban Policy [Symposium]." *Urban Affairs Quarterly* 19, no. 3 (September 1983):3–132.

Long, Norton E. "The City As a Local Political Economy." *Administration and Society* 12, no. 1 (May 1980):5–35.

Lovell, Catherine H. "Evolving Local Government Dependency." *Public Administration Review* 41, Special Issue (January 1981):189–202.

Luke, Jeff S. "Finishing the Decade: Local Government to 1990." *State and Local Government Review* 18, no. 3 (Fall 1986):132–37.

Lund, B. H. "Cutback Management in a City." *Planning and Administration* 9 (Spring 1982):25–32.

Lyden, Fremont J., and Ernest G. Miller. "Why City Managers Leave the Profession: A Longitudinal Study in the Pacific Northwest." *Public Administration Review* 36, no. 2 (March 1976):175–81.

———. "Policy Perspectives of the Northwest City Manager." *Administration and Society* 8, no. 4 (February 1977):469–80.

Lyden, Fremont J., Ernest G. Miller, and Leonard D. Goodisman. "Changing With the Times: The City Manager in the 60's and 70's." *American Review of Public Administration* 15, no. 4 (Winter 1981):295–307.

McDougall, Gerald S., and Harold Bunce. "Urban Service Distribution: Some Answers to Neglected Issues." *Urban Affairs Quarterly* 19, no. 3 (March 1984):355–71.

McEvoy, Robert D. "Ethical Challenges in Local Government." *Public Management* 63, no. 3 (March 1981):13.

McGowan, Robert P. "The Professional in Public Organizations: Lessons from the Private

Sector?'' *American Review of Public Administration* 16, no. 4 (Winter 1982):337–49.

McGowan, Robert P., and John M. Stevens. ''Local Government Management: Reactive or Adaptive?'' *Public Administration Review* 43, no. 3 (May/June 1983):260–67.

Markham, William T., and Joseph H. Pleck. ''Sex and Willingness to Move for Occupational Advancement: Some National Sample Results.'' *Sociological Quarterly* 27, no. 1 (1986):121–43.

Mars, David. ''Everyone Profits.'' *Public Management* 59, no. 8 (August 1977):2–5.

Mead, Timothy D. ''Identifying Management Capacity among Local Governments.'' *Urban Affairs Papers* 3 (Winter 1981):1–12.

Mendonsa, Arthur A. ''Council–Manager Relations and the Changing Community Environment.'' *Public Management* 59, no. 9 (September 1977):5–7.

Methe, David T., and James L. Perry. ''The Impacts of Collective Bargaining on Local Government Services: A Review of Research.'' *Public Administration Review* 40, no. 4 (July/August 1980):359–71.

Milkulecky, Thomas J. ''Intergovernmental Relations: Strategies for the Local Manager.'' *Public Administration Review* 40, no. 4 (July/August 1980): 379–81.

Miller, Lynn S., and Laurence Rutter, eds. ''Strengthening the Quality of Urban Management Education: A Special Symposium.'' *Public Administration Review* 37, no. 5 (September/October 1977):567–630.

Morgan, David R., and John P. Pelissero. ''Urban Policy: Does Political Structure Matter?'' *American Political Science Review* 74, no. 4 (December 1980):999–1006.

Mulrooney, Keith F., ed. ''The American City Manager: An Urban Administrator in a Complex and Evolving Situation.'' *Public Administration Review* 31, no. 1 Symposium Issue (January/February 1971):6–46.

———. ''Prologue: Can City Managers Deal Effectively with Major Social Problems?'' *Public Administration Review* 31, no. 1 Symposium Issue (January/February 1971):6–14.

Musolf, Lloyd D., and Harold Siedman. ''The Blurred Boundaries of Public Administration.'' *Public Administration Review* 40, no. 2 (March/April 1980):124–30.

Nagel, Stuart, and Marian Neef. ''What Is and What Should Be in University Policy Studies?'' *Public Administration Review* 37, no. 4 (July/August 1977):383–90.

Nalbandian, John. ''Local Government Professionals under Stress: In Pursuit of Economic Development, Efficiency, and Equity.'' *Public Administration Review* 48, no. 1 (January/February 1988):588–91.

Nalbandian, J., and J. T. Edwards. ''The Values of Public Administrators: A Comparison with Lawyers, Social Workers, and Business Administrators.'' *Review of Public Personnel Administration* 4, no. 1 (1983):114–29.

Nenno, M. K. ''President's Urban Policy Report: Findings and Observations.'' *Journal of Housing* 39 (November/December 1982):168–72.

Newland, Chester A. ''Council–Manager Government: Positive Alternative to Separation of Powers.'' *Public Management* 67, no. 7 (July 1985):7–8.

Northrop, Alana, and William H. Dutton. ''Municipal Reform and Group Influence.'' *American Journal of Political Science* 22, no. 3 (August 1978):691–711.

Northrop, Alana, William H. Dutton, and Kenneth L. Kraemer. ''The Management of Computer Applications in Local Government.'' *Public Administrative Review* 42, no. 3 (May/June 1982):234–43.

Oppenheimer, Martin. "The Unionization of the Professional." *Social Policy* 5, no. 5 (January/February 1975):34–40.

Ostrowski, John W., Louise G. White, and John D. R. Cole. "Local Government Capacity Building: A Structured Group Process Approach." *Administration and Society* 16, no. 1 (May 1984):3–26.

Oxford, Rebecca, Bruce Clary, and Mark Fetler. "Adversary Evaluation of an MPA Program." *Teaching Political Science* 8, no. 2 (January 1981):147–62.

Parmerlee, Marcia A., Janet P. Near, and Tamila C. Jensen. "Correlates of Whistleblowers' Perceptions of Organizational Retaliation." *Administrative Science Quarterly* 27, no. 1 (March 1982):17–34.

Parr, John. "The Council–Manager Form and the Future." *Public Management* 69, no. 2 (February 1987):4–6.

Perry, James L., and Lyman W. Porter. "Factors Affecting the Context for Motivation in Public Organizations." *Academy of Management Review* 7, no. 1 (1982):89–98.

Peterson, J. E., et al. "From Monitoring to Mandatory: State Roles in Local Government Finance." *Governmental Finance* 8 (December 1979):3–11.

Poister, Theodore H., and Robert P. McGowan. "The Use of Management Tools in Municipal Government: A National Survey." *Public Administration Review* 44, no. 3 (May/June 1984):215–23.

Pokorny, Gary F. "Training—Why Bother in an Environment of Increasing Demands and Drastically Reduced Resources." *State and Local Government Review* 13, no. 2 (May 1981):47–51.

Poole, Robert, Jr. "Objections to Privatization." *Policy Review* 24 (Spring 1983):105–19.

Preston, A. B. "Handling Ethics Charges." *Public Management* 63, no. 3 (March 1981):18–19.

Pugh, Darrel L. "Professionalism in Public Administration: Problems, Perspectives, and the Role of ASPA." *Public Administration Review* 49, no. 1 (January/February 1989):1–8.

Rainey, Hal G. "Perceptions of Incentives in Business and Governments: Implications for Civil Service Reform." *Public Administration Review* 39, no. 5 (September/October 1979):440–48.

Rainey, Hal G., and Robert W. Backoff. "Professionals in Public Organizations: Organizational Environments and Incentives." *American Review of Public Administration* 16, no. 4 (Winter 1982):319–36.

Rainey, Hal G., Robert W. Backoff, and Charles H. Levine. "Comparing Public and Private Organizations." *Public Administration Review* 36, no. 2 (March/April 1976):233–44.

Rawls, James R., and Oscar Tivis Nelson, Jr. "Characteristics Associated with Preferences for Certain Managerial Positions." *Psychological Reports* 36, no. 3 (June 1975):911–18.

"Responsive Citizens, Responsive Government." *National Civic Review* 66, no. 11 (December 1977):536–46.

Rice, Larry L. "The First Hundred Days: Or, What's the New Kid Like?" *Public Management* 59, no. 10 (October 1977):2–4.

Rice, M. F., and W. Jones. "Municipal Services and Service Equality." *Midwest Review of Public Administration* 14 (March 1980):29–39.

Riggs, Richard R. "The Professionalization of the Public Service: A Roadmap for the 1980's and Beyond." *American Review of Public Administration* 16, no. 4 (Winter 1982):349–69.

Roessner, J. David. "Incentives to Innovate in Public and Private Organizations." *Administration and Society* 9, no. 3 (November 1977):341–65.

Rosenbloom, David H. "Public Administrative Theory and the Separation of Powers." *Public Administration Review* 43, no. 3 (May/June 1983):219–27.

———. "Public Administrative Professionalism and Public Service Law." *State and Local Government Review* 16, no. 2 (Spring 1984):52–57.

Rowe, B. J. D. "Theory and Myth vs. Practice: What the Research Reveals about Council–Manager Government and the Principles of Public Administration." *Public Management* 69, no. 2 (February 1987):11–16.

Rutter, Laurence G. "Art and Magic: Local Government Management's Standards of Professionalism." *Bureaucrat* 6, no. 2 (Summer 1977):52–58.

Saltzstein, Alan L. "City Managers and City Councils: Perceptions of the Division of Authority." *Western Political Quarterly* 27, no. 2 (June 1974):275–88.

Savas, E. S. "An Empirical Study of Competition in Municipal Service Delivery." *Public Administration Review* 37, no. 6 (November/December 1977):717–24.

———. "Positive Urban Policy for the Future," with a discussion by H. C. White. *Urban Affairs Quarterly* 18, no. 4 (June 1983):447–53.

Schaefer, Thomas E. "Professionalism: Foundation for Business Ethics." *Journal of Business Ethics* 3, no. 4 (November 1984):269–77.

Schmidt, Ronald. "On Teaching Administrative Theory as Political Theory." *Teaching Political Science* 11, no. 2 (Winter 1983–84):78–83.

Schott, R. L. "Public Administration as a Profession: Problems and Prospects." *Public Administration Review* 36, no. 3 (May/June 1976):255–59.

Schrader, George R. "Establishment and Adequate Maintenance of a Comprehensive Training and Development Program in Local Government." *State and Local Government Review* 13, no. 2 (May 1981):43–46.

Seigel, Larry. "City, Consultant Join Forces for Management Audits." *American City and Council* 98, no. 3 (March 1983):31–32.

Sharp, Elaine B. "Citizens' Perceptions of Channels for Urban Service Advocacy." *Public Opinion Quarterly* 44, no. 3 (Fall 1980):362–76.

Shaul, Marnie S. "The Status of Women in Local Governments: An International Assessment." *Public Administration Review* 42, no. 6 (November/December 1982):491–500.

Shaw, J. B., and J. H. Riskind. "Predicting Job Stress Using Data from the Position Analysis Questionnaire." *Journal of Applied Psychology* 68 (1983):253–61.

Sink, David. "The Political Role of City Practical Implications." *State and Local Government Review* 15, no. 1 (Winter 1983):10–15.

Skaggs, Sanford M. "View from the Elected Official." *Public Management* 59, no. 9 (September 1977):8–10.

Slocum, J., and H. Sims. "A Typology of Technology and Job Redesign." *Human Relations* 33 (January 1983):193–212.

Smit, B., and A. Joseph. "Trade-off Analysis of Preferences for Public Services." *Environment and Behavior* 14 (March 1982):238–58.

Smith, Russ. "City Administrators as Policy Makers: Some Rules for Behavior?" *Midwest Review of Public Administration* 13, no. 1 (March 1979):3–18.

Sparrow, Glen, David Wanzenried, and Earl Campbell. "Modernizing Existing Local Government Units." *National Civic Review* 68, no. 6 (June 1979):295–98.

Stephens, Robert F., T. Scott Fillebrown, and Carol Miner. "City–County Unification." *National Civic Review* 68, no. 6 (June 1979):288–92.

Stewart, F. A. (Bud). "Ethics and the Profession." *Public Management* 63, no. 3 (March 1981):14.

Stillman, Richard J., II. "The City Manager: Professional Helping Hand, or Political Hired Hand?" *Public Administration Review* 37, no. 6 (November/December 1977):659–70.

———. "Status of the Council–Manager Plan: Continuity in a Changing Society." *Public Management* 67, no. 7 (July 1985):3.

Strauss, George. "Professionalism and Occupational Associations." *Industrial Relations* 11, no. 3 (May 1963):7–31.

Sullivan, James F., and Charles R. Adrian. "Urban Government Research: A View of Three Decades." *National Civic Review* 66, no. 9 (October 1977):437–46.

"Summary of the Interim Report of the ICMA Task Force on Women in the Profession." *Public Management* 57, no. 7 (July 1975):3–4.

Svara, James H. "Dichotomy and Duality: Reconceptualizing the Relationship between Policy and Administration in Council–Manager Cities." *Public Administration Review* 45, no. 1 (January/February 1985):221–32.

———. "The Rediscovery of Municipal Officials." *Public Administration Review* 48, no. 6 (November/December 1988):1005–1011.

———. "Is There a Future for City Managers? The Evolving Roles of Officials in Council–Manager Government." *International Journal of Public Administration* 12, no. 2 (1989):179–212.

Tashman, Leonard J., Robert Carlson, and E. Lauck Parke. "A Management Lesson in Curricular Development." *Educational Record* 65, no. 1 (Winter 1984):54–56.

Tewes, J. Edward. "The New Entrepreneurship." *Public Management* 63, no. 6 (June 1981):5–9.

Thompson, Dennis F. "The Possibility of Administrative Ethics." *Public Administration Review* 45, no. 5 (September/October 1985):555–61.

Trombetta, William L. "The Professions under Scrutiny: An Antitrust Perspective." *Journal of Consumer Affairs* 16, no. 1 (Summer 1982):88–111.

Upton, John G. "Bear Huntin' with a Switch." *Public Management* 63, no. 12 (December 1981):5–7.

Varardy, D. D. "Determinants of Residential Mobility Decisions: The Role of Government Services in Relation to Other Factors." *Journal of the American Planning Association* 49 (Spring 1983):184–99.

Von Oech, Roger. "The Mind as a Management Tool." *Public Management* 64, no. 1 (January 1982):7–9.

Walker, David B. "Intergovernmental Relations and the Well-governed City: Cooperation, Confrontation, Clarification." *National Civic Review* 75, no. 2 (March/April 1986):65–87.

———. "Snow White and the 17 Dwarfs: From Metro Cooperation to Governance." *National Civic Review* 76, no. 1 (January/February 1987):14–28.

Walker, Jack L. "The Origin and Maintenance of Interest Groups in America." *American Political Science Review* 77, no. 2 (June 1983):390–405.

Walker, Warren E., and Jan M. Chaiken. "The Effects of Fiscal Contraction on Innovation in the Public Sector." *Policy Sciences* 15, no. 2 (December 1982):141–65.

Walter, J. Jackson. "The Ethics in Government Act, Conflict of Interest Laws, and Presidential Recruiting." *Public Administration Review* 41, no. 6 (November/ December 1981):659–65.

Wang, Richard Pierce. "Problems in Evaluating Economic Development Politics: An Urban Perspective." *International Journal of Public Administration* 12, no. 2 (1989):305–29.

Warrier, S. K. "Values of Successful Managers: Implications for Managerial Success." *Management and Labor Studies* 8, no. 1 (1982):7–15.

Watson, Burford N., Jr. "Professional Conduct: The Clear and the Not-so-clear." *Public Management* 63, no. 3 (March 1981):12.

Weiss, Carin S. "The Development of Professional Role Commitment among Graduate Students." *Human Relations* 34, no. 1 (1981):13–31.

White, Louise G. "Improving the Goal-setting Process in Local Government." *Public Administration Review* 42, no. 1 (January/February 1982):77–83.

Whorton, Joseph W., Jr., Frank K. Gibson, and Delmer D. Dunn. "The Culture of University Public Service: A National Survey of the Perspectives of Users and Providers." *Public Administration Review* 46, no. 1 (January/February 1986):38–47.

Whorton, Joseph W., and John A. Worthley. "A Perspective on the Challenge of Public Management: Environmental Paradox and Organizational Culture." *Academy of Management Review* 6, no. 3 (1981):357–61.

Wikstrom, Nelson. "Mayor as a Policy Leader in the Council–Manager Form of Government; A View from the Field." *Public Administration Review* 39, no. 3 (May/ June 1979):270–76.

Wilensky, Harold S. "The Professionalization of Everyone?" *American Journal of Sociology* 60, no. 2 (September 1964):137–58.

Wilson, James Q. "The Rise of the Administrative State." *Public Interest* 41 (1975):77–103.

Wirt, Frederick. "Professionalism and Political Conflict: A Developmental Model." *Journal of Public Policy* 1 (1981):61–93.

———. "The Dependent City? External Influences upon Local Control." *Journal of Politics* 47, no. 1 (1985):83–112.

Wise, Jeremy A. "The Roles of the City Manager." *National Civic Review* 62, no. 6 (June 1973):306–10.

Wolf, James F. "Career Plateauing in the Public Service: Baby Boom and Employment Bust." *Public Administration Review* 43, no. 2 (March/April 1983):160–65.

———. "Public Management Careers—Understanding and Options." *American Review of Public Administration* 17, no. 2/3 (Summer/Fall 1983):91–101.

Wolfinger, Raymond E. "Why Political Machines Have Not Withered Away and Other Revisionist Thoughts." *Journal of Politics* 34 (May 1972):365–98.

Wooward, J. David. "Ethics and the City Manager." *Bureaucrat* 13, no. 1 (Spring 1984):53–57.

Worthley, John A. "Ethics and Public Management: Education and Training." *Public Personnel Management Journal* 10 (1981):41–47.

Worthley, John A., and Barbara R. Grumet. "Ethics and Public Administration: Teaching

What 'Can't Be Taught.' " *American Review of Public Administration* 17, no. 1 (Spring 1983):54–67.

Yeager, Samuel J., Jack Rabin, and Thomas Vocino. "Professional Values of Public Servants in the United States." *American Review of Public Administration* 16, no. 4 (Winter 1982):402–12.

———. "Sources of Information Used by Professionals in Government to Find Jobs: Effectiveness and Impact." *Review of Public Personnel Administration* 4, no. 1 (Fall 1983):100–13.

———. "Employee Perceptions of State and Local Government Evaluation and Reward Systems." *State and Local Government Review* 16, no. 2 (Spring 1984):58–62.

———. "How Do MPAs Find Jobs?" *Bureaucrat* 13, no. 2 (Summer 1984):48–52.

Zimmerman, Joseph F. "Ethics in the Public Service." *State and Local Government Review* 14 (September 1982):98–106.

Zody, Richard E. "The Quality of Rural Administration: A Symposium." *Public Administration Review* 40, no. 1 (January/February 1980):13–18.

## REPORTS

Andrews, Donna Lee, and Gregg B. Jackson. *Structure of Local Government Personnel Administration*. Washington, D.C.: Baseline Data Report 17, no. 6, June 1985. International City Management Association.

*The Balance Wheel for Accreditation: Annual Directory, July 1986*. Washington, D.C.: Council on Postsecondary Accreditation (COPA).

Bens, Charles K. *Strategies for Implementing Performance Measurement*. Washington, D.C.: Management Information Service Report 18, no. 11, November 1986. International City Management Association.

Burns, R. A. *Women in Municipal Management*. Washington, D.C.: Urban Data Service Report 12, February 1980. International City Management Association.

Connellan, Thomas K. *Management by Objectives in Local Government: A System of Organizational Leadership*. Washington, D.C.: Management Information Service Report 7, no. 24, February 1975. International City Management Association.

COPA Document: *Provisions and Procedures for Becoming Recognized as an Accrediting Body for Postsecondary Educational Institutions or Programs*. Washington, D.C.: Council on Postsecondary Accreditation.

Eadie, Douglas C. *Strategic Issue Management: Improving the Council–Manager Relationship*. Washington, D.C.: Management Information Service Report 18, no. 6, June 1986. International City Management Association.

*Fact Sheet on ICMA* (revised November 1987). Washington, D.C.: International City Management Association.

Farr, Cheryl. *Participative Management in Local Government*. Washington, D.C.: Management Information Service Report 17, no. 11, November 1985. International City Management Association.

Frankel, Laurie S. *Municipal Managers and Chief Administrative Officers: A Statistical Profile*. Washington, D.C.: Urban Data Service Report 7, no. 2, February 1975. International City Management Association.

Green, Roy E. *Local Government Managers: Styles and Challenges*. Washington, D.C.: Baseline Data Report 19, no. 2, March/April 1987. International City Management Association.

Green, Roy E., and B. J. Reed. *Occupational Stress and Professional Mobility among City Managers*. Washington, D.C.: Urban Data Service Report 13, no. 6, June 1981. International City Management Association.

Henderson, L. M. *Intergovernmental Service Arrangements and the Transfer of Functions*. Washington, D.C.: Baseline Data Report 15, June 1984. International City Management Association.

Henry, C. T. *Trends in City Management Career: A Profession under Stress*. Washington, D.C.: Urban Data Service Report 14, March 1982. International City Management Association.

Hoff, Ross H. *Salaries of Municipal Officials 1985*. Washington, D.C.: Baseline Data Report 17, no. 3, March 1985. International City Management Association.

Honadle, Beth Walter. *Capacity-building (Management Improvement for Local Governments): An Annotated Bibliography*. Washington, D.C.: Rural Development Research Report, no. 28, March 1981. U.S. Department of Agriculture, Economics and Statistics Service.

"Honesty and Ethical Standards." *Gallup Report*, no. 239 (August 1985):2–28.

ICMA Assistants Steering Committee. *Local Government Assistants—1983*. Washington, D.C.: Baseline Data Report 16, no. 4, April 1984. International City Management Association.

Jennings, Bruce, Daniel Callahan, and Susan M. Wolf, eds. *The Public Duties of the Professions*. New York: Hastings Center Report, Special Supplement, 17, no. 1, February 1987.

*Learning Lexis: A Handbook for Modern Legal Research*. Dayton, Ohio: Mead Data Central, 1986.

Mercer, James L., Susan W. Woolston, and William V. Donaldson. *Three Techniques for Better Decision Making*. Washington, D.C.: Management Information Service Report 12, no. 9, September 1980. International City Management Association.

NASPAA Document: *Policies and Procedures for Peer Review and Accreditation of Professional Master's Degree Programs in Public Affairs and Administration*. Approved by the NASPAA Executive Council, October 9, 1986.

*1984 Directory: Programs in Public Affairs and Administration, A Survey Report of the Member Institutions*. Washington, D.C.: National Association of School of Public Affairs and Administration (NASPAA).

Paul, Amy Cohen. *Local Government Managers: On the Job and Off*. Washington, D.C.: Urban Data Service Report 13, no. 9, September 1981. International City Management Association.

"Professions." *Gallup Report*, no. 193 (October 1981):15–53.

Schwabe, Charles J. *Personnel Appraisals in Local Government*. Washington, D.C.: Baseline Data Report 18, no. 1, January/February 1986. International City Management Association.

*Standards for Professional Master's Degree Programs in Public Affairs and Administration, Effective September 1, 1986*. Washington, D.C.: National Association of Schools of Public Affairs and Administration (NASPAA).

U.S. Department of Housing and Urban Development. *Developmental Needs of Small Cities: A Study Required by Section 113 of the Housing and Community Development Act of 1977, HUD-PDR–374*. Washington, D.C.: U.S. Government Printing Office, February 1979.

*Who's Who in Professional Local Government Management*. Washington, D.C.: International City Management Association, 1985.

Woolston, Susan, and Bill Donaldson. *Local Government Organizational Structures for the Eighties*. Washington, D.C.: Management Information Service Report 12, no. 3, March 1980. International City Management Association.

Zimmerman, Joseph F. *Ethics in Local Government*. Washington, D.C.: Management Information Service Report 8, no. 8, August 1976. International City Management Association.

# NAME INDEX

# SUBJECT INDEX

## ABOUT THE AUTHOR

ROY E. GREEN is an associate professor of public affairs in the Graduate School of Public Affairs at the University of Colorado at Denver, the director of research for the National Civic League, and president of the REG Management Resource Group. Previously, he has held appointments at the University of Oregon, the University of Wisconsin–Milwaukee, and the University of Alabama, and has been a visiting scholar at the University of Michigan. He has served as a legislative assistant to U.S. Senator John C. Danforth for community and economic affairs; as an I.P.A. visiting scholar with the Office of Community Development, U.S. Department of Housing and Urban Development; and on the Housing Finance Working Group of the Office of Policy Development and Research, H.U.D.

Professor Green coedited *The Homeless in Contemporary Society* (with Richard Bingham and Sammis White). He holds a B.A. from Chadron State College, Nebraska; an M.S. from Pittsburg State University, Kansas; and a Ph.D. from the University of Missouri–Columbia.